DAVID E. KLEMENT

'CONSCIENCE OF THE COMMUNITY'
MEMOIR OF A SMALL-TOWN EDITOR
1977-2007

ISBN For this edition: 978-0-5787208-0-7

Book formatting by: **Last Mile Publishing**

First Edition Published: July 2020

Published by Ivy Street Publishing

ACKNOWLEDGEMENTS

First, I want to thank my wife of 42 years, Jo Anne, for standing beside me during all of those years when the newspaper was like a mistress as well as during the last year as I holed up in my home office putting this book together. Now that it's finished, let's enjoy retirement.

Second, I need to first apologize to and then thank my daughter, Sara King, and son, Max Ramming – apologies for exposing parts of their private lives as well as that of their children in my columns over the years – without asking – and saying thanks for putting up with me without complaining too much.

Third, I want to thank the many readers who have told me since my retirement how much they missed my columns in the Sunday *Bradenton Herald*. They are a big part of the inspiration for this book.

And finally, I want to recognize and thank the many friends and ex-colleagues who helped me shape and birth this book, among them: John Cimasi, for his invaluable assistance in formatting the manuscript; Janet Kerley, a friend and former competitor, for her insights into structuring it; Marc Masferrer, *Bradenton Herald* President and Editor, who helped me with legal issues related to copyright, and Bill Bonney of Last Mile Publishing, my editor and publisher who helped me through the self-publication maze.

CONTENTS

'CONSCIENCE OF THE COMMUNITY': MEMOIR OF A SMALL-TOWN EDITOR 1

PROLOGUE: BEGINNINGS 5

INTRODUCTION 9

CHAPTER ONE: FAMILY 13

Part One: Christmases I Have Known 13

Part Two: Our Home, Our Town 21

Part Three: Parenting, Pets, Disaster Prep and Other Crises 27

Part Four: My Other Family, Back Home in Texas 49

Part Five: Wedding Bells and Grandchildren 66

CHAPTER TWO: MATTERS OF FAITH 87

CHAPTER THREE: ON DEADLINE 127

CHAPTER FOUR: MY BLEEDING HEART 193

CHAPTER FIVE: ON THE ROAD 255

CHAPTER SIX: TRIVIA OF LIFE 309

THE LONG GOODBYE 357

ABOUT THE AUTHOR 369

Aerial view of the Texas farm on which the author grew up | Courtesy Skypix Inc. Marshfield, WI

'CONSCIENCE OF THE COMMUNITY' MEMOIR OF A SMALL-TOWN EDITOR

An aged man is but a paltry thing,
a tattered coat upon a stick,
unless soul clap its hands and sing,
and louder sing for every tatter in its mortal dress.

--William Butler Yeats, "Sailing to Byzantium"

I am dying.

That's OK, no need to turn sad, or utter platitudes of empathy. And save your thoughts and prayers. I'm not going right away – at least I hope not. But it will be relatively soon, of that I'm sure.

That's because the terminal condition I have is incurable, untreatable, non-preventable.

It's called old age.

I am well into my 81st year on this earth, and Yeats' view of old age expressed above resonates as it did not when I first read it over 50 years ago. Eight decades is a long time. According to the Social Security Administration, I have 7.34 more years to live, if I am fortunate enough to make the average for male Americans my age, or age 88.3 years. If I want a slightly more optimistic diagnosis for my terminal condition, Dr. Dean Foster of the Wharton School of Business at the University of Pennsylvania says I have 'til age 90, or 1.6 years longer than Social Security's tables. Dr. Foster's projection was based on a study of 550,000 AARP members about 10 years ago. So maybe SS' projection is more up to date.

As my millennial grandchildren might say, whatever. I've got at best another decade to live, give or take a year or so. That's not a terribly long time, especially if it goes as fast as the last decade has. It's just one-tenth of my total years of life to date. It's disturbing, put in that context. Why, thinking back to my middle years, and having been born in a decade-ending year, 1940, a decade meant little, because there was always another one rolling along. Thirty? So what? Forty? Big deal. Fifty? Bigger deal. Sixty? Where did that come from? Seventy? Uh-oh. And eighty? The end is in sight.

And there's no assurance that, if I do luck out in the life-expectancy lottery, those will be *good* years. As in, good health. Retained mobility. Sound mind. Ah, yes, can't overlook the A-word. Alzheimer's. It's the old person's true enemy, more dreaded than the C-word – cancer. Perhaps it is even more feared than death. For I know from experience of friends and loved ones, it's a living death.

There's one thing about reaching this age: It concentrates the mind. Not unlike what is said of GIs in a foxhole, under enemy fire, finding a sudden interest in the Divine. Cut to the chase. I'm experiencing that, not just in regard to my hoped-for place in the hereafter as well as how I will spend those remaining 7.34 years. If I get them.

When I look at old family photos from the '40s and '50s or watch news clips from events that occurred in my lifetime, showing people I recognize, like members of Congress, news anchors, actors, singers, I can't help thinking: *They're all dead!* Along with all of my grandparents, parents, uncles and aunts, these people who were part of my life, even if vicariously, are long gone. Most of them were a generation ahead of me, or maybe just 10 or 15 years. They're dead. And soon I'll be among them.

And one other thing. What I will leave behind. How I will be remembered – IF I will be remembered. That's something we all think about as death approaches. I recently discovered that the 2014 movie *The Fault in our Stars* has some profound insights on that desire. It features two teenagers dealing with cancer who meet in a support group and fall in love. It's a sweet, sad story of young love bumping head-on into mortality as their cancers spread, with each wondering who will be stuck delivering the eulogy for whom. The two adorable teens, Gus (played by

Ansel Elgort) and Hazel (Shailene Woodley) discuss this issue at length. "I just want to be remembered, not go into oblivion," says Gus, echoing my feelings. "Oblivion is inevitable," replies the practical Hazel. "The only way to live a meaningful life is to be remembered," insists Gus.

In a July 2019 essay in *The Atlantic*, sociologist Arthur C. Brooks used an even more wince-inducing word to describe that fear: Irrelevance. The fear of being irrelevant drives many of my generation into unhappiness, depression, even to suicide. He cited a 2007 study by an academic team at UCLA and Princeton showing that older people who rarely or never "felt useful" were almost three times as likely as those who often felt useful to develop a mild disability and worse, more than three times as likely to have died during the course of the study.

So, being useful joins being remembered as a motivation for this book. Well, OK, being loved figures in there, too. In the movie, Gus and Hazel can't agree but ultimately find that love is the answer to being remembered. Will I have that? Perhaps, for a generation. But not much beyond, and not the whole me. Frankly, not many people who know me know much about what I have done. Of my family, my dear wife of 42 years, Jo Anne, is the only one who has shown more than a passing interest in my hopes, dreams, accomplishments. Or in my writing, including my own two children. She alone knows almost everything about me. But at 74, she isn't so far behind me, even though SS gives her an extra year and a half life expectancy over me.

I've written quite a lot about my life. As Editorial Page Editor of the *Bradenton Herald* for 30 years, I put my observations on life and living before the world daily, seven days a week, 50 weeks a year. Most of it was expressed in the *Herald's* editorials, most of the time focused on public policy issues. But I also wrote personal columns most Sundays. In those I tried to connect an issue of the day to an experience from my personal life. Many of those were about family, which will explain why that section is the longest in this book. Family was all I worked for, lived for, during all of those 30 years, so it is logical that the happenings in my family would often become fodder for my Sunday columns, whether members of the family liked it or not. Which they mostly didn't.

I reprise the best of them in the pages that follow because they speak for me better than I could express it today. And I do so because my fans – who were once numerous but of whom there are now not so many left – have repeatedly urged me to do so.

So, I write to avoid oblivion, if possible, as well as irrelevance. And because I think I have had an interesting life. All in all, I think it is not a bad accounting of the life I have made, at age 81. Here is how it began.

PROLOGUE
BEGINNINGS

Before I discovered journalism as the profession that would become a 45-year career, I was a naïve country boy, venturing into the universe with very little worldly knowledge or skills useful to survival in an urban environment. I was born in a clinic located above the town drug store in Muenster, Texas, a one-red-light town whose church and school were the hub of community life.

I was the third of four children born to my parents, who struggled daily to make a living on small dairy farm seven miles northeast of town that they had bought shortly after their marriage in 1933. The farm was reached by narrow, gravel roads that were rutted in rainy weather and dusty in dry. The town, whose population was around 1,100 in those days, was settled by German immigrants in the late 1880s, brought there by three German brothers who acquired a 22,000-acre ranch to establish a German-American colony in the rich soil of the rolling prairies north of Dallas.

Life was tough for farmers and their offspring in those days. Children were expected to pull their load from about age 6 or 7, when childhood essentially ended. There was a never-ending series of chores to do morning and evening, seven days a week, 52 weeks a year. We progressed from gathering the eggs in the henhouse – a scary job if an upset hen pecked at you – to feeding baby calves with a nipple bucket to bringing in the cows from the field to actually helping with the milking. By age 10 we were crouching beneath the flanks of 1,500-pound Holsteins attaching tubular vacuum pumps to pull the milk from their swollen udders and sometimes being sent flying by the kick of an angry cow's hind leg.

We also learned by that age to drive tractors, muck out the barns and spread the manure on the fields, lift 50-pound hay bales, deep-plow harvested cropland and, when the soil was too wet to go into the fields, to repair broken fences. By age 14 we were old enough to get a driver's license and euthanize ailing or unwanted livestock with our father's .22 single-shot rifle, the latter among my most vivid memories of my youth.

Love was tough, too, in our tiny frame home, which was three rooms when I was born but expanded to six, including a bathroom with indoor plumbing, by the time I started school. Mom didn't stand for back-talk or whining, issuing sharp rebukes for the former and her well-worn meme for the latter: "If you don't like it, your feet fit the road."

My escape was reading. There were no books in our home, only the daily newspaper that arrived by mail from Fort Worth one day late, plus farm and dairy magazines. I also read my older brother's reading texts when I could sneak it out of his school bag, worrying what would happen when I got to the older grades and already knew all the stories. Occasionally I was caught and scolded by Mom: "Why do you always have your nose in a book?"

I graduated third in my class of 17 from Muenster High School in 1958, and headed for the nearest state college, North Texas State, 45 miles south in Denton, on the highway to Dallas (now I-35). It was there I discovered journalism, which would become my career for the next 45 years. I was taught to write in Sophomore Reporting class, to lay out pages, edit copy and create headlines in daily labs, and to conduct interviews and take notes by instructors who had been seasoned journalists. By junior year I had become a page editor of our twice-weekly college newspaper, and by senior year I was editor. Though a humble state college, North Texas State was respected for the quality of its journalism program, and the region's big-city papers recruited heavily from its graduates.

It was through that network that I landed my first job at *The Daily Oklahoman/Oklahoma City Times*, 175 miles north on I-35. Well-equipped by my college experience, I quickly rose from writing obituaries to covering the police beat to general assignment reporter to Assistant City Editor. After four years I hit a pay-grade ceiling, so began a job search that wound up with an offer from the *Detroit Free Press*, a major metro five times the size of the *Oklahoman/Times*. I made the trip north with everything I owned in the back seat of my Plymouth Belvedere sedan.

I would spend 10 years at the *Free Press*, honing my journalistic skills at a newspaper that prized quality reporting and writing and provided the resources to produce it. I began as a Copy Editor, editing news stories and writing headlines, learning how to be an editor under the intense pressure of uncompromising bosses and unforgiving deadlines. Before the end of my first year there I would experience the worst race riot in U.S. history and the longest newspaper strike in history. Idled for nine months by the 1967 Detroit newspaper strike, I helped publish a short-lived strike newspaper, moved to Chicago for a temporary assignment at the *Sun Times*, and learned the basics of public relations.

Upon returning to work at the *Free Press* I picked up my Pulitzer Prize certificate awarded the news staff for coverage of the '67 riots and accepted a promotion to Picture Editor. In that position I had responsibility for creating a daily picture page and supervising the photo staff. Before long I again assumed the title of Assistant City Editor, first overseeing local reporting and laying out the local news front page. Within months I was the Night City Editor, solely responsible for local coverage on the night shift. But after close to 10 years of working second shifts and suffering the consequences of a blighted social life, I soon sought a position in the Business News Department and wound up as Assistant Business Editor. Besides supervising a staff of five writers, editing the daily business pages and a Sunday business section, I volunteered to re-energize the advertising beat and wrote a weekly column on the ad profession in Detroit's heyday as Motor City. In that beat I experienced a Detroit version of "Mad Men," the 2007 TV series centered on the Madison Avenue ad scene during the '60s and '70s.

But by 1975 Detroit had begun to sour on me. The level of crime, the post-riot race conflicts and the constant labor unrest simply made daily life unpleasant. And the winter of 1974-75 was particularly harsh.

Returning to Detroit Metro Airport from a vacation trip to Sarasota late in '74, I found my car encased in ice, the result of a night of freezing rain. Reliving the idyllic week of sunshine and warmth I had just enjoyed in Florida, I muttered to myself, "Life is too short for this." The deal was sealed a couple of months later when a two-foot snowfall kept the side streets impassable for over a week.

I inquired about transfers within the company, Knight News, which owned 35 newspapers scattered across the U.S. – including its newest acquisition, the *Bradenton Herald*, just 10 miles up Route 41 from Sarasota. I moved to Florida in early August, without securing a job at the *Herald* but confident I would soon get one. Within six weeks, I did. I started as Business Editor, quickly moved up to News Editor and, within a year, to City Editor. That last job almost drove me out of the profession. Even after enduring the mortal danger of the riot, the panic of long-term unemployment and the responsibility of overseeing the City Desk of a major metro, I was not prepared for the stress of being a small-town city editor with too-few resources. By 1977 I was stressed out to the point of quitting. Then I learned that the Editorial Page Editor had resigned. On a whim, I applied for the opening, and a new life opened up for me. The niche I found would sustain me for the next 30 years.

INTRODUCTION

Conscience (noun): the sense or consciousness of the moral goodness or blameworthiness of one's own conduct, intentions, or character together with a feeling of obligation to do right or be good.

--Merriam-Webster

How naïve I still was as I began what would become a 32-year career at the *Bradenton Herald* in fall of 1975. Sure, I was a lot more worldly-wise than the 18-year-old who had struck out for college 17 years earlier. I had faced the prospect of dying in a nuclear war. I had seen a city burn. I had covered horrible crimes and accidents with tragic loss of life. I had sent reporters out to do the same and directed the publication of their accounts. I had been part of exposing dirty cops and corrupt politicians. I had done my share of carousing in high- and low-life joints from Oklahoma City to Detroit to Chicago to New York to Sarasota. I was a carefree bachelor moving from job to job in pursuit of wealth, fame and happiness.

But I hadn't become a cynical, jaded know-it-all, the stereotype of a hard-bitten journalist. I took people at their word, and for the most part I trusted them to do the right thing. When they didn't, I felt it was my job as Bradenton's conscience to tell them where they were wrong, and what they needed to do to shape up.

Bradenton's conscience? Yes, that is exactly how I thought of my role as Editorial Page Editor. That was not a title I invented for myself. It was the role that newspaper journalism universally applied to the Editorial Page, which was considered the voice of the newspaper. And as the sole person on the editorial staff, I *was* that voice for the *Bradenton Herald*.

I learned of that heavy responsibility from the National Conference of Editorial Writers, the professional organization to which most opinion writers and editors in the U.S belonged and one I quickly joined in spring 1977 upon accepting the job of editing the paper's opinion pages. That fraternity – and it was mostly male, but women were accepted and treated as equals – provided me much professional guidance in the early days of my opinion-writing career. I learned of their standards for fair and constructive criticism and tried my best to put them into practice as I set about righting the wrongs of the world on a daily basis.

Naïve? Ho, boy, was I! But that didn't stop me from sticking my neck out day after day, telling our readers what the newspaper thought was the best course of action for any given problem or situation. Now, I wasn't doing this in a vacuum, with free rein to say anything I felt like saying about anything I felt like addressing. My editorials – as well as the topics to be taken up in them – were subject to approval by the publisher. Each week I submitted a list of potential topics I expected to address as well as the argument I planned to make for our position. Later there would be an Editorial Board that included the top two editors plus the publisher, and the position to be taken was decided by consensus of the board. But, as at most newspapers, the publisher always had the final word.

My first publisher – I would work under six during my 30 years in that role – was a man a few years older than me who had been sent to the *Bradenton Herald* by the Knight News organization to modernize its newest acquisition. Though from somewhere Up North, he was right at home in the good-old-boy culture of Bradenton. And like most of the community, he saw things from a conservative perspective, while I came from a more liberal one. Yet we had few differences of opinion during his tenure. I didn't go all radical on him, and he wasn't a right-wing fanatic.

But we did butt heads early in my career as an opinion writer. Early in 1977, the U.S. Supreme Court had ended a 10-year moratorium on imposition of the death penalty, and states – including Florida – were gearing up for a spate of executions. I proposed an editorial opposing the death penalty. The publisher advocated *for* the death penalty. We debated back and forth for quite a while, until I came up with what I though was a brilliant compromise. "How about if the newspaper's editorial position comes out against and you publish a personal column stating your support for the death penalty? Your name and photo will be in the article." An unspoken understanding: *I* would write both of the pieces, as he was not a writer.

He bought it. I had no trouble playing devil's advocate to make his case; a good journalist, like a good lawyer, can argue forcefully for a position whether he believes in it or not. The paper's position opposing reinstitution of the death penalty drew a good deal of opposition from readers, but its impact was softened by the publisher's personal viewpoint published right beside it. He had saved face, and I had established myself as a voice to be reckoned with at the *Bradenton Herald*.

I loved my new job. And I continued exercising my editorial influence to advocate for progressive causes as news developments put them in the spotlight. Gay rights soon became an issue. Abortion remained a perpetual one. Race, criminal justice, public prayer all made their way into the headlines and onto the opinion pages. And like Don Quixote, I naively kept raising my editorial lance and tilting at windmills. Then I decided to offer my opinions in a more personal way. The editorials were, by nature, anonymous – the viewpoint of the newspaper, not the individual writer. But in personal columns on the op-ed (opposite editorial) page I could let readers know what was on my mind and sign my name. It put my personal stamp on the opinion pages and established my reputation as a crusader.

Did any of it matter? Did all of my naïve do-gooderism make a dent? You decide. Herewith, a compilation of the best of my columns, published in the *Bradenton Herald* from 1977 to 2007. They, along with my asides printed in italics, complete the story of my life as Bradenton's conscience. The columns are sorted not in chronological order but rather by categories. The dates of publication are highlighted in boldface in my italicized comments preceding each.

CHAPTER ONE

FAMILY

PART ONE: CHRISTMASES I HAVE KNOWN

Christmas was always a big deal in our family. Here's how the tradition began. This column was published on **Dec. 25, 1977,** *the year I, a 37-year-old bachelor, met Jo Anne and her two children – my very first Christmas with my family-to-be.*

A Child's View Restores the Meaning of Christmas

How old is Jesus?"

The question is one of those stumpers that only a kid can come up with, and it left me fumbling for an answer.

"Gee, I don't know. I guess He's 1,977 years old. No, wait. He's 33 years old, because that's how old He was when He died, and Christmas is just the *anniversary* of His birthday, not really his birthday. . ."

It was a lame answer, because I'd never really thought about it. But it was the kind of thing on the minds of 4-year-olds last week, along with toys and trees and colored lights and reindeer and stockings and such. The story of Jesus' birth is a fascinating tale to a youngster hearing it for the first time, but it leaves out what a curious little boy considers some crucial details. Such as how old Jesus is today.

His question, dropped out of the clear blue as we were wrapping Christmas presents one evening last week, was a priceless souvenir of Christmas 1977, one of many I shall cherish in Christmases to come as the boy grows older and wiser – and, sadly, less curious about the mysteries of Christmas.

This Christmas I won't soon forget, for I am seeing it through the eyes of a child for the first time since. . . since I was a child. It has revived my flagging interest in Christmas, reminding me of how terribly exciting a brightly wrapped package can be – even if it contains but a necktie; of how enchanting a string of colored lights can make an ordinary living room or front door; how heady the smell and prickly the needles from a Christmas tree; how mouth-watering the aroma of cookies and fruit cakes coming from the oven, and how utterly delicious the anticipation of Santa's arrival.

"How do you spell Daddy?"

The question came as he put the finishing touches to a slightly dog-eared present which looked and smelled suspiciously like a bar of soap. It was a precious example of the real, true spirit of giving from one whose heart is absolutely pure.

"All by myself," as he defiantly put it, he had wrapped his presents to his mother, his sister, his father, showing far more skill with scissors, foil and tape than I imagined a 4-year-old could possess. It was only on the gift tags that he got stumped, his kindergarten-level facility with the English language not yet having progressed to the point of joining letters to form words. But he knew what they meant.

The results of his efforts were wonderful, only slightly-lopsided creations, with bits of paper sticking out here and there, the packages surely as interesting as the contents themselves.

"How do you spell 'Happy'?" And then: "How do you spell Christmas?"

I'd watched as he had labored over the piece of paper, coloring away with his red, blue and green Magic Markers between snatches of "The Nutcracker" on TV, thinking he was just scribbling out of boredom because he thought ballet was yukky. But no, the questions showed the true purpose behind his efforts: It was a Christmas card to me, a handmade, one-of-a-kind original more beautiful than any with Hallmark's logo on the back, and certainly more meaningful.

"If we have too many presents under the tree, will Santa not bring us any?"

It was a great worry as he watched the presents pile up from non-Santas, like Mommy, Grandma and Grandpa, and he wanted reassurance that Santa would still show up to fill the Christmas list he'd made up weeks before. There were special things like Mighty Mo's and electric trains on that list, not dumb stuff like clothes and underwear that were likely to be in presents from regular people.

He could not believe there should be this many presents for one household, and he sat under the tree for long periods, checking them out, trying to figure out by juggling what each contained.

One or two of those packages may be for me, but I'm not anxious to join this morning's orgy of unwrapping. For me, more happy memories went into them than will come out, and I'd just as soon leave them there for a while longer. Christmas, and its special moments, are over all too soon

He'll find that out one of these years, too – all too soon. At least, though, there are moments.

TWO YEARS LATER

That was the first of many columns I would write about my family over the next three decades. I tried in those pieces to relate my experiences in a way that readers might identify with their own lives, as well as to address universal feelings like love, heartbreak, loneliness or experiences of divorce, prejudice, poverty, corruption and death. I felt compelled to share my views with the world, not because I knew all of the answers but because I thought maybe my insights might help someone else see their situation with more clarity. Following is another take on Christmas, two years later, after I had *become an official member of the family, published on **Dec. 24, 1979.***

The Christmas Spirit: It Takes A Child

It came, as questions usually do from 6-year-olds, totally unexpectedly:

"Is there really a Santa Claus, or not?"

His father paused a moment, and then answered firmly, Yes, of course there is a Santa Claus. But he's not a person like you see in the stores. He's a spirit."

Proud of the ease with which he had handled this rather sensitive subject off the top of his head, he pushed on: "Because he's a spirit, Santa can get down chimneys and through doors that are closed. And that's also how he knows if you've been bad or good, because spirits can see you all the time."

"Oh." That meant he had had enough, that it would take a while to think over all that stuff before any more questions were raised along those lines.

Dad thought about it some more, too. He'd given that answer just to get off the spot, but when he considered it he decided that really IS what Christmas is all about. Spirit – the force inside you that compels you to be generous, that makes you feel joyful, that allows you to drop your ordinary pretensions and become childlike for a brief time.

It happens every year. You start out dreading the onslaught of the Christmas season – the crowded stores, surly clerks and picked-over merchandise; the stack of invitations to the same round of parties; the pressure of the postal deadlines and the cards that must be written, packages that must be mailed; the rubble from Christmas decorations in the unpacking stage and presents in the wrapping stage; the mess in the kitchen from cookies and muffins and fudge; the bills that will be coming along in January.

The bah-humbug fever is heightened by the commercialization that begins in October and builds to a crescendo by Thanksgiving. It is aggravated by the hedonistic flavor imparted by catalogs offering swimming pools filled with Perrier, sterling silver skillets, and his-and-hers blimps. Record albums like "Silent Night Disco" don't help much, either.

We would be grinches like that all year, most of us, were it not for the children. It is their enthusiasm, their spirit, that turns Scrooges into happy Christmas fairies by Christmas week. It starts with the Advent calendar. The first thing out of bed every morning, they head for the family room to open a little door on the Advent calendar. It's such a small thing to the sleepy parent – pull the tab, and there's a picture of a bird, reindeer, toy or Santa's workshop. But it helps the children count the days.

Then come the Christmas cards and wrapping paper, the ribbons and bows. The design of the Santa paper, the stripes on the fancy foil paper, the shade of blue of the Snoopy paper – all take on a significance far beyond the ken of an old grouch trying to read his evening paper amid all the confusion. Eventually, of course, he gives up and joins the wrapping brigade.

The Christmas records boost the spirit along, and snuggling around the TV set watching Christmas specials for a few evenings keeps it building. The turning point comes about mid-December, when the Christmas tree is purchased and the boxes with the decorations are brought down from the attic.

The tree must be one of perfect proportions, of healthy color and enormous height, with a spiked top and a big empty space on the bottom for presents to fit under. It is found after much searching, on the back of the lot, the tree that everyone agrees is worthy of greatness, and is hauled home and set up.

Out come the decorations, and each bauble brings a squeal of delight from the little ones whose short lives already contain a treasure of Christmas memories: the ornaments they got when they celebrated their first Christmas, the crayoned construction paper hangings they made in pre-school, the old-fashioned balls their grandparents had given them, the angels and elves and doves and bells and toy soldiers and Santas – each one a reminder of a previous Christmas.

Then Christmas becomes a magic time, the Christmas spirit real and contagious. Then you sing Christmas carols with gusto, get misty-eyed at school Christmas plays featuring off-key "Jingle Bells" and lopsided angel halos, and revel in the happiness around you.

Then you understand, as perhaps the 6-year-old cannot yet understand, what you really mean when you say Santa Claus is a spirit. He's the spirit of love.

TWO YEARS LATER

I wrote about Christmas a lot in those early years of our becoming a family. That's because it was all so new and wonderful for me – and also because I kept learning lessons about the meaning of Christmas from a child – my stepson, who by now was 8. This was my editorial for **Christmas Day, 1981**.

The Gift That Means the Most

*A*nd a little child shall lead them." – Isaiah 11:6

It was a typical pre-Christmas squabble in the Home of Divorce.

Long-distance telephone calls. Loud arguments. Telephone receivers slammed down in anger. The annual tug of war over where the children would spend Christmas was under way.

They should spend Christmas with me, she insisted. This is their *home*.

They should spend Christmas with me, he insisted. They haven't had a Christmas with me in six years. And my *home* is their home, too.

The boy listened as the voices of his parents got louder and angrier.

Finally, after his mother had once more slammed down the phone and stalked away, the boy followed her into her bedroom, tears streaming down his chubby cheeks.

"What does Christmas mean, anyway?" he asked his mother. "Jesus got born in a stable and he didn't say anything. So why is it so important where we spend Christmas?"

Her stomach sank as she pondered the question. My God! From an 8-year-old, here it was, the very essence of Christmas, stripped of the tinsel, ribbons, twinkling lights and rote-like carols, and she had missed it: The same gift that God had given on the first Christmas almost 2,000 years ago was now hers to give, too: her children. Her son and daughter. But not forever, and not to suffer and die, as God's son had. Only for a few days, to a man who, though she hated, would otherwise spend a lonely, sad Christmas, with only his memories of happy family Christmases past to warm his cheerless bachelor apartment.

How could she have missed it? What a poor example to her children, whom she was trying to raise by the principles that Jesus laid down during His brief life on earth. What a hypocrite she felt!

She looked at the thick piles of gifts under the tree, and knew that, compared to *this* gift she was being asked to give, they all meant nothing – that they were but hollow symbols of Christmas, which her children would quickly forget. But the selfishness she felt about the other gift, the one she did not want to give, that they would remember for years and years.

She waited until she had collected herself. Then she gathered her children around her and told them they could spend Christmas with their father.

Tearfully, she apologized to them for her anger and asked them to forgive her for the unkind things she had said.

Then they made plans for *their* Christmas. It would a special celebration on Christmas Eve, with dinner and opening of presents and everything, they decided. And the children shivered with excitement as they thought of opening of presents a day earlier than everyone else took center stage in their minds. It would be a good Christmas after all, she decided. . .

To all the Children of Divorce, even the Grandparents of Divorce, may your Christmas be as meaningful as this Bradenton family's. To you and to anyone who sees a lesson for himself in this family's example, may you find the charity and courage to give the gift that costs the most: Love. That is what Christmas means, really and truly. And it took an 8-year-old to point it out.

PART TWO: OUR HOME, OUR TOWN

The home in which we lived was the perfect place for creating all of these wonderful Christmas memories. A 1929 Florida farmhouse, it stood on a half-acre lot in northwest Bradenton, two doors off one of the city's finest, mansion-lined streets, Riverview Boulevard, and fronting McLewis Bayou, a tributary of the Manatee River. We lived on the water – albeit just a tiny stream that, unfortunately, as we would learn, was regularly polluted by the county's malfunctioning sewage lift station upstream.

The Bayou House: Our Secret Treasure

I have always harbored a secret delight in observing the reaction of first-time visitors to our house. They would squeeze through the tiny foyer with its arched entryway and then do a little double-take as their eyes swept the room with its white plaster walls, glistening pine floor and bookcase-lined fireplace flanked by sheer-curtained windows opening onto the back yard.

"Oh," they would say hesitantly, "What a NICE room!" Left unsaid, but in their minds, was the rest of their thought, "for such a plain-looking house on the outside."

I know that's what they were thinking because that was *our* reaction the first time we saw this house. It was so ordinary-looking, in fact, that after our first drive-by we told our Realtor not to bother setting up an appointment to tour it. We weren't interested. Set off from the road a good hundred feet and nearly hidden behind scrawny, overgrown shrubs and a massive palm bush, the house with its cedar-shake siding painted battleship gray had a look or ordinariness that invited rejection.

But our Realtor proved to be a better judge of houses than us. Plus she was a personal friend and knew if she didn't find us a house soon we'd be moving in with her, since our own home had already sold. She persuaded us to take a tour, assuring us the interior was much better than the exterior.

Once through the front door, my wife and I looked around, made the "What a nice room!" comment, then exchanged that knowing look and subtle elbow bump that house-hunting couples exchange when they've finally found the right one. And we knew, we had.

This house oozed character: Hardwood pine floors, plaster walls, crown moldings, 12-inch baseboards, heavy, solid interior doors, and old-fashioned, double-hung wood-mullion windows.

And space! A 15-by-28-foot living room; a 20-by-20-foot family room. A walk-in closet large enough to park a truck.

And, as we discovered as the tour progressed, it had charm: A window seat in the kitchen. Two fireplaces, including one in the master bedroom, both with decorative tiles inset into the mantle. There was a room off the back door that the owners called "the rumpus room," actually the original garage converted into a rec room big enough for pool table, darts, craft area and washer-dryer. A tiny room off the back, converted from an old porch, became our office. It had a French door leading out to the back yard and the bayou, in which mullet breached the surface and herons and pelicans stalked for meals. Covered breezeways, edged in vine-covered lattice work, led from the circular drive to both the front and back doors. And there was a stand-up attic, large enough to store all the junk we couldn't bear to throw out, plus room left over for the children to play on cool days.

Our most immediate neighbors were an eclectic collection of modern Florida ranches, older bungalows and cracker farmhouses like ours, along with a few weedy vacant lots. In other words, a neighborhood, not a tract housing development. It was just what I had been searching for, without really expecting to find it: a house with its own personality, one that said, "I'm not elegant, I'm not even a classic, but I'm reliable; I'm solid."

My wife and I loathed tract neighborhoods with their cookie-cutter layouts and hot, treeless yards. We wanted a story-book home for our children, and this was the nearest thing to vine-covered cottage we could find in our price range.

We've never regretted our decision, even as we coped with 60-year-old plumbing that accommodates no more than one faucet running at the same time, a bedroom with but one electrical outlet and no closet, an outdated air-conditioning system and a leaky roof. Over the years we've made lots of changes. One of the first things we did was change the exterior color to a soft green, the trim white, and installed new landscaping. That eased the foreboding look from the street, showing off the "Florida farmhouse" look to its maximum effect.

I latticed in the side of the carport to bring that look around to the side of the house, lined the circular drive in red brick and had white crushed shell brought in to cut down the dust from the old driveway. Whenever we redid a room, we found further proof of the wisdom of our decision. The studs were of heart of pine, so tough an ordinary nail would not drive in without a guide hole. The floors were of virgin pine, said the refinisher we hired. The asbestos slate roof, leaking in spots, had stood up to the Florida sun for nearly 60 years and could have been repaired if replacement tiles could be found. But they were no longer in production. Our fourth year there, we replaced it with asphalt shingles.

One summer a friend and I build a wooden deck off the back, and the family agreed that was the finest improvement we had made, for it opened the yard to outdoor living for the first time. Finally, we were able to appreciate the graceful oak, orchid and palm trees, some of them 50 feet tall, that populated the back yard.

But it wasn't until last year that our house finally came into its own. With interest rates low and home equity loans easy to secure, we added a pool, screened porch and promenade deck from the family room wrapping around the entire back of the house, overlooking the bayou. Four sets of double French doors were installed in place of the windows, opening the living room, dining room and family room onto the pool and deck. The porch is trimmed in white, the new fence is white pickets, and acres of new white lattice front the deck's superstructure, overlooking the pool.

We were concerned lest the addition detract from the basic character of the house. It did not. The brick-edged pool, the plank-decked, white pool apron and lattice trim were like a new wardrobe on a dowdy spinster. Our vine-covered cottage was transformed from cute to . . . well, sort of chic, what I call Useppa Cracker Beach House, for lack of a better description.

Now, when people come to our house for the first time, they say without equivocation, "My, what a beautiful home you have." And I have to agree with them, without seeming boastful: It's beautiful, but simple and unpretentious. Our house is just what we wanted it to be: our dream house.

BRADENTON: OUR LITTLE SECRET

*For years local officials have referred to Manatee County as "Our Little Secret" in Chamber of Commerce ads promoting the city and its environs as a good place to live, work and do business. And it was, back in the 1970s and '80s, before development erased lots of the Old Florida charm and tourism overwhelmed its beach communities. But that is just why I chose to stay in Bradenton, county seat of Manatee, to raise a family when I could have once again pursued a career at big-city newspapers. It was still a small-enough town that you didn't have to fight traffic to get places and you pretty much knew everybody who was anybody on a first-name basis. Here's what I wrote about that decision in **early 2001**.*

Manatee: A Great Place to Put Down Roots

Roots. It's a term and a concept that Alex Haley popularized in the '70s with his famous book and movie by that title which revolutionized the way we think of our heritage. My Random House Dictionary describes roots as "a person's original or true home, environment and culture, the personal relationships, affinity for a locale, habits and the like which make a country, region, city or town one's true home. . ."

Roots were on my mind the other night as I sat at the 38th annual Manatee Chamber of Commerce meeting and member appreciation banquet at Municipal Auditorium. As I leafed through the program and noted the directors, officers and members singled out for special recognition, I couldn't help but think back to my first chamber dinner, 26 years ago. I was new to Manatee County and new to the *Bradenton Herald*, having arrived from Detroit just five months earlier. As the paper's new Business Editor, I had the job of covering the chamber's annual dinner.

It was held in the dining room of what was then the Courtyard Motel (now a senior citizen residence). Back then, it was one of downtown Bradenton's favorite lunchtime restaurants, but it was barely adequate for the large chamber audience. I remember how crowded it was at the buffet, which featured fried chicken with all the trimmings.

What struck me the most from memories of that night, however, was this: I didn't know a soul. Here I was, assigned to cover Manatee County's premiere business group, and I didn't know a Blalock from a McClure, a Porges from a Bustle, a Taylor from a Harllee.

In contrast, on Jan. 16, 2001, I could look around the room and count hundreds of people whom I knew. For many my recognition was only by name and occupation, but it surprised me how many I could count as acquaintances and even friends. We socialized with one another; we worshiped and did volunteer work together. Our children grew up together. We watched them move through different peer groups in elementary school, play sports in high school, then scatter to colleges all over the country in pursuit of their dreams. And now we see many of them coming back, getting married, starting careers and buying houses in some of the same neighborhoods they came from.

Roots. That's what it amounts to, I thought. These are my roots now; this is my true home, environment and culture; my sense of place. That was more than a little startling to a native son of Texas, still holding on to that Lone Star pride, that yeehaw, cow-roping, bronc-riding spirit. But I couldn't deny it. Having left Texas for good at 22, I had now spent far more years in Florida than I had in Texas – or anywhere else, for that matter. This was – is -- now "home."

I can go back to my hometown in Texas, where everyone knows every member of three generations of every family in town and walk the streets in almost total anonymity. I have been gone so long that only immediate family recognizes my face. But in Bradenton, the opposite is true. Where once I knew not a soul, I now can't walk down the street without stopping to exchange news with friends. I can't walk into a restaurant without saying hello to acquaintances I pass en-route to my table. And I dare not try to slip into the hardware or grocery store in my Saturday grub-work clothes, for reports of my seedy attire will get back to my disapproving wife.

That's the definition of a hometown, of a place you want to claim as yours. Of roots. I see too many rootless folks these days, people who come and go with the changes of weather, it seems. I wonder what it is they are looking for as they job-hop from city to city, never getting involved or staying long enough to know the community that exists outside the workplace and favorite watering hole. To them Manatee County is just a way station on their journey to . . .what? The Big Apple, perhaps? Or, more likely, another dreary apartment in another dreary city full of rootless young people.

I was like that once, briefly, but I'm thankful I found Bradenton and Manatee County, where even a contrarian editorialist in the business of pointing out everyone's flaws and failings can find friends – and roots.

PART THREE: PARENTING, PETS, DISASTER PREP AND OTHER CRISES

Being a parent is a challenge, I soon learned – and perhaps made more difficult because I was a stepparent to the two children of my wife's first marriage, who were 8 and 5 when we officially became a family on Oct. 14, 1978. But this was a dream fulfilled: A wife, two kids, a cute cottage with a white picket fence (which I personally built from scratch). I had it all. And later, there came pets: a parakeet, cockatiel, gerbils, rabbits, and finally a dog, a beautiful black German shepherd.

Who first said: Be careful what you wish for? I thought of that admonition often in those years, although they were mostly good ones as we got used to living with one another and gradually bonded. It was not without stress, as sibling rivalry often produced squabbles and limits-testing, especially by my stepson, a button-pusher par excellence, which created frequent discipline issues. But I persevered. I talked to other parents. I read books on parenting. And I prayed for Divine guidance, for I knew I couldn't do this without God's help. I was only too happy to share some of the tricks of the trade with my readers.

Four Words to Successful Parenting

Want to know the secret to successful parenting? I have it, and I'm willing to share it, but you must not reveal it to your children, for if you do, its effectiveness will be lost. Make sure that this page does not fall into their hands.

Ready for the secret? Here it is, wrapped up in just four words: "That is not acceptable."

It may seem too simple, but believe me, those are magic words. I used them on my children throughout their adolescence, and they never failed to work. No losing your temper, no lashing out in frustration at an unruly child, no endless debate about the terms or conditions for correcting the situation. Just four words spoken in a calm but firm voice: That (or this) is not acceptable.

The beauty of the phrase is that there is no possible comeback for the child. There can be no debate about who was doing what to whom, no whining about the unfairness of your instruction, no drawn-out negotiations about alternative behaviors or activities. It cuts out all options for negotiation, and the child knows it.

Now, once you've stopped the conduct that prompted the statement, it may take time to decide on appropriate punishment. But if said in a calm, firm voice – repeated as often as necessary to get the child's full attention – the words never fail to calm the situation.

Say your two children are fighting over something – a toy, the TV remote, the last cookie – and you come into the room. You simply put both hands on your hips, get the attention of both, and announce: This is not acceptable.

They will sputter, "But he. . ." "But she. . ." You maintain the stance and repeat the phrase: This is not acceptable.

Believe me, they will stop the behavior and work it out themselves. They know that there is no comeback you will listen to because: This. Is. Not. Acceptable.

It works just as well – perhaps better – with adolescents. Say your teen comes home from the video store with a very R-rated movie of which he or she knows you do not approve. You know what to expect: "But it's not really that bad." "But there are only a few bad scenes, and I already know that stuff." This is not acceptable. This is not acceptable.

Same for broken curfews, bad driving, messy rooms, poor grades, annoying dinner-table behavior.

I don't want to come off as some kind of behavioral expert here, for I was like everybody else, groping my way through parenting by trial and error.

I just stumbled upon this phrase because I was so dumbfounded at some of the things kids try to get away with that I was afraid of what might come out of my mouth if had said what I really was thinking. It was a neutral way to avoid blowing my stack and to buy time to think about the appropriate reaction. And, as I learned much later, it was far more effective than a full-scale parental meltdown, complete with yelling, threats and table-pounding.

That knowledge came recently as my family was reminiscing over old times and my daughter, now a successful young woman, brought up the four magic words. "I used to hate it when you would say, 'That is not acceptable.' There was just nothing to say back. You couldn't argue, you couldn't try to squirm out of it. You knew the case was closed."

What could be more satisfying to a parent than to hear his children praise his child-rearing methods? Instead of going for counseling to try to work out the neuroses created by their screaming, neurotic parents, your kids could be looking back and laughing with you at the maddeningly pedantic way you dealt with their pranks.

A word of warning. The successful use of this phrase assumes you have established in advance what is and what is not acceptable.

If you haven't done that, then your kids can logically debate you when you use it. After all, it's up to you to set the standards in your home, because you're the parent.

And If you haven't done that, I have some more advice for you: That is not acceptable.

Setting the Stage for the Four Magic Words

Speaking of setting limits on what is and is not acceptable, here is a column I published in the mid '90s, long after our children left the nest. It was our set of standards for our son as he entered adolescence, the rules by which we decided whether something was acceptable or not.

Start of School Good Time to Set Rules and Expectations for Children

The start of a new school year means new beginnings for families with school-age children – new grades, sometimes new schools to get used to, new day-care arrangements, new morning routines to develop, new rules to follow.

The latter is especially important for parents of teenagers, who are going to be testing their wings – and the rules – at a new grade level, with the expectation of new freedom commensurate with their new status.

I remember this period as one of the most challenging for us parents. I was reminded of just how challenging the other day while cleaning out old files. I came across a memo I wrote to our son as his sophomore year was about to begin. Dated Aug. 23, 1988, the memo was a "summary of our expectations. . .for the coming year" to help us "avoid any misunderstandings about rules or conditions. . ."

I felt it necessary to put things in writing because our son had been a rule-tester from sandbox days; if he perceived any loophole in a rule he would take advantage of it instead of first clarifying whether his interpretation was OK. This of course led to . . .lots of groundings in middle school. This being the year he would learn to drive and, he assumed, get his first car, I knew clear understandings were imperative to avoid conflict for the coming school year.

Herewith, 10 rules for sane parenting of teenagers that worked for me:

1. You may apply for your learner's permit at the Christmas break provided there are no infractions of major rules AND your grades are A's and B's. It is impossible to list all of the possibilities, so if there is any doubt about whether something would be big enough to blow this, just say no.

2. After you have your learner's permit, you will need to practice under our supervision before going for your license – not less than six months, and contingent upon responsible conduct at

the wheel, that is, no speeding, traffic tickets, accidents or incidents of unauthorized driving.

3. We will help you get a car when we feel you are mature enough to handle the responsibility and not before. The kind of car will depend on safety, cost and insurability, not your wishes.

4. Weeknight curfew is 11 p.m.; weekend is midnight. One of us will be waiting up for you.

5. You may not spend time alone in the home of a member of the opposite sex without an adult chaperone being present.

6. You must ask permission before making plans to go anywhere. Do not assume ANYTHING is OK. You may not deviate from that plan without calling to ask permission first.

7. You may invite people to our home on short notice unless it interferes with plans already in place.

8. You must show respect for all school authorities and all fellow students.

9. You must keep your room and bathroom picked up and reasonably neat at all times. No pig-pen conditions will be allowed.

10. Expect us to check up on you without prior warning. Don't be surprised or offended when you see one of us wherever you say you are going.

Looking back at this list, it seems like we were really tough parents. But it was the best thing we could have done, for it established our expectations in advance. We had learned the hard way that failure to communicate expectations is the source of most conflict between parents and children.

The good part is, it worked. He knew what was expected, and for the most part lived up to the bargain. We enforced the curfews rigorously and followed through on our threats of surveillance often enough to keep him on his toes. I'm not saying there were no problems, but our family was not in a constant state of conflict as some families are.

Our son conformed to the rules sufficiently to become student body president his senior year, graduate near the top of his class, get admitted to a top-ranked university, earn his degree in four years, and immediately find challenging work. It's coincidental that, one week from tonight – almost 11 years to the day when I wrote that memo – he will make his national debut as a video editor when an hour-long documentary that he edited, *Ice Run: Submarine to the Arctic*, airs on CNN.

A proud parent? You bet. I like to think firm discipline in those crucial teen years had something to do with his success today.

There's a Teen-Ager in the House

*Obviously, I didn't record every highlight of our family life for all the world to read about. For one, they didn't like it when I wrote about them, and two, people would have grown bored reading about mundane daily life. But there were snapshots I felt compelled to share, such as this one when our daughter turned 13. Now I realize it sounds a bit chauvinistic, and it must have embarrassed her in front of her friends. At the time I was oblivious, taken up with my own thoughts and anxious to share them with the world. Sorry, Sara, I couldn't help it. The date: **Nov. 20, 1983**.*

A Father Struggles to Cope as His Little Girl Becomes a Young Lady

The words of "Sunrise, Sunset" from "Fiddler on the Roof" kept floating into his consciousness as he watched her handle the birthday accolades, first at the family party, then the next night with the half-dozen girl-friends invited to the slumber party.

"Is this the little girl I carried?
Is this the little boy at play. . .?
I don't remember growing older,
When did they?"

This beautiful, poised young lady with her silken hair and endearing smile framed captivatingly in the glow of the candlelight? This tall, graceful doe, blushing self-consciously in her new bright-red birthday dress that showed the blossoming figure of a woman where, it seemed like only yesterday, had been the tiny frame of a little girl?

His little girl – a teenager?

He had been dreading this 13th birthday for a long time. If she were getting older, so was he, and already on the other side of 40 he knew this represented a new, uncertain and not especially welcome phase for him. Middle age, for sure. Keenly aware, as was Tevye, of how quickly flow the years, he could count on one hand how many he had left with her under his roof. And that saddened him even as he basked in her happiness.

And he feared that even those precious years might be unhappy ones, marred by the same kind of strife he had seen tear apart once-happy families of so many friends and acquaintances. He was well-read on generation-gap issues – the normalcy of adolescent rebellion, the importance of peer acceptance, the casual attitudes toward sex and drugs, the prevalence of teen pregnancy.

Yet, he told himself, he really shouldn't have to worry. Things had gone pretty well so far. At 13 she had turned out to be just the kind of daughter he wanted her to be. Pretty, of course: big brown eyes with that mysterious Oriental quality that he never could quite explain yet found so entrancing about her; high cheekbones on an angular face; long brown hair curled under at the shoulder; nice, straight teeth (without braces) that you couldn't miss because of her almost perpetual smile.

She would be a tall woman, he knew – at 12 she had overtaken her mother and now was within an inch or two of him. She'll be a model someday, people were always telling him, a prospect which, while not exactly *his* choice of careers for her, secretly made him proud.

She was well-adjusted, a bright student, popular at school, fun to be around. He had never met a teacher of hers who hadn't commented about her cheerful spirit. That's how she had gotten one of her childhood nicknames, "Budgie Bird," after the Australian parakeet known for its pleasant singing and chirping. That fit her perfectly. He had seen that spirit cheer his family through difficult times and remembered the camping trip just the month before when the broken water pump had flooded the camper during preparation of dinner and set the family to snarling at one another in frustration. Her joking and light-hearted view of the soggy situation had everyone laughing within minutes.

She had always looked older than her actual age. At 6 she had looked 8; at 8, she looked 12, and just last week a sales clerk had mistaken her for an 18-year-old. Yet she had never acted like a precocious child-woman. She acted her age – and not, in the accelerated mode of the 1980s' standards, which start pushing children into teen activities at age 10. She was still playing with dolls at 10; she was still climbing trees and hanging from the jungle gym at 11.

Only in the last year had she begun to develop the unmistakable signs of adolescence: Frequent trips to the mall, telephonitis, awareness of popular tunes, much time spent worrying about clothing, fashions and hair styles. Boy-consciousness had not yet made its presence known, if it existed; film- or rock-star worship was not a factor. Val-gal slang was evident in her conversation, but not to the exclusion of normal language. If she said something was "Gaggy!" or "Awesome!" it probably was, and he had a hard time finding more descriptive words than those. And if she rolled her eyes and pleaded, "Spare my life," you couldn't help smile at the satirical exaggeration.

He tried, as Tevye had in "Fiddler," to think of appropriate advice to give her as she embarked upon her teen years. But this time the man with all the answers had none. Oh, he and his wife had tried to prepare her for this milestone ahead of time. They had long since given her the essential information about sex. They had over the years tried to instill in her the Christian values they believed in. They had had long discussions about drug experimentation, premarital sex, VD, peer pressure, selection of friends, self-esteem. She was ready for adolescence, he thought.

But was *he?* That's what troubled him as he watched her tear into the pile of birthday presents. The fear that their relationship would change was weighing heavily on his heart -- and, he knew, on his wife's.

"Don't change!" he wanted to say. "Don't let the trials of the world rob you of your happy smile, your sheer joy for living. Don't lose your ability to make people laugh. Don't let your peers tell you how you should feel or act; follow your own heart.

"And please, don't shut us out of your life. Even though you're going to become more independent and we're going to see less and less of you, don't stop needing us. For you'll always be our little girl."

The Best of Many Family Pets

Our pet menagerie began, as in most households, with gerbils. Herbie Gerbil was set up in a cage in a corner of the family room, complete with a tunnel, treadwheel and comfy nest of wood shavings. He was unimpressive as a pet, and the children soon tired of him. We donated him to the kindergarten class at their school, Bradenton Christian.

Next we tried cats. Each child got a kitten, one a calico and the other a brindle. They were the cutest — that is, until the kittens became cats. There was no space in our home for a litter box for two cats, so of necessity they became outdoor cats. The neighbors weren't happy to see cat pawprints on the hood of their shiny new Mercedes. They were even less happy to see the cats climbing up the screening of their pool cage. Eventually that problem was resolved, but in a not-so-happy way. One cat was hit and killed by a car, and the other simply disappeared. Years later I found the skeleton in a hedge bordering our and the neighbor's property. Whether the husband, who was known to be a hothead, dispatched the cat for climbing on his car or pool cage I'll never know. But I have my suspicions.

Next came birds. First was Ferd the Bird, a parakeet, which we inherited from my in-laws. He was an unusually friendly parakeet, responding to the human voice with what seemed like imitation

*sounds. He provided hours of entertainment for the entire family.
But parakeet lives are short, we learned. One day we went into the
kitchen, where his cage hung over the window seat, to find him
dead. We had a brief funeral in the back yard. A cockatiel followed,
and this was truly a fun pet. Ferd II actually talked. His attempts
to imitate our voices were hilarious, and he stayed with us for quite
a while*

*Then we tried a rabbit. The children had seen nature movies
featuring flop-eared bunnies called lops. So Babette Rabbit joined
our family. I built a cage in the back yard with a tin roof, feeding
trough, and waste collection system. It was the children's job to clean
the cage, dispose of the waste, and walk Babette. Yes, the rabbit was
leash-trained. That lasted only a few months, as the novelty of a pet
rabbit wore thinner with each day of the onerous chore of cleaning
a messy rabbit cage. But it did teach the children about
responsibilities, as we insisted they feed, clean up after and exercise
their pet. Babette eventually found a home with friends who owned
a farm.*

*And then came Maggie, the German Shepherd. The following
column, published in* **March 2001**, *describe our experience with
this loveable pet.*

Sad Farewell to a Faithful Friend

"Dogs' lives are too short. Their only fault, really."
— Agnes Turnbull, The Flowering

The posters of a cute puppy and a snoozing kitten seemed to
mock me as I sat in an exam room of my veterinarian's office,
waiting for the doctor to come in. It seemed like only yesterday
when my dog was like that puppy, so frisky and curious, so
loving and cute it almost broke your heart to go to work in the morning
and leave her in her pen.

Well, my heart sure was breaking now as I waited for the vet to come in. Bringing Maggie to this appointment had been one of the most difficult decisions I'd ever made. But it had to be done. At age 13, she was well beyond the average life expectancy for German Shepherds. Her arthritis and spinal problems made walking difficult and negotiating stairs impossible. She had lost her hearing, cataracts had dimmed her eyesight, and she no longer was much interested in eating. Incontinence was a frequent problem.

I thought back to that first time I spotted Maggie in the litter at the breeder' s home in Largo. In what seemed like a sea of puppies, she instantly stood out – the friskiest, the boldest, the most playful. And the final selling point: she had the pointiest ears of the litter. While the ears of her littermates only perked up now and then, this pup's big, black ears stood straight up all of the time. Which, I thought, was an important quality for a watchdog.

That's primarily what Maggie was being acquired for: Guarding our house. In recent months there had been burglaries up and down our block. And when the teenage son of our friends was tied up and robbed by home invaders just 20 blocks away, we decided it was either an electronic security system or a watchdog. We chose the latter.

I had resisted owning a dog in Florida for years, primarily because of the flea problem. A previous encounter with fleas on cats had convinced me I didn't want to bring a canine flea factory into our home. But fleas seemed somewhat less threatening than burglars, so in the face of a crime wave I relented and agreed to a dog.

But not just any dog. It had to be a smart one. I had had plenty of dumb mutts over the years. And, of course, it had to be a trustworthy watchdog. My wife and I researched the breeds and decided the German Shepherd fit the bill. While fearless in guarding its property, it was among the most-gentle of big dogs, and the most loyal. And it was one of the highest-intelligence breeds rated by the American Kennel Club.

Maggie was everything I had hoped for in a house dog. She was smarter than any dog I had ever encountered. Combined with her high energy level, it made for a challenging get-acquainted period. I had built a small pen out of lattice scraps in a secluded corner of the screened porch as her "den" for housebreaking training. She escaped within an hour – hopped right over a 3-foot-high barrier and began exploring "her" house.

One of the conditions upon which I had agreed to having a dog was that she be well-trained. So at six months, off we went to obedience class. She was a fast learner – finished as class salutatorian – and never tired of me showing off her mastery of verbal and even sign commands: Sit, stay, come, wait and down were the basics, plus an occasional special memory trick or two.

With 90 pounds of muscular German shepherd at the end of a leash, it was also imperative for this dog to walk correctly on leash so I wouldn't have my arm jerked from its socket. Not only did Maggie learn the precise position of staying parallel with my left knee when walking, she became my jogging companion, too. In her early years she was a 10-K dog as I trained for a big race, my faithful running mate from Northwest Bradenton across the Green Bridge and back.

For a dog of Maggie's energy, that wasn't nearly enough., At night there were endless games of fetching tennis balls in the family room. In later years, when she no longer enjoyed chasing balls, she amused us in endless chases of Dog #2 around the family room furniture, a game I dubbed the Canine Grand Prix. The main purpose of getting an auxiliary dog was to keep Maggie young, and it worked marvelously. She wore out the backyard lawn and the family room carpet chasing the puppy, never letting it be forgotten who was the Alpha dog of the family.

Maggie's most rewarding quality, though, was her loyalty. She was like my shadow, going from room to room with me; she followed me around the yard; she slept beside my bed. She instinctively knew what her job was: protecting us and our home. This docile, sweet-tempered dog turned into a ferocious wolf, with fangs bared and back-hair bristling, when strangers approached. One word of assurance from us, though, put her at ease.

It was that loyalty that made it so hard to make the call to the vet and then to go through with it last week. Having been raised on a farm, I was hardened to the coming and going of animal life. It is part of the natural cycle, and there is no place for emotion over an animal's death, even a pet's. I have previously written about my coming-of-age experience of shooting sick cows or worthless calves at my dad's order, around age 14.

But I had never felt this way about an animal before. To me, Maggie wasn't an animal – she was almost human. And for 13 years, she had been my closest friend.

Goodbye, old girl. I know you are doing a great job guarding the Pearly Gates. Have fun chasing tennis balls and chewing on endless rawhide bones until I see you again.

POST SCRIPT

The preceding column produced so much mail that I felt compelled to publish this follow-up, a week later:

I hate to stretch this dog-mourning issue out too much, but the reaction to my last column on the loss of Maggie brought such a reaction I feel compelled to share both my insights and some of the comments from readers who responded. I was overwhelmed by the outpouring of sympathy and empathy from dog lovers all over town and even from out of town who read it on the internet. I never knew there were special sympathy cards for the loss of a pet; I got several beautiful ones.

This brought home anew the amazing power of pets, especially dogs. to tap into the human spirit in a way that brings out the best in all of us. So many people wrote and called to share stories about their beloved pets who, like Maggie. were as loved as human members of the family and in fact, were almost human in intelligence. James Meier told of having a

German Shepherd like Maggie with almost identical health problems and facing the same decision that I had made. "I can't see myself doing this," he wrote, "but I will, though, because I owe it to her. It will be the hardest thing that I have ever done." Like Maggie. his Gallant Bess "is my shadow. Even now when I leave the room she tries to follow. When I leave the house, she sits and stares at the door until I get home..."

Donna Evans wrote of having had the same experience with her English Springer Spaniel, who was 16 when she had to make that difficult decision and said, "1 miss him desperately...." Another who signed only with initials "RR" told of dealing with cancer in his 12-year-old Lab mix, Riggs. He is a dog his wife rescued from the yard of a neighbor, who had chained him to a tree and neglected him. "I'm not looking forward to that trip to the vet," RR wrote.

And to prove how animals, especially dogs, have the ability to unite people across political and cultural barriers, there were a few notes from people who said that, despite sometimes sharp disagreement with the *Herald's* editorials, they could identify with me through my story about Maggie. I was especially touched by one from Gretta and John Holcom, who wrote that, though one never gets over the loss of a dog, "You learn to live with it." And they offered this consolation: "We believe that Maggie is in a happy place romping with our three collies, and if we all prove worthy, then someday we may once again enjoy long walks with those noble creatures."

PREPARING FOR DISASTER

If you live in Florida for any length of time, you become familiar with the drill during Hurricane Season. As the cone of probability bends toward your stretch of the coast, you race to the gas station, Home Depot, ABC Liquors and Publix, not necessarily in that order. By the time you get there, many of the shelves will be bare, picked clean by what I haughtily think of as scaredy-cats, panicking at the first warning of a slight disturbance noted off the Cape Verde Islands half a world away. But now, a few days later, calm, non-panicky people like me (otherwise known as irresponsible slackers) might find a few D-batteries left, or some warped sheets of plywood at the Depot, maybe some dented cans of tuna and beans at the grocery. The ice will all be gone, of course, as will the water. You might or might not be able to fill up the car before the Shell station's tanks run dry. But at least ABC never disappoints. There may be a line, but I've never seen them run out of inventory.

We had several hurricane scares during my 32-year stint at the Bradenton Herald. The first one I wrote about was Hurricane Elena, which was poised to strike Florida's west coast in early September 1985. Here is my account of the preparations for that storm, printed **Sept. 8, 1985.**

Near-Disaster Forces Change in Priorities

Almost from the start we agreed we should take the hurricane seriously. It required a few minutes for all the brain cells to resume functioning after having been jarred from deep slumber by the whoop-whoop of sirens and loudspeakers announcing, "This is a mandatory evacuation. You must leave your homes immediately and seek shelter on higher ground."

Shock, disbelief and confusion were our first reactions to this real-life drama. There was a surreal quality to the event, as if this wasn't really us sitting up in bed being told to get out of our home. "It makes you think of 'Diary of Anne Frank' or Corrie Ten Boom," said my wife as we watched the police car roll by with lights flashing and speakers blaring their orders to get out. It helped to call neighbors to see what they were doing and to confirm that it was happening to them, too.

It seemed silly to leave at that point. The night was calm, and a full moon shone through scattered clouds. We live a good seven miles inland from the Gulf, on a bayou that's only four or five feet deep and perhaps a hundred feet across at its widest. Our house is 12.3 feet above sea level and, being 60 years old, very solidly built. It's stood up to some pretty wicked storms in its time.

Yet there it was: A mandatory evacuation order. The warnings on Channel 10 (the only responsible TV station in the Tampa Bay area during those first frightening hours Friday night), were ominous: Hurricane Elena was headed in our direction. A direct hit at Manatee County was possible, given her unpredictable course. And I had read and seen enough about hurricanes to fear their awesome force and to reject the false sense of security that weather conditions preceding their arrival can generate.

Just two months earlier I had heard Neil Frank, director of the National Hurricane Center, warn at a meeting of Florida editorial writers that nine out of ten hurricane deaths are caused by the storm tidal surge, which sweeps far inland, flattening everything in its path. In the 1935 hurricane that devastated the Florida Keys, 500 died in the unprecedented 18-foot storm surge.

So even though no one came to our door and dragged us out, Anne Frank-like, I told my wife that we should take the order seriously and evacuate. And if we took it seriously enough to evacuate, we also should assume that our house could be damaged. Or even destroyed. So it followed that we should act as if we really *believed* it would hit us, and do everything the hurricane warning booklets tell you to do. She agreed, and we set about our respective tasks, she packing the supplies, I securing the outside of the house, our work made easier by the fact that our two children were visiting relatives in Naples for the weekend.

It was thus that I found myself on a ladder at 3 in the morning trying to nail 4-by-8-foot sheets of wall paneling over doors and windows – in the dark. Elena's timing was fortuitous in one respect: We were remodeling the family room and had just ripped out some old wood paneling. As long as the material was a hand, it made sense to board up the windows and really secure the house against hurricane-force winds, I thought; ours would be the only house on the block really battened down properly.

Ever try nailing a sheet of paneling while holding a flashlight and teetering atop a five-foot step-ladder – at 3 a.m.? Again, the surreal aspect struck me. "Am I really doing this?" I asked myself as I hammered my thumb for the third time. "Better yet, WHY am I doing this? I must be crazy. No hurricane's going to hit us."

But snatches of Neil Frank's warnings and images of Bangladesh kept going through my mind: 500,000 dwellers of coastal slums had been killed in a 1970 typhoon in the Bay of Bengal, and 10,000 had died in the same area just this spring. Frank had told us, "The rich in this country think that if they spend enough money (for their homes) they'll somehow be safe. Nature is no respecter of your economic status." So I kept struggling with the paneling. A short while later, a friend came over to help, and as a two-man operation the job went faster. "But next time," I vowed, "I'll have these boards fitted and ready to drop into place like custom awnings."

Meanwhile, my wife was busy putting together the things we would need to take with us to our evacuation shelter, which we decided would be her parents' vacant condo in Village Green, one of the highest points in Bradenton. She had a suitcase packed with a couple of changes of clothes for each of us and an overnight case with toiletry articles. "Good work, dear," I said.

She had two grocery bags filled with canned food, bread, cookies, cereal and the like. A picnic cooler was packed with milk, lunch meat, cheese, mayonnaise and a few cold drinks. "Excellent, dear," I said as I grabbed the bags to put them in the car. Every water container in the house was filled with water. "Do we really need all of these?" I asked, pointing to the assortment of jugs, pitchers, jars and Tupperwares she indicated I should put in the car. "I thought we were treating this seriously," she said. "If it hits, we might be out of county water for days." She was right, I acknowledged, as I trudged out to the car with the vessels.

"Well, is that about It?" I asked, surveying the house.

"No, the birds," she said, indicating the two cages in which our own pet bird and our in-laws' visiting parakeet were perched.

"The birds!" I bellowed. "We're not worrying about those birds at a time like this!"

"You don't think I'm leaving them, do you?" she responded testily. "They're part of our family. If we think our house might be blown away we're not leaving part of our family behind."

It was the wrong time to pursue the argument. I picked up the cages and added them to the growing mass in the station wagon. Then I noticed two bags she had taken out while I'd been occupied with the windows. One contained family pictures, baby books, albums. The other was stuffed with stuffed animals.

I tried to stay calm. "Dear, why are you worrying about these things at a time like this?" I asked. "What about the TVs and the computer and our furniture and really expensive stuff? Shouldn't we be worrying about that?"

"No," she answered. "Those things can be replaced. They're even insured. We can't replace our family pictures. They have no insurance value. But they're a very important part of us as a family. And the stuffed animals are the ones I had as a little girl, and they were our children's favorites, too. They part of our history. Either you aren't being serious about this hurricane or else you need to rethink what's important to us. Which is it?"

Both, I had to admit. Despite my throbbing thumb due to the boarding-up exercise, I was still mentally seeing the storm on a superficial level – as an abstract presence that wouldn't really hurt me. I had not accepted the fact that this might be the last time I'd ever see this house or its furnishings again. And that had distorted my thinking about what to take along.

On Monday, as I scanned the pictures and stories in area newspapers of Elena's destruction in the beach communities, I came across a picture of a St. Petersburg Beach couple, sifting through the rubble of their home for family pictures, now sodden and ruined by the saltwater. I thought of my mistaken priorities as well as my own hypocrisy about hurricane preparedness. Every year I dutifully editorialize against getting caught unprepared for hurricanes, and warning readers to take them seriously. Yet my own hurricane kit was sadly deficient, lacking such basics as matches, a flashlight, sterno, a mechanical can opener and fresh portable radio batteries.

And my mental attitude was deficient, too. I hadn't really taken Hurricane Elena seriously on that unforgettable Friday night of Aug. 30, 1985. I won't make that same mistake again.

19 YEARS LATER

We dodged a bullet with Elena. Her outer bands brushed the northern Tampa Bay region before a rogue band forced the storm into a northwestward turn, eventually hitting the area around Mobile, Ala., with deadly force.

*By 2004, when Florida experienced a blitz of hurricanes, I was a seasoned veteran of hurricane preparedness. On **September 4, 2004**, as the fourth hurricane in less than three months bore down on the Gulf Coast, I described what it was like to wait for impending disaster. Having missed the full fury of Hurricane Charley by only 50 miles just a few weeks before and having seen first-hand the destruction that Category 4 storm wreaked on towns just to our south, I took this one very seriously.*

The Waiting Is the Toughest

Is this what Death Row feels like?

Waiting for the sound of the executioner's jangling key ring, imagining what the end is going to be like?

Sitting around during a hurricane watch, it sometimes seems that way as we follow the little swirling propeller on the weather maps as it edges closer and closer to home, while forecasters issue dire warnings about the storm's size and strength.

Waiting for disaster to strike can be unnerving. Especially after Charley, with the images of smashed neighborhoods less than an hour's drive from our doorsteps. But here we all are, for the second weekend in the past four, hunkered down in front of the TV sets with our supply of tuna, Spaghetti O's, chips and dip and bottled water, waiting for Frances to decide, perhaps, who will live and who will die, who will have a home tomorrow and who will have rubble, whose lives will move on normally and whose will be turned upside down.

At this stage, the waiting stage, the adrenaline rush of preparing for the storm is past; weariness has set in. The house is secured, the potted plants taken inside, the garbage cans tied down, both cars squeezed into the garage. Inside, the battery powered radios have been located, the flashlights and candles set out, the coolers washed out, the vital documents put into plastic bins. The perishable food in the refrigerator has been cooked and frozen, the bathtub filled with water, the sliding glass doors sandbagged, the soiled laundry washed.

And we wait. We try to get our minds off the storm by watching old movies or reading, but we keep going back to the weather coverage. It's supposed to pass north of here, but what if it turns? We think about our home, splayed open like some we saw in videos from Port Charlotte just in the next county south, and get a sick feeling. We go outside and look at the sky. We check the plywood coverings on the windows. We look at the huge tree in the front yard and try to estimate the distance from its tallest limbs to the house.

We call relatives in other states and assure them everything is fine. We silently pray that it will be. And we wonder whether living in Florida is such a good idea after all. Yes, those blizzards were horrible – the icy roads, the stuck cars, the shoveling of driveways. Now they seemed less ominous. With a well-stocked home, hunkering down for those storms was a piece of cake – a treat, even. Get out the board games, kids. Who wants to do a jigsaw puzzle? Let's watch our family videos. Want to roast marshmallows in the fireplace? Come on, crawl under the comforter with me and snuggle.

It's heresy, of course. Despite such thoughts during stressful times like this, most of us wouldn't trade our Florida lifestyle for the peace of mind of life outside the hurricane zone. We'll get through this storm, this crisis, this hurricane season. The answer to hurricane anxiety isn't a mass exodus to Ohio or Michigan. Rather, it's to get smarter about construction. We learn from each disaster. Many buildings in Charlotte County constructed after Hurricane Andrew stood up well to Charley's Category 4 winds. That's because construction standards were stiffened after 1992. Doubtless Charley has provided more lessons about what works and what doesn't in hurricane protection.

Perhaps one day, when most homes have shatter-proof glass, securely-anchored roof trusses and reinforced walls, we will face hurricane watches with less of a sense of doom. Kids might even look forward to hurricane holidays like they do up North on snow days.

The blunt truth is, we would have to deal with Nature's wrath no matter where we lived. In the West, it's forest fires and earthquakes. In the Midwest, tornadoes and blizzards. In the Southwest, drought and killer heat. In the mountains, landslides, fog and icy roads. Here, the price of paradise is an occasional hurricane. We have no choice but to deal with it.

Please pass the chips.

Conscience of the Community

PART FOUR: MY OTHER FAMILY, BACK HOME IN TEXAS

While I was busy building my new family in Florida, I tried to maintain the bonds to my birth family back in Texas. With a wife and two children to consider, along with a job with a demanding workload and limited financial resources, I wasn't able to return for visits very often, maybe only every four or five years. But I phoned as often as possible and wrote long letters now and then to fill in my parents, brother and two sisters on our lives. They seldom came to visit me, and I can't say that we were close. But then we hadn't been when I was growing up, either. I just never felt that I fit in.

But we were family, and I was quite proud of my family's roots and accomplishments. They had risen from penniless immigrant refugees to respected community leaders in that insular community in just one generation.

Five years into my new family life in Florida, I was jolted back to my roots by a phone call. Here is what I wrote of that call on **Oct. 2, 1983:**

Dealing with the Phone Call You Dread: 'Your Father Is Dying'

The call came about 11 a.m. on a Thursday, as I sat staring at a blank computer screen waiting for an inspiration that might become Friday's editorial. If you're anywhere near middle-aged and your parents are aging, you begin to dread the phone call from back home, bearing bad news. But you expect such a call in the dead of night, when you're sound asleep, not in the middle of your workaday, when your thoughts are on the job at hand. . .

The call was, indeed, bad news. I just had enough time that Thursday morning to dash over to a travel agency for a ticket and home to pack a few clothes. By 1:25 p.m. I was aboard a People's Express puddle-jumper to Tampa International for a Delta connection to Dallas-Fort Worth Airport. By 5:30 that afternoon, instead of sweating off a few pounds at the racquetball court as I had planned that morning, I was standing beside my father's hospital bed in downtown Fort Worth, stomach knotted and tears streaming down my face, praying that he wouldn't die before I had a chance to speak to him once more, to say, "Dad, I love you and I'm sorry I haven't said that in such a long time."

But I could not say it then, because he was not conscious. He breathed with the aid of a respirator and oxygen; a tube ran into his throat; a heart monitor recorded his erratic heartbeat; a jungle of tubes ran from IV bottles into his arms.

The rest of the family was all there, having arrived earlier that day from other parts of Texas. There was nothing for us to do but wait; doctors would not be able to tell more until his condition stabilized. That first day it appeared he had had either a stroke or a heart attack, or both, exacerbated by his long-standing diabetic condition. His condition was critical.

We turned, then, to each other for comfort: two brothers, two sisters and our mother, as we had not for perhaps 25 years. Scattered across the country, living our separate lives with our own individual families, we exchange letters, phone calls, even occasional holiday visits in which we try to cram conversations between reunions, sightseeing, cooking, shopping and the like. It is too often small talk; too seldom real, heart-to-heart talking, listening, sharing.

But that day in St. Joseph Hospital, and in the ensuing days of that week of waiting, we had time to talk, to listen, to hug and to cry. Life-or-death crises, besides upsetting one's secure routine of work-play-sleep and living happily ever after, help to knit the tattered threads of a family's fabric back together, to tear down emotional walls that can build up between grown children and parents, and between brother and sister.

Why they get there I'm not sure. Once we were a complete circle, closed against the outside world, relying upon each other to supply every physical and emotional need. But as the years fly by, and one by one we leave the nest, we grow apart emotionally. We give – and find – our affections elsewhere. But there is no good reason not to maintain the old family bonds, too. I've done a lousy job of that over the years – weeks passing without a phone call; months without a letter. I resolved to do better in the future.

The third day of our vigil brought hope. Dad's vital signs stabilized, his color returned, he could breathe on his own, and awoke for short visits and meals. It had been a stroke, the doctors finally agreed, and though he had some impairment of his right side, there was no paralysis.

He didn't want to talk much at first and had to be helped with his meals. My soul was stirred to its depths and tears once again welled up the first time I held a forkful of food to the mouth of the man who had once cradled me in his arms. It was at the same time a tender act of love and a shared confrontation with his mortality; it was sadness over our switched roles mixed with joy over the fact he was even able to eat!

Other revelations emerged from my Dad's stroke that week. One of the most significant was how your own loved one's need alters your views of the medical profession. I have in recent years become somewhat cynical about the medical technology race and highly critical of medical costs, including doctors' fees. With my father's life hanging in the balance, there was no procedure we would not have authorized, no specialist we would not have consulted, no expense we would have spared to help improve his chances of recovering.

He was, fortunately, adequately covered with Medicare and two supplemental hospitalization policies. But I wondered if we'd have felt the same way if he hadn't had insurance – if he were among the "medically indigent" who must rely upon the charity of others for such superb care. Would we draw a line on medical expenses for him? Or what if the hospital did? You don't want to have to face those questions; I'm glad we didn't have to. I have always supported our own Manatee

Memorial's strong commitment to indigent care; now I really understand why it is so vital to the community.

I was better able to see, during our hospital vigil, why hospital costs are so astronomical. The highly complex electronic equipment, the highly trained doctors (he required three specialists), the labor-intensive personal care (one nurse for every two patients in ICU) all add up. And no one had to tells us that had he not had that care – had he become ill at his small-town rural home instead of while visiting my sister in this city – he probably would not be alive today. Even 10 years ago at this hospital he might not have made it.

As it was, he was well enough within a week to leave intensive care, a sign to me that I could return home to my own family, to the blank computer screen, the leaking roof, the foot-high lawn and all the mundane details of daily life. But returning changed: More conscious of the tenuous grip each person has upon life, more appreciative of the fragile ties that bind families together, and lighter-hearted for having restored those ties.

Especially with my father: to hold his hand, to hug his neck, and just to say, "I love you, Dad." Thank you, Lord, for letting him be with us awhile longer.

Post Script

That column produced one fan letter that I have in my file of memorabilia to this day. I feel it is worth sharing this letter here, for its rich poignancy. But first the background. At this time my wife worked as a reporter at the Manatee bureau of the Sarasota Herald-Tribune, *the chief news competitor of the* Bradenton Herald. *The Manatee Bureau editor was John Hamner, the epitome of the curmudgeonly editor, countless examples of whom I had worked for and with in newsrooms across the country. He intensely disliked the* Bradenton Herald *and its publisher, for good reason. Fifteen years earlier, he had been fired as its Editorial Page Editor.*

Indeed, he had held the very job I now claimed title to and was forced to move back to his home state of Alabama to find work for a few years before he landed the Manatee Bureau position back in Bradenton in the early '70s. His offense: Publishing a cartoon critical of American military troops for the My Lai massacre. I once looked up the offending cartoon. It was mild by today's standards, showing a GI holding a rifle with a bayonet dripping in blood, with the figures of a slain woman and child in the background. That was it. As I inquired further, I was told that the cartoon was merely a convenient pretext for the publisher to get rid of an editorialist whom he considered too liberal.

So sensitive was the subject that in her early days on the job Jo Anne mostly walked on eggs in the H-T office, lest she set Mr. Hamner off on a rant about The Mullet Wrapper, the pejorative term for the Herald in those days. I had never met the man, as fraternizing with the enemy (unless you were married to one of them) was a firing offense. But I greatly admired his writing ability. His Sunday columns were literary treasures, combining wry humor and encyclopedic knowledge of Florida, Manatee County and the South in general to make points about the issue of the day. Putting my Sunday offerings up beside his was humbling. He was a superb wordsmith.

So it was with great surprise one day in the week following publication of the column above that I opened my mail to read the following letter:

Dear David,

Your column this morning brought back some memories, with a startling similarity and a major difference.

On a Thursday morning in late January 1957, I was sitting at my typewriter trying to produce editorials for a future edition of The Herald (I think it was for Sunday) when the phone rang. It was my brother, telling me that our father had died that morning.

I had many of the feelings you described. They'd visited us in December. The last time I saw him he was waving to me as Della

(John's wife) and the kids, and my parents, pulled away from the curb at the front door of The Herald. . .

But when I got to Huntsville the next morning, Mother told me of his last moments.

I was sending them The Herald. *I had written an editorial a few days before about the retirement of a Salvation Army couple here with the same service record as my father's -- who for 40 years was a Methodist preacher. I had, you may imagine, written with some warmth and personal knowledge of a dedicated lifetime.*

Mother said Dad had a good breakfast and she was reading him that editorial (he was debating a cataract operation). She said that when she finished reading it, he said, "We know who he's really writing about, don't we?" She agreed and looked up to see him handing her his pipe. "I think you'd better take this. I think this is it." And with a gesture, as if trying to blow her a kiss, he leaned back on the couch and was gone -- without a grunt or a grimace.

The point is, that while it is nice to tell them, they know anyway. Mine don't have to tell me, though a note my son wrote me for Father's Day just before he was shot and almost killed is one of my most treasured possessions. Your Dad knew, too. Thanks for being the sort of writer who can share such things with his readers.

(Signed) John

Post-Post Script

Turns out John really wasn't a curmudgeon after all; that was just his public façade. Years later we became friends, and I realized that he was one of the warmest, most compassionate men I had ever met. His compliment about my writing gave me a much-needed boost to keep raising the editorial lance to tilt at windmills.

Nine Years Later

My father lasted another nine years, though never fully recovering from his stroke. He was able to shuffle-walk with aid of a walker, and to feed himself if someone cut his food into bite-sized pieces. But he never was the same; he only spoke with difficulty, and some words were slurred. He and Mom built a new house in town, to be closer to the hospital and to doctors. In his last year, it became too difficult for Mom, dealing with her own health issues, to care for him by herself, so he was moved to an assisted-living facility nearby. He suffered a fatal heart attack there in **late June 1992**. *Here is what I wrote following that sad event.*

A Death in the Family – and a Lesson in the Importance of Fatherhood

We're hearing a lot about fatherhood and families these days. They are subjects I feel I have some expertise in as I had good ones – father *and* family.

I learned just how good this past weekend when I buried my father. His death and the family gathering together to mourn his passing brought fresh insights regarding the role of dedicated parents and loving families to the shaping of healthy, well-adjusted children. I had not thought too much of the importance my father played in shaping my life. To be honest, I had probably taken him for granted – as too many of us do about too many of those who love us most.

But as I sat disconsolately during his wake service in my hometown funeral parlor July 3 and 4, listening to family members and friends eulogize him, I experienced moments of insight: My father epitomized what Vice-President Quayle was talking about in the Murphy Brown speech and all the weeks since. My dad was the role model for me and my siblings as we grew up. Without him would I be where I am today? Of course I can't say for sure, but the chances are I would not.

Now this may not seem like a forehead-clapping revelation, but it became so to me as I listened to the tributes and heard stories from his life told and retold. For they showed me a side of my dad I had not known – a side of compassion and concern for others that his stern German demeanor belied, but which has surely rubbed off on me.

There must have been two dozen who mentioned how he made them feel special as children by always having a lemon drop, stick of Juicy Fruit or a quarter – plus a warm greeting – for them when he'd bump into them around town with their parents. And there was somber, taciturn Uncle Ed, seven years younger, who revealed my dad had been his "bestest friend" when they were youngsters growing up in a family of nine children – his confidant and protector.

There was the mentally challenged elderly woman who hobbled forward to say she also considered him her best friend, because he had befriended her and didn't make fun of her like so many others had done over the years.

And there was my cousin Kenny, one year younger than me, who said he always thought my dad was "a notch above the others" because he was responsible for his being able to play football as a freshman. Too young to drive, Kenny had no transportation to twice-a-day practice that year because his parents couldn't spare the time from their dairy operation to drive the 14-mile round trip to school, twice per day. Recalled this cousin, "Uncle Johnny came over and said David (me) had his license and he would come pick me up and take me home if my folks could spare me from milking. And I got to go because of Johnny."

I had long since forgotten that incident, as well as others that recounted by many others among the hundreds who came to pay their respects that weekend. That's when the realization of my pride of sonship really hit me. I was extraordinarily proud to be Johnny Klement's son, and I always had been. Many is the time as I was growing up that an adult asked me, "And who are you, boy?" And I always answered, without apology or hesitation, "I'm Johnny Klement's son," assured that was the only

56

credential I needed for validation as a person, as a member of the community.

And it was. I never encountered a negative response to that announcement, never a snicker of under-the-breath disparagement. Johnny Klement, respected not because he was a man of means or power, was simply a man of integrity, whose character and reputation were without question in the community.

I thought about that in relation to the "character" issue bedeviling so many presidential candidates. It's one controversy Dad would have avoided had he run for office, for he had no hidden past for which to apologize or explain.

And I thought about all of the fatherless boys and young men in south Los Angeles who couldn't relate to a father like mine – indeed, who have no father figure at all, good or bad, in their lives. No wonder they turn to gangs and drugs for their validation as they reach puberty. I have no doubt that, in the same situation, I would turn out much differently than I have.

And it dawned on me, as I pondered all this, how much like him I had wound up, and how without thinking about it I am trying to model the same qualities that Dad had modeled for me. How I have sought to be a father who would never bring shame upon his son, about whom he could proudly say, "I'm David Klement's son."

And I silently, tearfully, prayed, "Thank you, Dad, for being such a wonderful father to me. Now I understand. You gave me everything I needed."

Another Take on Fatherhood

*Jumping forward to **June 17, 2001** – Father's Day, and one of the most significant days of my life.*

Sweetest Word to Stepfather Is 'Dad'

I don't know what I was expecting – perhaps some high-sounding justification for the role that many men fill today. But what I found in the dictionary was mere confirmation of society's stereotype of such men. "Stepfather: a man who occupies one's father's place by marriage to one's mother," said my Random House Dictionary.

As they say on the street, that's cold! But quite accurate, in the literal sense. Hey, you're not my father; you're just the man who married my mother. My *real* father is. . ."

How many men today are feeling that situation, if not hearing those actual words, I wonder? Caught in a lose-lose bind where, no matter how hard they try, they don't quite measure up to the role of father to their stepchildren because. . .you're not my *real* father. They are legion in this country – the surrogate fathers who have stepped into the vacuum left by that *real* dad – the one who walked out on Mom because he found a new sweetheart. The one who felt too tied down by a family and needed his space. The one who found booze and drugs more rewarding than shaping lives of precious children. The one who assures the kids that yes, he really loves them, but. . .

I've known quite a few of those kinds of fathers. And I've known quite a few of the other kind, the stepfathers. Fact is, I am one myself. So when I write about the pain and glory of stepfather-hood, I can truthfully say: Been there, done that.

And it can be painful. The first years are the hardest. When you are desperately trying to fit in, to make them at least like you if not love you. When you want more than anything to hear them, just once, say, "Daddy." To you. Not the other one.

Eventually, you stop trying so hard. You discover that the most you can do is just to be there for them. You can't take his place. You can't make them love you like they love him. You can only hope that, if you hang in there with the kind of unconditional love that every child desperately wants from a parent, they will understand. And perhaps someday accept you as something more than a "stepfather." Perhaps as a good friend, a confidant – someone they can go to no matter what.

For any man reading this who may be in that situation, let me offer this assurance: It can happen. As the children mature and begin to figure out the adult relationships around them, they are able to understand for themselves. They see the difference between words and actions. They weigh their reality against the stereotypes that society puts on role titles.

And then, you may look forward to Father's Day cards like these, plucked from my private treasure chest of memories:

"Dad, so much of what I am today I owe to you. As I was growing up, you created a nurturing environment. . .a perfect balance of guidance and freedom, gentleness and strength, discipline and love. From you I learned the confidence to create goals for myself, the persistence to pursue them, and the understanding to accept disappointments along the way. . .So now, whenever you start telling me that I've made you proud, I hope you remember that much of what I am today is a reflection of all the qualities I learned from you. Love, (Daughter's name)."

Here's one from my son, who recently honored me by inviting me to be the best man at his wedding:

"Dad, If I spend the rest of my life trying, I'd still never have enough chances to tell you how much your love, your guidance, and your trust in me have always meant to me. There will never be enough words to say or enough ways to show how very much I love you, and how proud I am to be able to call you my dad."

And this, a religious one containing a quote from Proverbs 20:7: "The righteous man walks in his integrity; his children are blessed after him." An arrow points to that verse from a handwritten note that says, "That's you!"

No stepfather – or father – could ask for more. Happy Father's Day, stepfathers.

THE PAIN, IT KEEPS ON COMIN'

*I never got involved in public demonstrations, and I didn't often advocate in my personal columns as I did in editorials. But I made an exception on **March 11, 2001**, when I made my birth family's health challenges the focus of a plea for public support of the fight for a deadly disease. The headline said it all:*

Striking a Blow Against Diabetes, the Silent Killer

A t first glance, the woman looks like a normal 65-year-old. A little overweight, but not obese, she is neatly groomed and wears stylish clothes in colors that flatter her. She listens intently to the conversation buzzing around her and smiles pleasantly when addressed.

You wouldn't know until you spoke to her that something is wrong. It will take several seconds for her to respond to a simple question. If she is able to comprehend at all. Chances are it will have to be repeated several times. Her answer will more than likely be one or two syllables; she has difficulty speaking in complete sentences. Occasionally someone will have to wipe the drool off her mouth.

That woman I'm describing is a shell – a medicated, zombie-like version of the person she used to be. Until recent years she was a vivacious leader of her community – a dedicated school teacher, church worker, neighborhood activist, family matriarch and life of the party. If there was a good time to be had, she would be the first to arrive and the last to leave, and she could tell stories all night.

What has brought her to this pitiful state is the silent killer: diabetes. She has been fighting it since age 20, and now after 45 years it is winning. She is virtually blind. She undergoes dialysis three times a week, because of her failing kidneys. She has lost a big toe, and the ugly purple tone of her lower legs betrays the signs of poor circulation that indicate more amputations may be necessary. She shuffles around with a walker only with great difficulty. She needs the constant care of her family, mostly provided by her husband. She is incontinent.

She is my big sister. Over the years of my growing up, Joan was the one member of my family who understood me, who defended me to our parents when I needed a defender. She was the ambitious one, the first-born who paved the way for the rest of us to attend college by stubbornly demanding a chance to go. She became the glamorous career woman with friends in highfalutin' Dallas social circles. She married a wonderful guy who became like a second older brother to me, and they honored me as a skinny high school freshman by asking me to be in their wedding.

I have lived with diabetes most of my life – as a family member, not thankfully as a victim. It began with my dad when we were all still young children at home. This trim, muscular, even-tempered man who worked 15-hour days and was never sick suddenly started gaining weight and becoming quite irritable at times. Tests soon turned up the cause: diabetes. Deficiencies or excesses in his blood sugar level – a new term with which we soon became intimately familiar – affected his metabolism, including the supply of blood to the brain, which caused the mood swings if out of balance.

Soon it became routine for us to watch him prick his finger for a blood-sugar test, then administer himself a shot of insulin in one of his arms. Less routine but often enough to cause constant worry were the middle-of-the-night runs to the emergency room, when my mother would awaken to find him in the middle of an "insulin reaction," unconscious and as stiff as a log because his brain had shut down. When we kids were still small we had to call neighbors to help get him in the car. Later my brother and I could half-carry, half-drag him to the back seat, 911 not yet having arrived in our rural setting.

Finally when I was the oldest at home it fell to me to trundle this 200 pounds of dead weight to the car and race at 100 m.p.h. to the hospital, praying each time that if he pulled through he wouldn't have any permanent brain damage. The last such trip, when I was in college, I still remember the chill I felt when he told us after coming out of the coma,

"I heard the angels singing that time." He lived with diabetes 30 more years after that, progressively deteriorating with diabetes-induced strokes, heart disease and failing eyesight draining most of the quality from his last eight years of life.

Now it is my sister's turn, and I hate seeing what this disease has done to her. I also hate seeing the statistics about how it is increasing, rising by 70 percent among those aged 30 to 49 in the last 10 years – including another family member, my sister's own son-in -law, my nephew by marriage, a 40-year-old father of three who undergoes kidney dialysis while he awaits a transplant. It is especially prevalent among minority groups, with the diabetes death rate in Manatee County for non-whites 62 percent higher than that for whites.

There isn't much I can do for Joan, but I can help others by helping raise funds to promote research that leads to a cure for diabetes. That's why I will be at the Sarasota-Manatee chapter of the Juvenile Diabetes Research Foundation 5k Walk on March 31. I'll be walking for my dad and my sister and my nephew and anyone else whom you would like to designate with a pledge. Let's join together to lick this insidious disease that works so silently and steadily to destroy the human body.

A Personal Loss – and the Tragedy of 9/11

The year 2001 was perhaps the most traumatic of my life, beginning with the death of Maggie, our family dog; two months later my sister Joan and, just two months after that her husband Dick, my much-loved brother-in-law. And then, on Sept. 5, I got a call from my surviving sister, Betty Jean. Mom was dead. I didn't write about her death at the time, for it occurred just six months after the column above was published. There had been too much grief to absorb, too much sorrow to even try to put into words or to seek cause for comfort. And only two days after my return home from the funeral, America went into mourning, for that was 9/11. It took a full year to put the events into perspective. Here is my attempt, published on **Sept. 7, 2002:**

Time Heals Loss of Loved Ones – If You Avoid Regrets

Time, they say, is the great healer. It's demonstrated over and over as families grieving the loss of a loved one gradually move on with their lives. Pain that was so great they were sure they couldn't endure it begins to subside. Widows and widowers begin to date. Often they remarry and start new lives. Children adapt to stepparents, go off to college, marry and start families of their own. The missing one is never forgotten, but the hole in the lives of those they left is slowly filled with other people and concerns. Life, as they say, goes on.

And so it is with Sept. 11. One year ago Wednesday, we as a nation suffered a terrible loss when terrorists used airliners as guided missiles to kill and destroy. We have begun to heal from that loss, but it will take far more than a year to fill the hole left by the events of that day.

The first anniversary has special significance for me personally. One year ago today I buried my mother. She died of natural causes after a long and full life, with family members and medical professionals at her side. While her death was sudden, it was not unexpected; she had suffered from a congenital heart condition for years and needed oxygen to breathe. Yet the news, when it came, was devastating.

I was comforted by the knowledge that she had had a peaceful death, and that we had said goodbye. Only a few weeks before, passing through north Texas for the funeral of a much-loved brother-in-law, I had made the 150-mile round trip to see Mom, who hadn't been up for a long ride into the city for the funeral. Knowing this might well be the last time I saw her, I made a special effort to listen to every one of her stories and to accommodate her every wish. When I left, I gave her an extra-tight and long hug and looked right into her eyes when I said, "Goodbye, Mom, I love you."

On Sept. 11 and in the days following, I thought of that farewell in the context of the 3,000 families who didn't have that chance – the thousands of sons, daughters, husbands, wives, moms, dads and lovers who parted that Tuesday morning without any significant leave-taking –

not knowing it would be their last chance. A lucky few got a second chance in wrenching phone calls from doomed passengers in the hijacked airliners or trapped workers in the World Trade Center, before the towers crumbled. The sudden loss with no chance for goodbyes – that has to hurt more than anything.

My enormous relief at my farewell to Mom was tempered by the knowledge that I had almost missed the chance. For the truth is, I hadn't wanted to go. After the physical ordeal of a hurried cross-country flight and the emotional drain of a funeral, I just wanted to blob with my niece and nephew, reminisce about their parents, and catch my flight home next morning.

But thanks to the urgings of that nephew – the one who had just lost his father and two months before his mother – I got in a car he loaned me and drove 75 miles to say hi to Mom.

Was I happy that I did? Was I grateful to that young man? Do I understand why the survivors of the 9/11 victims haven't begun to "get over it?" You better believe it.

Truth is, as a nation, we haven't begun to get over it, either. Even if we didn't lose a specific loved one on 9/11, we suffered a very real loss. It wasn't so much the "innocence" that people talk about. We haven't had that for a long time. Vietnam, Watergate and Monicagate, among other national traumas, long ago took away a sense of national innocence.

What we lost on 9/11 was our faith in our nation as an impregnable fortress, safe from threats by outside forces with evil intent. We learned of our naked vulnerability to random attacks when suicidal fanatics can choose any target at any time to try to kill and destroy. We saw that our security precautions, even when working perfectly – which they seldom do – aren't enough to thwart holy-war zealots who are willing to die for their beliefs.

Now we must incorporate that loss into our lives and to rebuild around its reality. It's scary knowing that terrorists may strike again, in even more diabolical ways. We can't be complacent about it; each of us must be alert to potential threats. But we can't let that fear paralyze us. Life goes on. And time heals. The important thing is to make the best of it. Don't squander chances to spend time with loved ones and to tell them how much they mean to you.

PART FIVE: WEDDING BELLS – AND GRANDCHILDREN

*We got through the adolescent years of the children, the deaths of both my parents and Jo Anne's, and before we knew it we were empty-nesters. But that wasn't all bad, for it opened the possibility of travel. But it also opened up the possibility of enlarging our family, with a son-in-law and a daughter-in-law and, in time, even grandchildren. It all happened in the late '90s and early 2000s. This one is from **mid-1995**.*

Daughter's Wedding Prompts Reflection

I'm living the *Father of the Bride* story these days. No, not the current sequel – the 1992 remake of the Spencer Tracy classic in which Steve Martin plays a befuddled father trying to cope with his only daughter's impending wedding.

No, I haven't been up in the attic trying to squeeze into a 20-year-old tux humming *What's New, Pussycat?* as Steve Martin did, (although I'm sure I still *could* fit into a tux from my bachelor days – I just never owned one).

But I have found myself in some familiar scenes ever since my only daughter told her mother and me in June that she was planning to get married.

It was exciting news. At 25, Sara is ready for marriage. She is finished with her education, has a real job, and is a mature, responsible young woman. And her intended, Joe, is as fine a young man as a parent could hope to have as a son – or son-in-law.

But a wedding? Gowns! Flowers! Photographers! Videographers! Invitations! Cakes! Wedding consultants! The whole nine yards of wedding whoop-de-do that makes people smile sympathetically and pat you on the shoulder when they hear you say you're having a wedding.

Well, not quite. In our wedding there's no Martin Short as the ditzy wedding consultant bedeviling the father of the bride with ruinously expensive preparations. In fact, Sara is so responsible that she's acting as her own consultant and doing an outstanding job of planning a tasteful formal wedding while staying within a modest budget. Still, the house is filled with wedding talk these days, and I feel extremely useless. For one who has played an integral role in every important family matter, it's an uncomfortable position to be in.

A friend who went through this crisis last summer offered what I trust is sage, if somewhat chauvinistic, advice: "Weddings are strictly for women," he said. "Just ignore all the fuss and let them do their thing. All you have to do is stay calm when you walk her down the aisle. Oh, and keep your checkbook handy."

Which leaves me time to contemplate this mind-boggling aspect of parenting. This wedding ceremony will mean, I think, that our job essentially is complete. When children are ready for marriage they truly are on their own – adults in every sense of the word.

And it is then that you really wonder if you've done everything you could to prepare them. It is then, I suspect, that the parents who haven't made their children's well-being their top priority will have their regrets. If they have deluded themselves with the quality vs. quantity time defense for making their kids just another entry in their day-planners, they may regret the way their kids' lives are turning out.

No parent is without some regrets. We all wish we could go back and relive some of the moments when we've yelled, made unfair decisions, or not listened closely enough. But we hope those times are minimal; that the "parent ledger" that's inside the heads of our children will have far more credits than debits when they're making decisions that will affect the rest of their lives, such as who they marry.

When that time comes, it's too late to assert your parental influence. You can't redeem the lost time, can't relive the wasted opportunities to be a strong, positive influence on their lives.

I still marvel at how the years have flown. And, now that the hectic pace has slowed somewhat, I cherish the thousand and one joys and trials of child-rearing, the bedtime stories, the complicated car-pool schedule, the sometimes-cacophonous school band recitals, the pets not always fed and cleaned up after, the messy rooms, the chore lists, the spring-break camp-outs, the first floor-length dress, the first date, the driving lessons, the teen party chaperoning. . .

Now they're just memories. But *what* memories! As Frank Sinatra so aptly phrased it in one of his classics: Regrets? I've had a few. But then again, too few to mention.

Five Years Later, Another Wedding

So, one wedding down, and one to go. Our son Max told us he was engaged in fall of 1999. We weren't so sure about his choice. His fiancé had been one of our daughter Sara's dorm-mates in college, which meant she was a few years older than him. They had met when we all went to Sara's college, Furman, for Parents Weekend one year, and she needed a date for the big college dance. They had not corresponded for years but reconnected when both found themselves working in Atlanta. And, love blossomed. Here is my take on their wedding, published **Feb. 11, 2001.**

A Moving Event for the Father of the Bridegroom

I am standing in a hidden alcove at the front of the church, waiting for the signal from the minister, and I think of a little boy in shin guards and cleats on a practice field at Jesse P. Miller Elementary School, so shy he wouldn't go onto the field unless his father would help coach his 6-and-under soccer team.

Now I am following the procession of men into the church to the steps of the altar, and I think of a brainy but scatter-brain kid who made it into the State Science Fair competition – but forgot to bring the science project to the bus taking him to the fair.

I am standing at the front of the sanctuary now, watching the bridesmaids in chic silk gowns walk slowly down the aisle, and I think of a rapscallion of a teenager who pushed the envelope on every parental policy and every school rule, suspended from school in eighth grade but elected student body president in 12th.

I catch my breath as the great pipe organ swells into the familiar chords of the "Wedding March" while the sanctuary doors open to reveal a beautiful young woman in an elegant white gown, and I remember a surfer dude with flowing blond hair who had his pick of upper-class women from his freshman year on and think, "He's lucky she picked him."

I stifle a gasp as the bride reaches the altar rail and the handsome groom advances to take her hand and face the minister, both radiating such happiness that you wish you could freeze this moment forever. I think back 12 years, at their chance meeting as teenagers far from home, and how miraculous it is that God has brought these two together today, to become husband and wife.

Now as the minister joins the hands of the bride and groom and asks, "Who gives this woman to be married to this man?", I think of an idealistic young intellectual who was too preoccupied to remember to pick up his cap and gown on university graduation weekend, now embarking on the final step of adulthood.

My reveries are interrupted as the minister begins the recitation of the vows, for my big moment is close. I have had the rings on the little finger of my right hand for the last 20 minutes, and I must fight the panic of "What if I drop them?" while I wait for my cue. Finally, the minister turns to me for the gold bands that will unite my son to this wonderful young woman "till death do you part," and I place first one, then the other, into his hand, and I haven't embarrassed myself or anyone else.

But while all heads are bowed during the blessing of the couple, I grab for the Kleenex in my pocket to deal with the sudden allergy attack that comes over my eyes and nose, way too early for my spring pollen season. I hope nobody notices my eye-daubing and that the video camera is on the minister and bridal couple, not me.

And then the vows are completed, the final prayer of blessing prayed, the minister introduces the beaming couple to the congregation, and I stand in relief and awesome realization that my job is truly done. He is grown up at last.

How the time has flown in the 24 years since I first met him as a winsome 4-year-old, torn between a father who had left and me, a stranger who stood ready to take his place. He was a hurting child of divorce who wanted only for everything to be the way it used to be, unaware that it would never happen. There were several years of heartache in between – for both of us ––– as he sought to assure me I could never be that replacement and I tried just as hard to prove that I could.

Eventually we both figured out that I wasn't a replacement father; I was an additional one, and we built a relationship on that basis. It deepened over the years as he began to trust me, to accept that I would always be there for him and to test my unconditional love in some rather creative ways. And though I was never officially "Dad" to him in personal address terms, I believe I became it in intellectual and emotional ones. I became the soccer coach to get him onto the practice field and the crazed parent dashing back home for the science project, the meanie busting him for driving with only a learner's permit, and the nagger who made sure he changed the oil in his car and, yes, picked up his cap and gown to graduate. Along with his mother every step of the way, of course.

Wonderful memories of a young lifetime that brought us to this joyous day, and now he has rewarded us first by consenting to this formal wedding, in this cathedral-like church, the dream of every parent, and also by inviting me to stand beside him as his best man.

No father could ever be prouder.

And Then Came the Grandchildren

*I had looked forward to becoming a grandparent for quite a while. "Spoil 'em and send 'em back to their parents," I boasted to friends of my intentions once I actually had grandchildren. I dreamed of the special relationships I would develop with my grandchildren, a trusted confidant if they were having difficulties at home, school or the playground: You can confide in Grampa; I'll keep your secret. So I guess I went overboard when the first one arrived on May 20, 1999. I waited until Grandparents Day before putting into print my reaction to this miracle, on **Sept. 12, 1999.***

Grandparents Day Acquires New Meaning for Proud New Grandpa

Today is Grandparents Day, my first as a genuine grandfather. I find I'm as surprised at the mystery of this status as any new father holding his baby for the first time. Grampa David – it's a name I never expected to hear in reference to myself, but here I am after almost four months thoroughly enjoying the role as I begin to grow into it.

It does take some getting used to, I mused the other night as I sat and rocked this darling baby, Emma, to sleep. Dear Emma, I thought, why is it so pleasurable to just sit here and look at you? Why have eight otherwise intelligent adults – your parents, grandparents and great-grandparents – suddenly gone ga-ga over your every twitch and sound? Why do the hearts of every adult who sees you melt like butter at your rosy cheeks, lush head of black hair and bright hazel eyes staring out in wonderment?

A lot of it is those eyes, I guess, so inquisitive, so full of wonder at the strange new world before you, mesmerized by ceiling fans and dangling Big Bird rattles, yet so piercing when looking into my eyes that sometimes I feel as if you are looking into my soul and may find me unworthy of the task of grandfather-hood.

And part of it is your miniature perfection, so soft and endearing that we just can't get enough of you. The dimple of your right cheek, of course, is adorable, as is the arched left eyebrow, just like Great-Grandpa's. But until you came along I had no idea that babies also had dimples on their knuckles, elbows and wrists – well at least you do, and they are, as your Uncle Max used to say when he was only a little older than you, "Too cute to talk about" (his interpretation of some adult's expression 'Too cute for words.")

We keep remarking, your Nana Jo and I, at the miracle of your birth and your development – at how you, now almost 15 pounds and 17 inches of waving, kicking, cooing and crying humanity, could just 16 weeks ago have been inside your mother's body, like a caterpillar in a cocoon waiting to emerge as a butterfly. Of course, 14 years and eight months from now we'll probably still be making stupid observations like that as you get ready for your first date. But humor us, will you, kid? This is what grandparents do.

Dear Emma, I have to admit that I am fighting my '90s work ethic impulses to do something else but just sit here and rock you. I feel like I should be doing something "productive" – reading a periodical, making notes, doing a home-repair project, drilling the puppy on her obedience lessons – something. But even as I think such thoughts I realize that's part of what's wrong with the world today. Too few of us are willing or content to just sit and focus on a child to the exclusion of everything else. We delude ourselves that brief snatches of "quality time" will make up for the lack of much quantity in the time we spend with children like you. And look at how many of them are turning out, growing up as aimless adolescents unable to make commitments because they never knew unconditional love.

I feel you're going to be good for me, Emma, in forcing me to just sit here and spend time with you. (I've already learned the hard way that you require the full attention of your rocker-person to hold the pacifier, rock at the right pace, hum lullabies and stroke your arms and shoulders, to make the proper exit into slumber.) Sitting here like this, watching your eyelids droop lower and feeling the steady rhythm of the rocker, puts a new perspective on the rat race most of us run every day. Now, here, I am forced to slow down and smell not the roses but the baby, which in your case is a warm, heavenly fragrance of soap, powder and sweet-breathed innocence.

As I sit here and look at your pink-cheeked health, your precious pink-flowered nightie and your cozy nursery, I can't help thinking about other babies being rocked to sleep in far less comfortable circumstances. I think of all the wailing, traumatized babies I've seen in TV news footage from the world's conflict points: Kosovo, Iraq, Kuwait, Somalia, Bosnia, Rwanda. I think of the hauntingly thin babies I've seen on trips to Mexico, Puerto Rico, Honduras, even the migrant worker camps of rural Manatee County.

You are truly blessed, Emma, in so many ways that we seldom think about. Just the fact that you had excellent prenatal care gives you a big head start over most babies in the world. Then to have two devoted parents, two sets of grandparents and a huge network of uncles, aunts and cousins backing them up assures you that you will never fall through the cracks. I will never let it happen, I promise you that.

What will you grow up to be, Emma? A doctor, like your Grandpa Bob? A professor, like your Great Grandpa Patterson? Perhaps a senator or governor, even a president? (You have the genes for the latter from your great-great Grandfather Rosales in Honduras, by the way.) You can be any of those, you know, if you want. You have been born into the most prosperous period of the world's most prosperous nation, and no one stands in your way to the heights of any career field. But you can also choose motherhood, as your mother, grandmothers and great-grandmother have, and I will be proud and happy. I am thinking ahead 25 years, when I hold your beautiful daughter and once again marvel at the miracle of birth and the fascination of a newborn baby.

I hope I will be as fascinated with being a GREAT-grandfather as I am at being a grandfather.

One Year Later

*Emma was the only grandchild for three years. So naturally I kept writing about her, and probably went overboard at times. But I kept gaining new insights about children, the way they learn and grow, and about generational passages, one coming of age as the previous one succumbs to age. The latter was me, I began to realize, and I wanted to slow down in order to savor life as it was lived by a child. Herewith, my tribute to Emma as she turned 1, published on **June 18, 2000**.*

Discovering the Purest Love: Grandparent and Grandchild

One year old! It seems impossible that it has already been a year since Emma joined our family and redefined my concept of grandparenthood, life and love. This human dumpling who seemed as fragile as an orchid blossom 12 months ago is now walking, making her first word-association sounds and asserting her will on all around her – especially pliable grandparents who are suckers for smiles and who melt at jutting lower lips and teardrops.

I introduced Emma to readers in this space not long after she was born. The reaction to her introduction last summer was so gratifying I thought an update might be of interest at this milestone.

Emma has come quite a way in her first year: She has more than doubled her birth weight, to a bit over 20 pounds, and measures about 22 inches, close to a foot taller than when she arrived. Almost two feet tall in one year! Surely if the ranks of brain surgeon, concert pianist or rocket scientist are all oversubscribed in 20 years, she can always fall back on the

Women's National Basketball Association for a few years to build a nest-egg.

Emma still has her melt-a-heart-of-granite smile, now made more winsome by her habit of scrunching up her nose as she grins, as if to subtly say that she's sharing this special look just with you. That nicely shows off the two little bottom and matching top teeth that have sprung up in the last month, which she has learned to put to good use at chow time.

And she eats prodigious amounts, showing no signs of food-pickiness. I'm still amazed at how quickly she progressed from milk to formula to regular food. She now feeds herself – only with her fingers so far. And her generous side is already showing as she offers to share a bit of food or a Cheerio with her grampa.

Having completed the transition from rolling to crawling to drunken-sailor toddling in only a couple of months, she has become a confident explorer of every corner of the house. We're wishing she'd stayed in the sitting-up stage a big longer, as someone must now follow her everywhere to be sure she isn't going outside to hitchhike.

Though an accomplished walker, she is also content to sit in laps for long periods, mouthing her "binkie" and staring out at the world around her. Staring is her specialty – she drinks in everything with her eyes without any visible reaction. That can be disconcerting when it's your eyes into which she's staring, as if she is trying to read your mind. What if she can tell what I'm thinking?

Now we are waiting for the next big advance, talking. That, I think, will be the ultimate treat for a grandparent who can sit for an hour or two listening to the rich fantasies of a child's mind but avoid the wearing down of all-day exposure to baby-talk that Mom and Dad face. A side benefit of being a grandparent: You can walk away when you get tired.

Emma is anything but shy. At her christening a few months ago, she was undaunted by a church full of people watching her every move. She almost lost it when the water was sprinkled on her head, but when that part was over she seemed to revel in the spotlight as the minister walked the full length of the church, holding her high for all to ohh and aah over. This is cool, she seemed to say; let's take another lap.

I am reminded in thinking back over the past year how after each advance I couldn't wait for the next stage of her development. First it was to get her to focus her eyes on me, then to hold her head up, then to sit up, then to crawl and then to walk. And always when a new phase began I sort of wished the old one could have lasted a little longer, for I knew it was gone forever. Doubtless I will be feeling this way for the next 20 years.

Kids grow up too fast, darn it, and the hectic pace we all keep makes us all the more oblivious to the process – to our eventual dismay. I remember marveling at how fast the years flew by as our own children were growing up and wishing I had taken more time to enjoy the precious moments of their childhood. Oh, I tried. I was there for all their games, concerts, plays and so forth. I sweated over the science project and homework, driving lessons and SATs. And all of a sudden it was over. They were out of the nest and flying on their own.

Now it begins again with Emma. And despite my best intentions to slow it down, to savor the day-to-day times when she just sits in my lap and turns the pages in her books, I am often torn by guilt that I am not doing enough. I get wrapped up in my affairs and before I know it a week has passed since I've seen her. And that means I've missed some priceless moments with her, time when I should have been strengthening our bonds. I'm grateful that she at least knows who I am and gives me a fair share of lap-time.

I'm learning that grandparenting is a very special relationship, much different than parent-child. Cultural anthropologist Margaret Mead said it exists partly because grandparents and grandchildren are "united against a common enemy – the parents – (as) partners in crime" – the "crime" of pure love, without the psychological baggage created by discipline, anger or other unresolved conflicts that are almost inevitable in any parent-child relationship.

In her book "Another Country," psychologist Mary Pipher puts it more benignly than Mead: "Parents have the job of socializing children and of raising them to be emotionally sturdy, responsible and independent people. Grandparents mostly have the job of loving children for who they are at the moment." It is, she says, the purest relationship humans have.

Well, I accept the job enthusiastically – and vow to do better in Emma's second year than in the first. What makes it more relevant this time around is that at age 60 I understand that life has limits, that, as Pipher put it, "we all get a finite number of harvest moons, sunsets and walks by the sea." So I want to make each one count.

As soon as Emma starts talking, I'll begin to tell her all of this. And hope that the feeling is mutual.

TWO YEARS LATER

*Of course I couldn't stop writing about my granddaughter. As seen in this column published in **June 2001**, I continued to be fascinated by watching her grow and develop new skills. And current events kept offering hooks on which to hang new insights about child development, as demonstrated by Emma.*

Terrible Twos: A Terrific Time for Discovery

I never went through the Terrible Twos with my kids. Because they were 7 and 4 when I came on the scene, I avoided what is supposed to be one of the most difficult phases for parents as their sweet, adorable baby turns into a stubborn, independent-minded tyrant.

Twenty-five years later, I'm having my chance. Granddaughter Emma hit the Big 02 last week. So far, I'm wondering, "What's the big deal?" So far, I would call this the Terrific Twos. In the space of the last three months or so, Emma has changed from a helpless, single-syllable, babbling baby into a talking, thinking person. She now speaks in sentences expressing complex ideas and using multi-syllable words. Already she can count to 6, and she can say the ABC's to at least "P." She still likes to walk on her toes instead of the soles of her feet, and she loves to play dress-up in old hats, scarves and jewelry.

And she has grown! She's now 26 inches tall and weighs 36 pounds. I still have my sights on the Women's NBA in 20 years.

Her Nana and I are amazed at her progress on our visits week to week. It was only a short while ago that a request for a drink would be simply, "Juice." Now it is, "Nana, I need some juice . . .pease (please)." The other day, listening to a tape of '50s classic rock-and-roll songs while riding in the car, she exclaimed with a grin, "This is fun, Nana." Carrying a bin of plastic toys that is half her size from bedroom to living room, she stopped and said in the most pitiful voice, "This is too hard, Depa (grandpa)." Walking into a fast-food restaurant, she informs, "I like French fries."

How does she know such concepts? How did she learn "fun" and "need" and "hard" and "like?" How does she associate subjects with verbs? More ominously, how is it she already knows most of the characters from "Sesame Street" by sight? And her favorite, Elmo, just by seeing the printed name?

By observation, of course. By paying attention to the world around her and mimicking it. If she hears adults around her, "Pass the milk, please," she soon learns the words as well as the concept. When she sees an Elmo video come out of a case with the word "Elmo and Friends" on the back, she learns to associate that image and word with the name of her cartoon friend.

It has been awesome to see over the past year what sponges for knowledge little children are. Watching Emma's progress has shown me how crucial parental influence is in the development of a child. Of course, I knew that, both from my experience as a parent and even as a child. But to see the process of development, of becoming a person, on the fresh slate of a new baby, especially a first grandchild who lives close by – it is a renewing and joyful experience.

And a cautionary one. I do not want to be the one from whom she learns poor grammar. Or negative attitudes. Or four-letter words. Far be it from me to be her inspiration for "I can't" or "She's ugly" or "He's not as good as me." Oh, she'll hear such things soon enough, but because her parents have tried to establish a positive, affirming atmosphere in their home, she will grow up with solid, positive values. The 2-year-old who learns "hard" and "please" will also learn "love" and "share" and "help."

Of course, this experience has also been all too illustrative of the reverse side of the coin: The children who grow up in homes filled with fighting, profanity, substance abuse, hate and violence. What are they learning? Exactly what they see around them. Do we wonder why we have such troubled kids in the public schools? It's because they come from troubled homes. Of course, *their* parents probably also came from troubled homes, so we are repeating a cycle that expands exponentially.

President Bush campaigned on a theme of "No child left behind." But we're deluding ourselves if we think many children growing up in such home environments won't be left behind. Somehow, we have to find ways to break the cycle of violent behavior in the home, to train adults how to be supportive, positive parents.

One of my biggest joys is to watch Emma play with her mother's old Fisher-Price toys, carefully saved all these years by her Nana for just this purpose. Watching Emma create scenes with the doll house and accessories, it is almost like being taken back in time 25 years. A sensitive, very bright little girl who likes sparkly jewelry and French fries plays with the little wooden figures while the adults talk. A family member comments on something that seems outlandish, and I exclaim, "No way!" From the corner I hear a tiny echo: "No way!"

Playing – and listening. A 2-year-old sponge for knowledge is learning lots these days. And so are we.

THREE YEARS LATER

As long as Emma kept growing and providing new insights on child development, I felt I needed to share those insights with my readers. So naturally, on her third birthday, I had plenty of new insights to share. This is from **September 22, 2002** *– a little after her third birthday.*

Granddaughter at 3: Curious, Precocious, and Full of Giggles

The things you notice taking a walk with a 3-year-old:

- The tiny flowers on scraggly weeds
- The shiny oyster shells in driveways paved with shell
- The holes that gophers make in lawns
- The way schedules go by the board.

Indeed, taking a walk with a 3-year-old, you are likely to literally stop and smell the roses if there are any roses along your route. Being only about two feet tall, a 3-year-old notices lots more stuff on or near the ground than an adult does. With a natural curiosity and not yet a captive of schedules, a 3-year-old has an entirely different concept of time than a harried grandpa does.

Yes, the 3-year-old is my granddaughter, Emma – 3 going on 8, I tell friends. The past 12 months have been an amazing year of growth and discovery for Emma. She has developed from a shy toddler into a precocious little girl with strongly held views on many subjects and very discriminating tastes in clothes and accessories. Elmo is no longer one of the most important people in her life. Madeline, the little French girl, and Angelina Ballerina, the dancing mouse, have taken the fuzzy little red monster's place in recent months.

In fact, most of the classic nursery story heroines are now on Emma's radar screen – Cinderella, Sleeping Beauty, Snow White and Goldilocks, among others. She has gone through a princess phase, having spent a good deal of the past year in various princess costumes, complete with flowing diaphanous gowns, jeweled tiaras and glittery slippers. Not just playing at home, either – she likes to wear those outfits in public.

The 2's were difficult at times, but not terrible – at least for me. Emma asserted her independence in a number of ways. Hugs and kisses were no longer automatic – they were given when *she* felt like giving them. I learned not to assume anything about a 2-year-old's preferences or moods. Best to ask first. For example, a highlight of my bonding time occurred one day when I was permitted to take her to lunch at McDonald's, on my own. We did fine on the drive to the store and in ordering our food: cheeseburger, fries and shake. Of course, I assumed she needed help with her food, so I proceeded to unwrap her burger and to tear open the paper sleeve holding her fries so she could get at them. As she watched me do that, her face clouded over and she literally turned her back to me, without a word. I felt the entire lunchtime crowd was looking at this old guy pleading with a sullen little girl facing the back of the booth to turn around and talk to him.

Later I learned I should have *asked* if she wanted help with her food, as she liked it done a certain way.

The 2's were a rich learning experience for Emma. She already has one year of "school" under her belt – two mornings a week of nursery school to help with socialization and structured activity. She can count to 10 and recognizes some letters and the sounds they represent. She is taking ballet classes – from the same teacher her mother studied under 16 years ago.

Most astounding to my wife and me is her vocabulary. Emma constructs complex sentences with lots of multi-syllabic words, precisely pronounced. We marvel at her grasp of complex ideas and situations. How did she learn that, we wonder? But as I noted in last year's report when Emma turned 2, children are sponges and observers. They absorb knowledge and imitate adult behavior. They copy what they see and hear.

Emma loves to draw and paint. While her works are abstract in content they are precisely arranged and intricately detailed with color selection and multiple media: Crayons, pens, markers, glitter tubes and stickers.

On the reading front, during the year she has graduated from the simple picture book phase to more complex stories that hold her interest for considerable periods. One of my greatest pleasures is to snuggle into the couch with her and read "Cinderella" or "Snow White" all the way through and to know that she gets it.

And now Emma has a new status: Big Sister. Baby brother Matthew was born at the end of March, giving her a living toy to play with. And some competition. No longer are all eyes on Emma; now she shares the spotlight with her brother. It has taken some adjustments for her to deal with the new family dynamics and for the adults to take care not to overlook her in ga-gaing over the new baby.

What I love most about Emma – even more than slow, interesting walks or cozy story times – is hearing her giggle. She does it often – when she feels like being silly, when you tickle her, when she's bobbing in the surf at the beach, or sometimes when she just feels happy. There is something about the sweetness and innocence of a child's giggle that is irresistible, a pure sound that melts sadness and relieves stress.

Sometimes, watching the news, I think that what the world needs is more giggling children. I wonder what would happen if someone made a tape of children's giggles and sneaked it into a high-level diplomatic setting, say the U.N. Security Council, and played it. I like to think there'd be less talk of war and more of caring for needy children who have little in their lives to make them giggle.

FOUR YEARS LATER

Just one more grandchild column, I promise. This one heralded the arrival of my son's first child, who was Grandchild No. 3. Since he lived in Atlanta, I saw him rarely and thus was not able to gush over him as I did for Emma, and probably my readers had tired of *it by then. Which I acknowledged up front: Don't expect me to keep doing this. But I felt the need to share some of the experience of being a grandparent – and my reaction to the awareness that I was getting older. Of course, I'd give anything to be that age now – all of 63, when this piece was published on **June 8, 2003**.*

Third Grandchild Offers New Insights to Proud Grandpa

Four years old!
One year old!
One week old!
Now what?

When I began sharing my insights about being a first-time grandfather four years ago, it didn't occur to me that I might have a problem if other grandchildren came along. As any parent knows, the shock and awe of the first child tends to diminish in direct proportion to the repetition of the event.

After all, how many ways can you ooh and aah about your grandkids without becoming boring? Now, that is my problem. In the space of a few weeks, I have celebrated the fourth birthday of grandchild No. 1, Emma; the first birthday of Grandchild No. 2, Matthew, and the birth of Grandchild No. 3, Connor.

So now I must try to do for three in the space formerly reserved for one. Which, now that I think of it, is not a bad metaphor for becoming a repeat grandparent. At the first you think your joy could not possible be greater or your heart fuller. I recall my wife saying, "When we had only Emma, we thought we could never love a child as much as we loved her."

Then with the arrival of the second you find you *can* – that this precious new life is an entirely different person, with a different personality and whole new set of charms. Matthew, a blue-eyed redhead with a single dimple, smiles easily and readily opens his arms for long lap-time. Compared to his bubbly, chatty older sister, he has been a quiet, studious baby, silently observing his universe. I take that as a sign that he will be a writer, like his grampa. In fact, even at 1 he is holding a crayon and pencil to "write" – in a code I am still trying to decipher.

And now, there's grandchild No. 3. You wonder that your horizon was so limited before, for of course there is room in your heart for another baby, another unique creation of God who stares into your eyes with a look of wonder and fascination. I am reminded, while holding Connor for the first time, just how sweet is the breath of a newborn and how soft the feel of its pink skin against your cheek. He, too, is a quiet one, only rarely voicing his feelings of hunger above the level of a coo. Another writer, perhaps?

The birth of this new grandchild reminds me of the ever-changing pattern of life as I age. Each new grandchild in a sense represents a claim against my own mortality, for they will someday supplant me even as I did for my parents and grandparents. Indeed, my children are taking their place in the world, well-embarked on careers, established in homes and taking on volunteer roles formerly held by my generation. In one year, Emma will start kindergarten, and Matthew will do part-time nursery school this fall.

Time marches on. I am aware that the nuclear family of four that existed under my roof 10 years ago has, with marriages and births, now increased to nine. But in that same span the nuclear family of my birth has been reduced by half, to three.

I am learning that new grandchildren also mean new family dynamics. A pair of almost newlyweds is now a family of three, with new interests and new priorities. That means expectations to be revised, family rules about holiday visits and vacations to be renegotiated. It dawns on me that, when they speak of going "home" now, they're speaking of *their* houses, not ours.

It's neat being a grandparent, but it's not easy, I've learned after four years. Sure, you get to spoil them, but you've also got to learn to be a kid again – to pretend you're a chicken, if that's the game Emma has invented, or to endlessly retrieve objects thrown on the floor by a toddler practicing his hand-eye coordination. And babysitting, while very rewarding, can be tiring to a 60-something.

But for the new parents, there is a steep learning curve, too: Round-the-clock feedings and changings, unrequited crying episodes, sleep deprivation, work schedules, day care issues – the whole package of responsibilities that comes with parenthood. I look forward to seeing my parent-testing son assume that role. Early indications are that he's going to do just fine. The kid who I had to yell at and threaten loss of major privileges to get the garbage taken out or the lawn mowed has become a domestic wonder. He dotes on his wife as much as his new son. He not only takes out the garbage without being told, he cooks meals, washes the dishes and mops the floor. He has transformed their fixer-upper house into a cozy nest. His favorite weekend haunt is no longer the beach; it's Home Depot.

Would I trade places if I could? Yes. No. How wonderful it would be to start over with a new baby, to have another chance at writing a better book on this human blank slate that a baby represents. But then I remember the hard work of parenthood – the stresses and heartaches and disappointments.

And I think no, it's their turn. Being a grandparent, especially a serial one, suits me just fine.

CHAPTER TWO
MATTERS OF FAITH

I *was 37, a life-long bachelor who never thought he would find a soulmate, when I met Jo Anne. I had a brief engagement in my early 20s, but we broke it off by mutual agreement when we both realized we weren't ready to settle down. Lucky for both of us that we did, because not long afterward I headed to the big city of Detroit to find my fortune and Sue joined the Navy. But that's another story.*

The author at age 40 | Courtesy Bradenton Herald

I wanted to get married, but I just never found the right person, someone to whom I was both physically and intellectually attracted. For a long time I carried the stereotypical fantasy in my head: Married to a beautiful woman with dark hair, living in a cottage with a white picket fence, with two adorable children, a boy and a girl, playing in a shady back yard.

I was a fallen-away Catholic at that point, and Jo Anne was a professed atheist. But because of the gentle but persistent prodding of relatives and friends, we separately found ourselves at a non-denominational prayer meeting at Sacred Heart, a Catholic church near downtown Bradenton. I went because my brother Jerry had personally asked me to go — "as a favor to me." Not that I felt I owed him any favors, for we had never been all that close. We rarely called one another, and certainly not in the middle of a workday.

But there he was, calling me in mid-morning of a weekday about two years after I left Detroit and took up small-town journalism at the Bradenton Herald, *"just checking to see how you're doing." As a matter of fact I was not doing well, not well at all. In fact, I was seriously considering leaving the profession I loved so much, just to get out of the situation in which I found myself. I was the paper's City Editor at the time, and it was the most thankless, frustrating job I had ever held, even tougher than being Night City Editor at the* Detroit Free Press, *a paper at least 30 times bigger in circulation than* The Herald. *That's because I was solely responsible for all local news content, and I lacked the resources to cover all the bases. The authorized staff was maybe 12, but a couple of reporters had recently left, and management had been slow in advertising for replacements, let alone actually hiring any. Trying to fill seven days' worth of news-hole on a five-day work week was frustrating – and exhausting. Later I told people that I felt like the Jews in Exodus 5, 6-14, held in bondage and forced by Pharaoh to make more bricks while being given less straw and clay.*

I told Jerry how things were and told him that Steve, a reporter friend, had been pestering me to go to a Thursday night prayer meeting at Sacred Heart. But I really didn't want to go. That's when he pleaded, "Do it for me." So, I said OK.

I went – and liked the experience. There was a quite professional musical quartet, with a couple of soloists leading the singing of praise songs in between sessions of communal prayer. I found the weight of my unpleasant job slipping away and began to feel happy for the first time in a long time. I continued to go with Steve on Thursday nights, and my faith deepened with each evening's experience.

But I was not yet ready to go all-in for this Jesus business. Despite my unhappy work situation, I had an active social life. I had invitations to go out to dinner with friends almost every night if I wanted to. I closed the bars many a night – and was up at 5 a.m. to put out the next day's paper. I partied hearty even as I continued to attend the prayer meetings and go to church on Sundays. I renewed my belief in God, but as a Protestant, not a Catholic.

I was in that state of one foot in church and one foot in hedonism when I had my conversion experience. Sound asleep in my bachelor apartment, I was awakened in the middle of the night by pounding on my door and a loud voice demanding, "Let me in! Let me in!"

I sleepily arose, went to the front door and looked out. There was no one in sight, no drunken idiot who couldn't find his own apartment pounding on random doors to be let in. The parking lot was deathly quiet – as it should have been at 3 a.m.

So who pounded on my door? Then the thought struck me: What if the voice I heard was the Lord, asking me to let Him into my life? Staggered by the thought, I went back to my bedroom, fell to my knees, and prayed. "Yes, Lord, I'll let you into my life," I said between sobs. "I'll stop my carousing and go all in as a Christian. I'll change."

Meanwhile, Jo Anne, as a recently divorced mother of two young children, was anxious to meet new people, especially of the adult male gender, and confided as much to her friend Maureen, the mother of her kids' best friends – and who just happened to be the wife of my friend Steve. Jo Anne didn't want to hang out in bars, she confided to Maureen, so how was she supposed to meet decent guys?

"Come to our Thursday night prayer meeting," Maureen urged. "I understand Steve has a guy he works with named David who attends, and he's single. We'll introduce you." To this day Jo Anne tells the story: "There was just something about that name, David. I liked the way it sounded. So, I got a sitter for Thursday night and went with Maureen."

So she went to church to meet guys. *Not because she felt a spiritual void in her life, or was deeply depressed, as I had been. She wanted to meet "this guy named David."*

And meet we did. Not that night; she first checked me out to be sure I wasn't a loser. We introduced ourselves to one another a few weeks later at a beach cookout for singles from the church I had been attending the last couple of months. She stood out from so many of the other single and divorced women in the group: tall, slender, beautiful, with shoulder-length dark hair and a lovely smile. When I found out she was a journalist to boot, I became much more interested.

So, we began dating as we continued to attend the prayer group and not long after, we both joined the non-denominational, charismatic Church of the Cross, of which many of the prayer group attendees were members. We grew closer to God together and closer to one another at the same time. About three months in, we made a commitment to become "born-again Christians" by accepting Christ as our Savior and the Holy Spirit as our spiritual resource.

We dated for 15 months before I asked her to marry me. How I got to that point is a story in itself. I had been agonizing about the decision, unsure of whether I was ready to take on not just a wife but two small children in the bargain. I was making peanuts at the time – a bit over half of my salary at the Free Press, so wide is the wage gap between North and South – and wasn't sure I could support a family. So I prayed about it, every day, asking God for a sign that this would be the right move. One evening in June, as we were preparing dinner in her kitchen, which we did almost every night during our courtship, I "heard" a distinct voice in my head say: "Now is the time to ask her to marry you."

The voice of God, again. I believe that to this day. It was so clear, so out of my thought process, that it could be nothing else. It was the second and last time I heard God speak to me audibly; it hasn't happened again in that form for 43 years. So, just as in the middle-of-the-night encounter in my bedroom, I said OK, Lord, I will do it. But not right then. I made a date to have dinner the following Saturday night at what was then the Pier Restaurant, now Pier 22, on the Manatee River in downtown Bradenton. And there, in a booth in what is now the bar, I popped the question. I can't remember her reaction at this point, whether it was shock, or tears, or merely calm acknowledgement of what she had heard. What I do remember is that she said yes.

We delayed our wedding until fall, and the reason we did that is another story. She was working as a part-time temp at the Manatee Bureau of the Sarasota Herald Tribune, *the* Herald's *arch-enemy competitor, reporting to the man who had previously been fired from the job I held. (See Chapter One for more on that point.) At the time she was waiting to learn if she would be promoted to a full-time reporter's position that had recently opened up, a salary bump that we would need to make ends meet. We were sure that if her boss knew his employee was going to marry his nemesis at the competition, she would never get the promotion. So, we waited — and waited. Finally, by August we agreed that we couldn't wait any longer. Wedding plans had to be made, attendants had to be invited, at least one house had to be sold, and on and on with the logistics of combining two households into one. So, in our second act of stepping out in faith, the first being accepting the Lord in the first place, we agreed: "We just have to trust the Lord that I will get the promotion."*

So we went public with the news of our engagement and set the date for Oct. 14. A few weeks before the wedding, after the news was out, Jo Anne got the promotion. We said a prayer of thanksgiving.

And thus it came to be that, within two years of making my commitment to become a committed Christian, not one in name only, I had realized my long-held fantasy: A wife, two adorable children, living in a vine-covered cottage with a white picket fence (which I built with my own hands). That is the background of my faith, the context for the columns related to faith that I published from time to time. I didn't wear my faith on my sleeve; it was rare when I made reference to my faith, or to matters of faith in general. I was quite aware I wasn't working for a religious publication. And that the Bradenton Herald *had readers of many faiths besides Christian. But at times, matters of faith intersected with public policy, and I simply had to speak out. The best example is the column that follows, written sometime **during the 2000 presidential*** *campaign (Bush vs. Gore); I don't have the exact date. Reading it today, I am struck by how similar the political atmosphere in the Trump era is to that of 20 years ago, differing only in degree. Today social media has heightened the problem by quantum degrees. But it was bad enough in 2000.*

Terrorists Among Us Hate in the Name of God

There are terrorists among us – perhaps sitting next to you in the church pew, with hands raised, praising the Lord.

You won't recognize them by their clothing or ethnic features – they look nothing like Osama bin Laden or Muhammad Sadiq Howaida, the suspected mastermind and bomb-maker, respectively, of the bombing of the U.S. Embassies in Nairobi, Kenya, and Dar es Salaam, Tanzania. They look like ordinary Americans because they are – as ordinary-looking as Timothy McVeigh or Terry Nichols.

Unlike those two terrorists, who are now in prison for the Oklahoma City Federal Building bombing, the terrorists you might encounter in church or the grocery store haven't yet acted on their hate-driven impulses. They lack an organization, a leader, who will turn their hate into an assassination, an exploding package or, God forbid, a truck bomb.

I hear from these would-be terrorists often, usually after a terrorist incident like the bombing of an abortion clinic or an act of violence against the government by a militia group.

"Too bad they didn't kill more of them," is the common message from these callers, who inevitably refuse to give their names and hang up before you can get in too many words.

The most recent such call came from a woman who wanted to share her views on the U.S. missile attack on terrorist facilities in Afghanistan and Sudan in retaliation for the embassy bombings.

"We blew up our own embassies," she announced. "It was done by the CIA and FBI to make it look like Islamists, but it was our own government."

"But why would we want to blow up our own people?" I asked incredulously.

"It's the Jews," she replied. "They are behind it to make the Arabs look bad and to gain more power for themselves."

President Clinton, she declared, is but a tool of the international Jewish conspiracy. After all, Secretary of Defense William Cohen and Secretary of State Madeleine Albright are Jewish, so Clinton is merely following their orders, instead of the other way around.

I would have left it there, thanked her for expressing her opinion, and rung off, if she hadn't added a statement that made my blood boil.

"I wish they'd have bombed the White House. We have to do something about Clinton and the Jews."

"What?" I bellowed into the phone. "I can't believe you would say that about your own country. You're as bad as them (terrorists) – you're no better than Timothy McVeigh."

"Oh, I'm a Christian," she assured me.

"Oh, no, you're not!" I shot back, anger rising in my voice.

"Yes, I am," she answered confidently. "I'm a born-again Christian, and when the Rapture comes, I'll be among the first ones to be raised up to heaven, and the greedy Jews will still be down here killing people off."

I probably should have left it there, realizing this poor woman was so propagandized by some splinter white-supremacy sect that she had no concept of the Christian tenets her rantings were violating.

But I didn't; I couldn't let her blasphemy of my religion go unchallenged.

"Oh, no you won't!" I fairly shouted into the phone. "Come the Rapture (the belief that at the second coming of Christ the faithful will be raised up bodily into heaven) you'll be so far down they won't be able to dig you up. What nationality do you think Jesus was?"

"Jewish," she admitted. "But he. . ."

"A Jew!" I interrupted. "Jesus himself was a Jew. And what teachings did he give us about Jews and Christians (meaning Gentiles in New Testament vernacular?)"

"But he. . ." she began.

"And what did he say about love for one another? What about First Corinthians 13 (the "Love Chapter" in the Bible)? How can you hate Jews so much and call yourself a born-again Christian?"

She stood her ground, arguing about Christian superiority over the Jewish faith, until I finally slammed down the phone in disgust.

And promptly felt miserable for how I had acted. I certainly wasn't practicing what I believe, to say nothing of following our company's customer-service policies, and my heated argument hadn't changed her mind one iota about our country, terrorists or Jews.

But as I have thought about it over the last week, I believe I did the right thing. It is important, I believe, to confront evil in strong terms and call it by its name. Terrorism is evil. Wishing harm on our president and other leaders of government is evil. Blaming Jews for the world's problems is evil. Surely, we learned that from the Holocaust, didn't we?

So, I didn't change this poor woman's mind. But I didn't sit there and pretend that political or religious ends justify the means of terrorism or genocide. Maybe I planted a seed of doubt in this true believer's insular world of intolerance. At least I tried.

Maybe one day she'll even drop into my church, where the common bonds between Jews and Christians are celebrated, not condemned, and hear the truth expounded – but hopefully in a more loving way.

LATER THAT YEAR

During summer 2019, as I watched cable news talking heads discussing Republicans' refusal to condemn President Trump's racist comments about four Democratic congresswomen who have criticized his administration's policies, the feelings expressed above came rushing back. Many of those Republican politicians profess to be evangelical Christians, but few have spoken up to denounce this or dozens of other racist, homophobic, misogynist and downright pornographic comments Trump has made in rallies and in his ever-active Twitter feed, not to mention his thousands of lies. They echo the sentiment of the majority of evangelical Christians across the country, according to reliable polling data. They rationalize their abandonment of the most basic teachings of the Christian faith by the support Trump professes for their position on such social issues as abortion, public prayer and gay rights, as well as on traditional conservative issues like environmental regulation, tariffs and taxation. We went through the same thing 20 years ago, and I felt compelled to follow up on the message expressed above with the following column, published during the primary season of 2000.

'Becoming a Christian' – It's More Than Words

Suddenly it has become very *in* to be a Christian. Candidates in the presidential primaries are outdoing one other to be the most public professor of faith. And in good timing with the political buzz, no less an ex-political persona than Jane Fonda is reported to have had a religious experience that has made her a Christian.

The buzz causes many to wonder: What does it mean to "become a Christian" in the born-again context? It's a question that a lot of people who think of themselves as members of the Christian faith ask – people who were born into Christian homes, baptized as children and raised in Christian-denominations' traditions and beliefs?

So what's with this "I'm a Christian" business, which always seems to carry a holier-than-thou connotation when revealed in public – especially by politicians.

I attempt to answer this question with great trepidation, for I know it is an emotional minefield. Anything I say will likely be misunderstood or misinterpreted by some. But with so many presidential wanna'-be's draping themselves with the Christian mantle, it's relevant to ask – and try to answer – the question: What does it mean?

When someone says to me they have "become a Christian," I interpret that to mean he or she has come to know the Lord in a personal way. It is a knowledge that goes beyond memorized doctrinal principles, scripted prayers and prescribed rituals. It is an intensely personal relationship – no third-party authority figure oversees it. It is, simply, a commitment to God. A comparable commitment in public life would be a marriage ceremony. One faces another persona and solemnly pledges love and faithfulness to that person "til death do we part." So one does with Jesus in the private heart ceremony by which one "becomes a Christian."

My experience in 25 years as a Christian is that that generally occurs during a time of personal crisis. People have reached the end of their ability to handle a certain situation, whether it is addiction, bankruptcy, health crises, marital problems, depression or whatever. In desperation, they cry out for help from a higher power.

During war they call such crises "foxhole conversions," as soldiers facing the possibility of death make deals with God. But truly becoming a Christian means more than making a quickie bargain with the Lord. It means changing one's lifestyle to conform to the model of the namesake, Christ. It means not just talking the talk but walking the walk as well.

Once you've made your decision, no one is going to be checking up on you. No one is going to grade your degree of success as a Christian. As I said, this is an extremely personal relationship. It's between you and the Lord.

Now, if one is a public figure and is making public statements about his Christianity, one risks having his faith graded by others. After all, Jesus said, "By their fruit you shall know them."

Thus, one can reasonably wonder whether George W. Bush truly "gets it" when he peppers his conversation with four-letter words, as he did in a revealing interview with *Talk* magazine recently. One wonders how Al Gore reconciles some of his campaign rhetoric with his professed Christian beliefs. Or, for that matter, whether Jane Fonda will renounce the hedonistic values she has epitomized for many years.

But again, this isn't our deal – it's theirs – theirs and the Lord's. Sure, when it comes to the voting booth we may make a judgment on a self-professed Christian candidate's sincerity. That's the risk a candidate takes in wearing his religion on his sleeve.

But in the end, this Christian business is what's in your heart. If you want to make that a public issue, it's OK. But you'd better be sure what's there is genuine.

20 YEARS EARLIER

*Faith didn't exactly fit in with the column I wrote during the 1980 presidential campaign, but prayer did. It was, as were the first three columns in this book, inspired by my stepson Max, then age 7. It was published on **Nov. 2, 1980**, as America prepared to vote in a three-way race between incumbent Jimmy Carter, Republican Ronald Reagan and Independent John Anderson.*

Need Help Picking a Candidate? Try Asking a Child

" ...And please, help Reagan to be president, so he can make bombs. Amen."

The prayer of a 7-year-old can tell you more about campaign perceptions than a month's worth of David Broder (veteran *Washington Post* columnist) columns or Harris Surveys. How our son got the idea that Ronald Reagan "likes to make bombs" I don't know. He does not read newspapers or magazines, not even the editorials of the *Bradenton Herald*. He does not watch television news; reruns of *Happy Days* are the preferred show at 6:30 p.m.

Yet there he was, in his earnest little-boy prayer, with the clear idea that Reagan would be more likely to get the country into a war. That's appealing to our son not because he's a warmonger but because he likes the sounds firecrackers make and thinks of bombs as big firecrackers, knowing nothing of the destruction they produce in the process.

Well then, he was asked after explaining the closing line of his prayer, what do you think of Jimmy Carter?

"I think he thinks Russia is sort of like a snake," was the dead-serious reply.

A snake? Why?

"Because if you don't bother a snake it won't bother you."

Perceptions – just a little boy's perceptions of issues and people he is too young to understand. Yet when translated into an adult context they are quite accurate in reflecting the adult view of the candidates' posture – at least the view of many adults.

Perceptions – perceptions of John Anderson as loser, of Reagan as simple-minded, of Carter as gentleman-turned gut-fighter. How do people get 'em? From the candidates' opponents. From TV commercials packaged by professional image-builders. From the polls. From talking to each other.

And from the press. We get our perceptions from listening to the candidates, from examining their records, and from watching the polls.

Perceptions are what each of us will take with us into the polls Tuesday. Perceptions are about all we have to guide us in our decision-making process, for we can't know for sure how a candidate will serve if elected. Certainly, the last four years under Jimmy Carter are proof of that. We thought we knew him in 1976; we perceived him as being a forceful, dynamic leader who would guide America to new heights of greatness.

Our perceptions were wrong, of course – as well they may be this year toward Reagan, Anderson, or any other candidate for state or local office. Even with the revised perception of Carter as weak, indecisive and even mean, many people will vote for him because they perceive Reagan to be worse.

Perceptions are also colored by individual experience and preference. Like our son praying for Reagan to win because he likes the bang from fireworks. Some will vote for Reagan because they like the "bang" from his promised tax cut, without thinking of the fiscal destruction that might accompany it. Some will vote for Carter because they like the federal programs he stands for, without thinking of who will pay for them.

I've been called a pragmatist, one who worries about the practicality of ideas and plans. So I'll vote for Anderson because I perceive him to be more pragmatic about America's problems, more willing to make the hard decisions that are going to have to be made to restore economic order to this country.

Strange as my son's perception of Reagan is, it's at least as valid as some adults with tunnel vision. Like the letter last week from the Citizens' Crusade, which sought to espouse the "Cocaine Connection" of President Carter. Among the evidence cited: That two White House aides rent a townhouse in Georgetown, an upper-class Washington neighborhood which allegedly has a high incidence of cocaine use. And Miss Lillian once visited Studio 54 in New York.

If presumably mature adults can perceive Carter as a coke addict from that, I'll take the 7-year-old's word. He's at least as well-informed.

Faith and the Waging of War

The country was extremely divided when the U.S. invaded Iraq on March 20, 2003, in response to President Bush's assertions that Saddam Hussein was able and willing to use weapons of mass destruction to punish America for its invasion of Afghanistan over that country's role in 9/11. We learned after the fact that the so-called evidence of WMD was highly exaggerated if not entirely fabricated, making the stated purpose of the war bogus. But at the time there was an intense debate about the justification for invading a sovereign country. I decided to weigh in on it from a Christian perspective, inspired by a sermon I heard in church shortly after the invasion. Since Pastor Mark Alt is responsible for the meat of this piece, I give him full credit for the inspiration. The date was around the end of March, 2003.

When's It Right to Go to War? Check the Bible

Everybody has an opinion about the war in Iraq. They range from people marching in the streets in opposition, to those so supportive they would repeal the First Amendment to stifle criticism of the president.

Somewhere in the middle are many people like me, totally agreeing with the need to remove Saddam Hussein but worried about the long-term consequences of President Bush's decision to pre-emptively attack a sovereign nation. And all of us are heartsick at the loss of life among our fighting men and women as well as among the Iraqi people.

It thus was a welcome intellectual exercise last Sunday when Pastor Mark Alt led the congregation of which I am a member, Palma Sola Bay Baptist Church, in considering the vexing question: When is it right to fight a war? The answers he provided, of course, are from a Christian perspective. But given the fact that our nation's foundations are based on universally accepted Judeo-Christian principles, I believe that almost anyone could find them relevant in the war debate.

The first point, Alt emphasized, is that the Bible provides guidelines for communication with people and nations. Citing Psalm 122: 6-8, Matthew 5:9 and Colossians 4: 5-6, he noted these are instructions "always to speak with grace. . .always to seek peace and pray for peace." Today we would label that concept diplomacy -- which, many would argue, Bush diligently pursued for months until the United Nations Security Council refused to honor its own resolutions for political reasons.

Next, Alt tried to answer the question: Does the Bible condone pacifism? Some cite the Sixth Commandment as forbidding war in the statement, "Thou shalt not kill." But, said the pastor, a more accurate version of the commandment is: "Thou shalt not *murder*." "Murder is not the same as killing someone in battle," he said. "War authorized by legal government authority is not the same as murder."

In Luke 3:10-14, when various groups, including soldiers, ask Jesus, "And what shall we do" to be saved, he didn't tell them to lay down their weapons, Alt pointed out. Revelation 19: 11-13 portrays Jesus as returning as a warrior on a white horse who "in righteousness judges and makes war." Romans 12: 18 instructs people, "if it is possible, to live peaceably with all men" – emphasis on if, said Alt. And from the Old Testament the well-known verse from Ecclesiastes Chapter 3 says that sometimes it is proper to fight: "To everything there is a season," the chapter begins, working its way to Verse 8 with ". . .A time of war and a time of peace."

Next Alt cited the writings of St. Augustine, the fifth-century scholar who wrestled with these questions and came up with the concept of a "just war" doctrine. That doctrine, often cited by modern-day secular leaders in debates about war, holds that there are four standards for a war to be just:

- It must be approved by proper authority.
- It must be for a just cause.
- There must be a reasonable chance of success.
- The military response must be proportionate; that is, no decimating a weak enemy.

Those conditions are present in this war, he suggested. Applying the principles to Scripture, Alt cited three justifications for going to war:

- To punish evil. In Chapter 32 of Numbers, God berates two Hebrew tribes for failing to join the rest in destroying the evil nation of Midian, where child sacrifice was practiced. Does anyone doubt that Saddam qualifies as evil?
- To liberate the innocent. Proverbs 24: 11-12 begins, "Deliver those who are drawn toward death." Could anyone argue that the oppressed Iraqi people don't qualify for "deliverance"?
- To bring peace and order to society. "God gives power to government authority to bring peace and order to society," Alt said, citing Romans 12: 1-5, which instructs that we are to "be subject to the governing authorities, for there is no authority except from God."

Drawing these principles into the current conflict, Alt reviewed Bush's stated goals for this war: to free the people of Iraq from Saddam's cruel reign, to bring peace and prosperity to Iraq as well as to the rest of the world by preventing his use of weapons of mass destruction.

What is the bottom line for Christians? First, he said, pray for our national leaders, the troops in the battlefield, and the enemy, too. Second, seek peace and pursue it in all dealings with our fellow humans. That would preclude ugly confrontations between opposing sides on the war.

And finally, he cited Psalm 20: 7, which states, "Some trust in chariots and some in horses; but we will remember the name of the Lord our God." While it is fine to rely on America's sophisticated military machines to beat the Iraqis, "Victory will not happen apart from God," Alt warned. "Make your own peace with God, through Jesus."

I left church feeling much better about the moral justification for the war. Perhaps others who share my ambivalence will find these answers comforting as well.

TWENTY-TWO YEARS EARLIER

Regarding the words above, in hindsight we know that the war failed to meet at least two of President Bush's goals: Bringing peace and prosperity to Iraq and bringing peace to the world at large. And because the war was based on the false premise that Saddam had WMD, it also failed to meet Scripture's requirement that it be for a "just cause." Lying about evidence of WMD negates the "just-cause" clause, in my opinion.

*Changing focus, I'd like to go back to my early days as an editorialist and a Christian by recalling one of my most moving experiences up to that point in my life. Always willing to learn about other cultures, I jumped at the invitation by my church's prison ministry team to join them on a visit to a state prison in Avon Park, a small city about 50 miles east of Bradenton. A bit longer than my typical columns, this one was published **on May 24, 1981**.*

Prison Revival Rebuilds Lives from the Human Scrap Heap

AVON PARK, FLA. – John "Big Moose" Curry looks the part he played most of his life, right down to his nickname. A great, barrel-chested hulk with arms and legs as big as tree trunks and a belly that could hold a side of beef, he was a minor hoodlum in New Jersey -Pennsylvania labor unions, a tough guy who "learned how to hate" from the frequent beatings his father gave him as a child.

On a Florida visit on Christmas Day 1976, high on booze and pills and crazed with fear that his ex-wife would no longer allow him to see their son, he pulled out a gun and shot her and her boyfriend to death. Today he is serving three to 15 years for manslaughter at Avon Park Correctional Institution here.

But Big Moose Curry is no longer the hate-filled, violent man he once was. Having joined the small community of born-again Christians in this prison, he is a gentle, peace-loving man who has taken or is taking three college courses and 11 Bible courses, has served as president of the prison's Jaycee chapter and who is allowed to go to area schools to talk sense to today's confused kids.

A man to whom a gun "was a way of life" now has as his main goals in life 1. To serve God; 2. To make a decent life for his son; and 3. To try to "make my Mom's last few years on earth happy."

Moose is the best example I saw on a recent visit to this state prison of the way the born-again experience can turn vicious, hardened criminals into role models for society. It may, in fact, be the most effective form of criminal rehabilitation that this crime-plagued nation could hope for.

Though I would have accepted that concept on my own faith, I could not have been so convicted of its truth had I not seen the evidence for myself. Here, inside the high chain-link fence of Avon Park Correctional Institution, I saw the healing power of God's love free the human spirit that hate and bitterness had kept shackled in the souls of inmates – the hate that had landed most of them here in the first place. Though the state said their bodies must stay behind that steel fence for 7, 10, 20 or 30 more years, their spirit was free to begin a new life as a newly-reborn Christian.

I went into this prison with Abe Brown Prison Crusade. Brown, a Tampa high school dean and former Florida A & M football coach, takes his crusade to a Florida prison nearly every weekend. Witnessing one day of it was perhaps the most emotional experience of my life. To be locked up, if only for a day or two, is a frightening, demeaning thing. Even though I knew I was not confined – that I could, in fact, have walked through the gate any time I wished – I felt what must be a natural human revulsion against captivity.

And I could not help but empathize with the 1,200 inmates who could not leave at day's end, who faced year after year of the stupefying monotony of prison life. I shudder to think of standing in a line of blue-uniformed men three times a day to eat, of limiting my personal space to a two-foot-long wooden shelf and metal cot surrounded by 39 others, of waiting without real hope for a letter, a visitor, a parole.

Preconceived notions about criminals and justice tend to undergo drastic changes under such circumstances. Whatever you think about the laws, the courts or the prisons, make no mistake about one thing: Prison is no picnic. Locking a man up is a terrible thing to do. Even under the best of conditions – and the "old unit" of Avon Park is considered a country-club prison by the inmates – it is a depressing, lonely, violent place to live.

Country club? I thought it more resembled a World War II concentration camp with its fences and ancient wooden barracks, uniforms and rules. But because the "old unit" is a minimum-security section, there are no cells. Prisoners have relative freedom to move within the prison grounds and sleep in barracks. Some are permitted to go outside the prison for daytime jobs. Compared to the hell-holes of Raiford or Starke, where many of the inmates here came from, Avon Park must, indeed, seem like a country club.

But it is not without its hazards. "It's a battle for survival here every day," said Moose. "A guy with a grudge can pick up a lead pipe or a piece of wood and jump you any time." And, he adds, "Anything you can get on the outside you can get in here," including drugs, knives and guns.

"Prison is a jungle – it messes up your mind, it makes you sick," adds "Preacher" John Bouldree. "Only the joy of the Lord can keep our spirit up in here."

Bouldree, a backslid minister before his incarceration, was first in line on death row in 1972 for killing his wife and father-in-law when the U.S. Supreme Court ruled capital punishment unconstitutional.

Alive today by what he considers a miracle, Bouldree is able to accept the crushing burden of 23 more years in prison (he will be 80 before he is eligible for parole) with hope and joy, not bitterness and despair. "The love of God keeps me from being bitter," he said. "He has the master key to my life. If He can open the doors of Death Row, why should I worry about these little gates here?" Bouldree wants to be free, of course, but until he is, "I'm here to help any way I can to do the Lord's work."

Though the state could not officially acknowledge its efficacy, "regeneration" (the code word here for being born again) produces precisely the effect that prisons strive without much success to achieve while spending jillions of dollars for walls, guards, steel bars and alarms. Evangelists like Abe Brown are able in a weekend to do more to change men's lives than years of incarceration have.

And why not? Being rehabilitated by state standards requires accepting the blame for one's crimes, asking for mercy, making amends if possible, and proving by subsequent behavior one can follow society's rules.

Regeneration is a similar process: Acknowledging one's sins, repenting, and accepting Christ as master over one's life. The Bible says, and Christians believe, that is sufficient to merit forgiveness, provided the confession is sincere.

Few prisoners get rehabilitated through the regular prison channels. According to Chaplain Warren B. Wall, the recidivism rate for the prison population as a whole runs from 60 to 75 percent. For the born-again prisoners, however, the rate is about 1 or 2 percent.

Rev. Wall, a Southern Baptist minister with 19 years in prison ministry, 13 of them at Avon Park, has more trust in God's rehabilitative powers than the state's.

"My experience is that the factor that has made a difference in men's lives is that they have found the Lord. The big word here is rehabilitation. But it's not the most effective. Regeneration is."

Regeneration: It seems so apt a word to describe what happens in the born-again experience here, where new, productive lives emerge from the human scrap heap collected in prison.

To rehabilitate a criminal, "you must change a man's attitude, his outlook," said Rev. Wall. "And most of the time that comes through Jesus Christ. Before a person can get his act together he has to want to. Most don't. They're mad at the judge, their lawyer, the sheriff, their wife. They don't realize it's their fault – that they are adults and have to change themselves. Accepting the Lord also causes them to accept the blame for their actions. And that's the first step in rehabilitation."

Rev. Wall welcomes evangelism teams like Abe Brown's because they are able to get the message to many more men than he can reach. With only one assistant helping him minister to 1,200 inmates in the two units of Avon Park, he admits that he generally spends more time *ad*ministering than ministering.

"We feel that if we had enough of us (chaplains) to go around, we could touch so many more of them. As it is, we can touch only the hem of the garment. And most don't care. Look at the turnout," he says, gesturing toward the small knots of inmates gathered before a flatbed truck on which Abe Brown is preaching.

Though all regular prison activities have been suspended for the crusade, perhaps 90 to 100 men have stayed through the musical program to hear Brown's message, out of 700 in this section of the prison. And many of these are already Christians, so it seems a disappointingly small audience.

Yet, when Brown gets to the altar call, pleading for the unsaved to signify their willingness to repent and turn over their lives to Christ by raising their hands, nine hands go up. Nine men who have tried everything else are ready to try God. Nine men have started on the road to rehabilitation. (Before the weekend is over, 37 men in both sections of the prison will have made that decision.)

It was an emotional experience.

A DIFFERENT KIND OF REVIVAL

Fourteen years later, I again went on the road with a faith-based group. But this was an entirely different kind of revival. It was the peak year of the Promise Keepers movement. This was a movement founded in 1990 by Bill McCartney, head football coach at the University of Colorado Boulder. It was described by its founder as "a Christ-centered organization dedicated to introducing men to Jesus Christ as their Savior and Lord, helping them to grow as Christians."

As it turned out, the 1990s became the Decade of the Men. Many, especially women, considered it a kneejerk reaction to the women's rights movement of the '60s and '70s, when women fought for equal rights much as blacks had done in the '50s and '60s. But in my opinion, it was not an angry campaign by male supremacists seeking to maintain their dominance in the social hierarchy. It was a genuine grass-roots movement to get men to shape up and accept their responsibilities as husbands and fathers, through a commitment to Christ.

It was energized by the Million Man March, which was a secular crusade launched by Nation of Islam leader Louis Farrakhan for black men to "declare their right to justice to atone for their failure as men and to accept responsibility as the family head." At the crusade's signature rally, on Oct. 16, 1995, more than one million African American men descended on the National Mall in Washington, D.C. to "convey to the world a vastly different picture of the black male" and to unite in self-help and self-defense against economic and social ills plaguing the African American community.

*Almost exactly two years later, on Oct. 4, 1997, Promise Keepers' Stand in the Gap: A Sacred Assembly of Men open-air gathering at the same National Mall drew a crowd between 600,000 and 800,000. But the two groups were not in competition; rather, they complemented one another, as the goal of each was to motivate men to shape up and fulfill their role in society. At the rally I attended at the then-named ThunderDome in St. Petersburg (which four years later would become the home of the Tampa Bay Devil Rays Major League Baseball Team), white, brown and black men created, as I put it, "a mosaic of diversity that sociologists only dream about." Here's my column on that experience, published **Aug. 13, 1995.***

Promise Keepers: A Revival That Could Rebuild American Society

Two feature stories and an editorial in *the Herald's* local section in recent weeks, then a news story atop the front page Aug. 5. Big spreads with color photos in the St. Pete and Tampa papers. A 14-mile traffic jam on I-275 Aug. 4. All because a group of men were heading to the ThunderDome for an event that had nothing to do with sports, tools or tractor pulls.

By now, many newspaper readers are no doubt wondering: What is this Promise Keepers business all about, anyway?

Having read the group's seminal book *Seven Promises of a Promise Keeper* and having sat on the hard plastic seats of the ThunderDome for all 16 hours of the Promise Keepers Tampa Bay-area conference last weekend, I am prepared to tell you precisely what Promise Keepers is all about. It is, fundamentally, a Christian religious revival. Of the 13 hours of actual scheduled conference sessions (lunch and dinner breaks excluded), I estimate one third of the time was devoted to formal presentations and two thirds to songs, praise and prayer. You know you have "been to church" when you leave a Promise Keepers conference.

But it is also a concert, a course in personal development, a father-son bonding marathon, a marriage seminar, an emotional journey out of race- and class-based comfort zones into the lives of other men, and a junk-food bonanza where fat-content labels don't count. In other words, a regular guy-fest, only without drum-beating iron men in loincloths hunkered over campfires in the woods.

T-shirts with slogans plastered all over them are very popular at Promise Keepers, only they don't say things like Party 'Til You Drop" or "S---Happens" or even cruder four-letter words you have to shield your kids' eyes from at typical stadium events. Here the T-shirts say things like "Bent-Knee Society," "Life Is Short . . .Pray Hard" and "Real Men Love Jesus."

They toss beach balls around the stands during lulls at Promise Keepers, just like at regular stadium events, and they do the wave even without a team on the field to pump up. There are no co-eds body-surfing down the stands on fans' hands, but there are chants that threaten to blow the dome off the Dome. The most popular one heard last weekend was, "We love Jesus, yes we do. We love Jesus, how about you?"

As I said, it is a religious revival, with long and frequent prayers, lots of hymn-singing, sermons, and two altar calls. There are no punches pulled here; they want you to experience salvation first and foremost. If that is not your cup of tea, then you might not be thrilled at attending Promise Keepers' conferences. On the other hand, you will have missed out on some things rarely experienced in the fast-paced, sophisticated society of the '90s. Such as the awesome sound of a 50,000-voice men's choir singing *Amazing Grace* a capella. Or the awesome sight of 50,000 men being served lunch in 24 minutes, with no pushing or complaining and zero litter when the meal is over. Here you see a sea of hands raised in tribute – not to a grungy rock star but to God. And here a 15-minute ovation of such thunderous dimensions that the ThunderDome literally became its name – in honor of overworked, underappreciated pastors, many of whom were brought to tears by the demonstration.

Here's one you surely can't imagine unless you were there: White and black and brown men bear-hugging, tears streaming down their cheeks, burying ancient prejudices and forming a mosaic of diversity that sociologists only dream about.

But I have not yet gotten to the meat of the meeting – the call to men to "seize the moment" to become "men of action," "men of integrity," "men who keep their promises to wives, families, churches and communities." This is the essence of the Promise Keepers' message, to transform the wishy-washy men of America into spiritual leaders and moral guides for their families. I listened to every single speaker who took the podium on Friday and Saturday. Here are the main points of each, paraphrased by me:

- So you've messed up, big time. You can start over. God gives second chances – Greg Laurie, pastor of Harvest Christian Fellowship, Riverside, Calif.
- So you've got a personal problem – an addiction, a weakness, a character flaw – that keeps you from achieving real joy and success in life. With God's help, you can overcome the problem. – T. D. Jakes, founder of T. D. Jakes Ministries, Charleston, W. Va.
- Realize that prayer is a powerful spiritual tool. Get into the praying habit. – Joseph Garlington, pastor of The Covenant Church of Pittsburgh.
- Don't just read and study the Bible, do what it says. Get with a small group of men and tackle real projects like helping poor people buy homes or becoming involved role models for fatherless boys. – Dr. Juan Carlos Ortiz, Pastor of Hispanic ministries, Crystal Cathedral, Garden Grove, Calif.
- Raise the standard in your marriage by honoring your wife, becoming the spiritual leader of your home, renouncing

procrastination and keeping commitments. – Dr. John Trent, president of Encouraging Words, Phoenix, Ariz.

- Be a real father to your children by modeling the qualities of a good son, by telling *and* showing your children you love them, by listening to them, by giving "meaningful touch" to them and by praying for them. – Gary Oliver, clinical director of Southwest Counseling Association, Littleton, Colo.

- Seek out mentors who can help you meet your needs and become a mentor for others. – Howard Hendricks, distinguished professor, Dallas Theological Seminary.

- Wipe the slate clean by forgiving every person who has ever offended you. Put your wife's needs first, to help her realize her dreams. Make a real effort to befriend a man of another race and/or culture. Discover the pain that oppressed peoples have lived with for decades, centuries. Read current books that deal with racial divisions and reconciliation. Get your church to become a partner with a church from the minority community so members may get to know and help one another. Support your pastors. – Bill McCartney, co-founder of Promise Keepers and former football coach of the University of Colorado at Boulder.

What in these messages is controversial? I know I come with a male perspective, but I heard nothing over the entire weekend that I considered threatening to women. Rather I heard answers to most of the problems that plague our society today in the calls for brotherhood, repentance, commitment and love. Men were asked to become servants – to their wives, children, churches and fellow humans. The closing song summed up the spirit of the event:

"Brother, let me be thy servant,
"Pray that I might let you be my servant, too."

REALLY HITTING THE ROAD – ALL THE WAY TO JAMAICA

How far we are in 2020 from that 1995 ideal, with overt racism on a resurgent upward spiral and deep political divisions the norm – especially among evangelical Christians. Promise Keepers and Million Man both faded by the late '90s, the evangelical spirit of both apparently spent as most Americans' attention turned to the approaching millennium.

But before I leave the topic of serving others, I want to share my experience on my first and only mission trip. The church I was attending in 2003 regularly offered to take groups of volunteers on mission projects in foreign lands, giving individuals the opportunity to witness for the Lord while at the same time doing something concrete, such as building a school, digging a water well, rehabilitating a run-down clinic. That year the mission trip was to Jamaica. With my wife's blessing, I decided to join the group of 15 who would travel at their own expense to the Caribbean Island to help repair a pastor's sagging house and upgrade the electronic technology of a small Christian divinity college. The following account of that trip was printed on **March 16, 2003.**

On Mission Trip, You Get Far More Than You Give

KINGSTON, JAMAICA – I came to Jamaica intending to be of service to others. But I leave with the awareness that I have gained far more from this beautiful island than I have given.

I have spent the last week here as a member of a mission team from Palma Sola Bay Baptist Church of Bradenton, doing construction work for a suburban mission church and computer upgrades for a theology college in the northern section of the city.

My contributions here, I'm afraid, have been minimal: Ripping out rotted plywood soffits and putting in replacements, painting concrete walls, pulling computer cable through underground conduits, and hauling computer equipment up and down stairs. Basically, I have been a gofer.

But what I take away from the experience: A new awareness of universal human values – indeed, a life-changing view of the basic goodness of people when not consumed with the need to *consume*. A glimpse of a culture where "No problem, mon" is a genuine lifestyle. Friendships with people whose joy and generosity shame well-meaning American visitors. An appreciation for – and not a little guilt at – the creature comforts we take for granted in the United States.

And, oh yes, a whole new set of skills if I ever decide to stop writing editorials and get into the computer hook-up business.

I have also relearned forgotten lessons from childhood about family sharing of limited facilities, like bathrooms, kitchen utensils, bed linens, and food. The 15 of us from Bradenton came as virtual strangers to one another. We have lived together for seven days as one family, sharing two guest houses and a communal kitchen -- adults ranging in age from 21 to set-in-their-ways 60-somthings. Somehow, we worked out a system of boiling water for ice cubes, chopping vegetables for stews to feed 15, washing and drying dishes by hand, sleeping on mattresses as thin as monks' cots, sharing a bathroom with seven others.

Only through divine assistance could we have pulled that off without steady squabbling. It was not for nothing that the Christian song *Bind Us Together with Love* became our theme song in travels about the city and island. Impromptu verses helped defuse stressful situations quite a few times.

Jamaica is a beautiful but poor country. Almost everywhere you turn, poverty mars the natural beauty. Rusted sheets of tin serve as a universal construction material. The streets are potholed and narrow. Trash litters sidewalks and empty lots, which are wastelands of bare dirt with patches of weeds and brown grass. Ramshackle thatched fruit stands line the roadways.

Economic conditions are severe, the people struggling to stay ahead of inflation that has devalued their currency by quantum leaps in recent years. The exchange rate of 20 Jamaican dollars to one U.S. dollar five years ago has soared to 50 Jamaican to one U.S. dollar today. And for those who think there is a heavy tax burden in Manatee County: Jamaicans pay 15 percent sales tax on most items, including groceries, and 25 percent income tax.

Yet the Jamaican people, by and large, maintain their dignity and their incredible *joie de vivre*. The smiles and gentle manners can be disarming to Americans accustomed to surly attitudes and rude gestures among our own people. I have seen no road rage in Jamaica – most drivers politely make space for others to merge. And there is *no* red-light-running.

No doubt religious faith accounts for much of the people's stoicism. The island is 70 percent Christian, and every block seems to contain at least one church – even the narrowest, most twisting, tin-lined alley. It is in the churches that the Jamaican spirit really bursts forth. At the Cumberland Community Church last Sunday, our team was swept up in the pure joy of a Jamaican Pentecostal service. It was a tin-roofed, concrete-block building with open grille-work walls and plastic chairs for pews. But once the service started, this humble church became a virtual cathedral as the music of drums and synthesizer pounded out a reggae beat and a female vocal duo led in singing of traditional hymns and contemporary songs with a rhythm and spirit that shook the rafters. These folks know how to pray and sing!

On our last full day in Jamaica, the lesson of true, unselfish service is brought home to me in an unsettling way. It occurs at an orphanage run by the Salvation Army on Manning Hill Road. The place is clean and neat but painfully threadbare: Whitewashed concrete walls, mostly bare concrete floors, tin roof, room after room of steel and wooden bunks with battered wardrobes holding the children's meager clothing. Andrea, a 13-year-old with an angelic smile whose mother has died of AIDS and whose father has abandoned her and her four siblings, proudly takes us on a tour of the dorms, bathrooms, laundry and playroom, pausing to show off her school uniform and "church dress."

Majors Ishmael and Marie Ixmail Polusca have been the house-parents at the orphanage for five years. While our group distributes Happy Meals and sodas to the orphans, Mrs. Polusca talks of the difficulty of finding enough food to keep her 36 charges adequately fed and of the loneliness of the children, some of whom are physically handicapped. Yet, she concedes, they are much better off than the thousands of street children in the city. We cannot help them all, she admits, but we can help these 36.

It is painful for me to be here for one hour, surrounded by such beautiful, happy children who have so little. The bolder ones clamor for a hug or an extra treat, even a handshake, and in the eyes of some, especially Andrea, I see a desperate longing for us to take them with us. I am torn by guilt as we leave. Compared to the Poluscas, who have given their lives to these children, our effort is pitifully small. But it *is* a gesture, I think – hopefully something to build on.

MOVING ON TO A NEW CHURCH

We left Church of the Cross in 1992, after 15 years, because we felt it did too little to minister to children, putting the majority of its resources on music and worship. It bothered us to see uncovered diaper pails, infants watched by middle-school girls, and Sunday School classes with no teachers. As Sunday School superintendents, Jo Anne and I pleaded with the leadership for a full-time children's minister, to no avail. The straw that broke this camel's back came in 1992, when my father died and not a single word of sympathy was offered by any leader or member of that church. Being part of a church community ought to mean more than music and worship, I thought.

So, we began church-shopping. After visiting one charismatic church after another and not finding a good fit, we visited Palma Sola Bay Baptist. This church on 75th Street West was Baptist in name only;

116

it was a spirit-filled, warm and friendly place that had a great band and outstanding vocalists to lead worship. But it also cared for its children, and since its free-wheeling services appealed to young couples, there were plenty of kids who needed ministering to. After a few weeks of visiting, I said to Jo Anne as we drove out of the parking lot one Sunday, "I feel the Lord releasing us to join this church." Unbeknown to us, that was the very Sunday that the elders of Church of the Cross publicly confronted the pastor for adultery with a female church member and demanded his resignation. It was an ugly time for that church, which many of our long-time friends still attended. But we had been spared from the bitterness and back-stabbing that followed, once again by the prompting of the Holy Spirit.

Years later, I dredged up some of the memories from our years in that church, published in the following column sometime in the year 2000.

Pages from an Old Church Directory: Reflection of the Secular World

I wanted to phone an old acquaintance recently but didn't have his number and couldn't find a listing in the phone book. So, I turned to a very old source: a membership directory from my old church, which I left eight years ago.

I found the phone number I sought in the circa-1984 directory. But I also found something that left me feeling confused and sad. As I flipped through pages of photos of family groups, I was struck by how many were broken – or worse.

"They're divorced," I said to myself, turning pages, recognizing a couple who had gotten married around the time I did. Another page:

"They're divorced." And another:

They're divorced."

Then: "That cute little kid in that picture – committed suicide last year at 19, I heard."

"I remember her – one day she left her children and moved in with her lesbian lover."

"That guy – he decided he was gay but wanted to continue living with his wife and children in an 'open' marriage."

"This one had an affair with his best friend's wife."

"She left her husband of 40 years to join a cult."

"He went to prison for incest."

"Oh, I remember that kid – he killed his mother during an argument in the kitchen."

"Good Lord," I thought, as page after page yielded a dismaying collection of dysfunctional families, messed-up kids, ruined lives. "And this was a *church*. These were people I sat near Sunday after Sunday, for years. People I prayed with, sang with, fellowshipped with. How could such people, whom I thought I had so much in common with, have messed up their lives so badly?"

I realize the family disintegration that I saw on those pages is all too typical of American society today, where about one out of two marriages ends in divorce. Yet I had always assumed that people who professed to be born-again Christians, as most members of this church did, wouldn't conform to society's dismal standards of greed, promiscuity and deceit. These are people who have committed their lives to Christ, which means living their lives according to His example of love, selflessness and piety.

In its defense, this congregation is known as an "emergency room church" because it seems to attract some of the worst victims of wrecked lives. They come seeking answers and hope. Many find both in the exuberant, music-oriented worship style, friendly congregation and no-

nonsense preaching they encounter from the first time they step in the door.

But as in any emergency room, not every "patient" through the door of this church can be saved. Some do just fine until they get their lives back in order, then backslide when the temptations of their old lifestyle beckon. Some have spouses who don't attend and thus are gradually pulled away from church by their mates.

Others are just posing – playing a game with themselves and their fellow church members. "Carnal Christians," they're called, and eventually the carnal side wins out.

But as I flipped through the pictures a second time, other faces from the past began to stand out.

"That couple became missionaries," I remembered.

"That one adopted four sibling foster children who were going to be split up. And this one – they adopted two orphan babies from a Haitian orphanage."

"That guy successfully raised three children as a single father."

"Oh, this couple, they headed the hospital visitation team for years."

"She sang in the choir every Sunday for as long as I can remember."

Thankfully, the weight of failure began to lift from my spirit as I kept turning pages and looking for the positive things that my former fellow-congregants had done. I realize that the church, like the world, is made up of imperfect people. Some find there the answers to life's most vexing questions: Why was I born? How can I be happy? What is my destiny?

Others do not, so they keep searching – through drugs, sex, material goods, fame. They become part of our society's depressing slide into hedonism —and faded memories in old church directories of lives that once touched mine.

AN ANSWER TO PRAYER

*Obviously, I didn't win many friends at my old church for the column – although most of our close friends had joined us at Palma Sola Bay Baptist by then. After a few years, I was asked to join the Deacons, the board that governed the financial and physical functions of the church. By this time, we had become empty-nesters; our children were both in college, and I had a tiny bit of free time to devote to outside service. But it had not been easy getting to that point. As previously noted, our son was an envelope-pusher, and as he entered adolescence the pushing took on greater consequences than it had for childish pranks. The fact is, he was suspended from school twice in eighth grade, and I had to personally appeal to the School Board to prevent him being expelled. So, you can see why the following column recounting that time meant so much to his mother and me. It was published on **Nov. 7, 1999.***

When a Kid Needs a Friend, Pray That Young Life Is There

The message from the Columbine High School team who came to Bradenton last month for Project Safeguard couldn't have been clearer: If you want to do your part to prevent a deadly Columbine-type rampage in your local schools, get involved in a young person's life. Support an organization that caters to teens' needs, become a mentor, spend time one on one with a young person.

Just two weeks later I saw that message being walked out by a dedicated group of volunteers right here in Bradenton. And they were doing so long before two angry young men took bombs and semi-automatic weapons into Columbine High in Littleton, Colo., last April 20. The group is part of the Manatee chapter of Young Life, a Christian organization that has served teens nationally for more than 50 years.

At the local group's annual banquet in Municipal Auditorium, I saw a group of close to 300 middle and high school students express with youthful exuberance and respect for God, church, family and friends that belies the scary headlines about out-of-control youth turning their schools into terror-filled hell-holes. These kids did silly skits, sang spiritual songs and gave emotional testimonies about how Young Life had changed their lives until you just wanted to cry in gratitude for the work their leaders are doing in our town.

I was among those daubing at teary eyes that night as I thought about what Young Life had done for my family. It was 11 years ago when Young Life came into our lives in the form of a surfer-dude minister whose charisma attracted teens like a magnet attracts iron filings. With his long blond hair and killer tan, Jim Nelson was a youth minister who understood kids and offered a program that reached them on their level.

Little did he know that he was an answer to prayer for us. Our son was an independent type whose march to the tune of his own drummer left him with few friends his own age and the ability to get along with older kids. And around 15, he was at a vulnerable age for influence from the wrong type of friends, especially dropouts or seniors who were "cool" but deficient in the values we emphasized in our home.

Our prayer was for a friend for our son – someone who would share our values and appreciate his uniqueness rather than make fun, someone who would help him say no to the inevitable temptations of drugs, alcohol and sex that teens face as they emerge from under their parents' protective wings.

Our prayers were answered – and don't tell me God doesn't have a sense of humor. Our son came home from surfing at Manatee Beach one day to tell us about this neat guy he had met. He said the man was here to start something called Young Life and it might be something he'd want to check out. Well of course that's just what we did, and when we met Rev. Jim Nelson, our mouths literally dropped open. Here was a 25-year-old man who could have been our son's older brother. Same surfer haircut, same build, similar facial features, and same interest in water sports like surfing, skiing, windsurfing, beach volleyball and tanning.

This was too good to be true, but it got better. Young Life met weekly at a local church fellowship hall for what is known as "Club," which is an evening devoted to games, Bible study and worship. It also offered a weekly small-group Bible study in individual homes. And it gave our son a gang of friends to hang out with, people who accepted him for himself without judging his labels, hair style or taste in music. And always in the background there was Jim Nelson and a small core of adult volunteers who would show up at school for lunch, at sports events and school dances.

Through Young Life our son successfully negotiated the difficult sophomore and junior years, when rebellious tendencies are the strongest and trouble easiest to find. By his senior year he himself was a leader, helping tutor a middle-school small-study group of boys.

It took a while for me to get the hang of the Young Life method. Most of the kids in my son's group were from intact, churchgoing, middle-class families. And this was the exact group Nelson was targeting. Why? Because of the alienation that inevitably develops between parent and teen during adolescence as the child tries to establish his or her own identity. And also because some of the homes that appear so "normal" from the outside prove to be anything but normal when a troubled teen starts to unburden himself to trusted friends. Divorced parents. Alcoholic parents. Drug-using parents. Absent parents. From some of the best neighborhoods in town.

The press reported that the homes of Dylan Klebold and Eric Harris, the two Columbine High killers, came from in Littleton fit the "ideal" image. I couldn't help thinking about them as the high-spirited Young Life kids, glowing with health and optimism, crowded onto the stage to share their love of God and life with the audience. Was there a Young Life for those two troubled boys, I wondered? A Jim Nelson or someone like him to listen to their tales of torment and perhaps guide them to a more positive outlet? Probably not. And what about all the thousands of other kids out there in this very community who don't have someone like Nelson to step in at just the right time to be a buddy? Who go through their school day angry and alienated, picked on or shunned by the in-crowd and never seeing a friend who will say, "I understand, I care?"

The challenge is real. The need is great. There is a youth organization at virtually every church, there are youth sports leagues, Boys and Girls Clubs, all kinds of groups crying for volunteers to help them reach young people and plug them in to wholesome activities. We can't all be Jim Nelsons, but we can follow his example of showing youth that we care. As I was reminded by Young Life's presentation, watching the results is an uplifting experience.

LIVING THE PARABLE OF THE TALENTS

*Palma Sola Bay Baptist was a fun church in the '90s, under the pastorship of Rev. Jim Killoran. His sermons used scripture to clarify issues involved in daily living, and vice versa. Sometimes he used daily living to clarify scripture. As he did one Sunday when he issued a challenge that many of us accepted. Of course, I had to write a column about it. I'll close this chapter on faith by offering the following column, originally published **Dec. 3, 1995**.*

Muffin Project Shows It Doesn't Take Much Talent to Help Others

"Are you *sure* this is the way Tony Rossi started Tropicana?" I asked my wife as the sweat from my brow threatened to fall into the batter I was stirring.

Not that I was comparing my tiny muffin-baking project to the founding of the beverage giant by the visionary Italian immigrant who was an icon of entrepreneurial success in Bradenton. But Rossi *had* started with a pushcart and kept expanding until Tropicana became a global corporation which he sold for something like $500 million. So, my inspiration for a cottage industry to raise some fast money was valid, if somewhat presumptuous.

"I wouldn't quit my day job, if I were you," responded my wife, amused at my bafflement at the mysteries of baking.

No need to panic, Duncan-Hines. I'm not likely to cut into your pastry market anytime soon. My muffin project wasn't *really* a bid at entrepreneurship. It was simply a response to a sermon preached by my pastor Oct. 8 on the theme of stewardship.

I've always known the lesson of Luke 19, verses 12-26, in which a rich ruler entrusts his servants with one talent (a currency denomination) each while he goes off on a long journey, then comes back to see what they've done with the money. But I've never personally considered which of the servants I would be: the speculative one who made 10 talents and was rewarded with rulership over 10 cities; the more conservative one, who raised five talents and got control of five cities, or the fearful one, who hid the money in a handkerchief for fear of losing it and found himself royally chewed out by his master.

On this Sunday in October, though, Pastor Jim Killoran challenged the entire congregation of Palma Sola Bay Baptist Church to test their stewardship in a tangible way. As he completed his sermon on Luke 19, ushers passed through the aisles with baskets filled with bank cash envelopes and, in a reversal of usual church practice, congregants were asked to *take* rather than *give* an envelope. Inside each was a one-dollar bill.

The sermon had a three-fold purpose, explained Rev. Killoran: First was to "put into practice an actual Biblical parable. . .to understand the basic truth of what the Lord was talking about: responsibility." Second was to raise money that the church would use to spread the gospel. Third was to challenge church members "to connect in a practical way to their responsibilities at home or on the job. . .in other words, to be good stewards, responsible citizens and responsible Christians."

We were given 60 days in which to put the $1 to work and, hopefully, to avoid being regarded as "wicked servants" who get their "talent" taken away.

Thus my slaving over a hot stove baking muffins. By pooling our two dollars with another couple and giving ourselves a 58-cent loan, my wife and I were able to buy, at $2.29 each, two boxes of Duncan-Hines bakery-style muffin mix, one blueberry and one honey nut butter.

I measured the batter into the muffin tins so each box made 10, a compromise between the eight "jumbo" and 12 "regular" sized muffins the directions said each box would produce. I put them in two locations at the *Bradenton Herald* priced at 50 cents each, payable on the honor system. They sold out by mid-morning, and the office coffee-breakers were clamoring for more.

The first day's take was $10.86. Not only had the honor system worked perfectly (thanks for your honesty, fellow employees), someone had paid more than was asked. I had more than doubled our investment!

Buoyed by that success, I repeated the muffin sale a week later. Again, I sold out. And now I had turned our original $4 investment into $16.66.

By Luke 19's standards, we were in line to rule four cities each! And we now had the capital to really get big. Why not add cookies to the selection? Better yet, why not expand to sandwiches? I even thought of joining with a couple of other church families and investing in the stock market. We still had more than a month left, and if we picked a hot stock we could really make some serious money for the Lord.

Alas, it is now Dec. 3, just a week from the end of the 60-day challenge – and the $16.66 has lain in an envelope atop my dresser, uninvested, ever since. I got busy with work, and none of my partners took the initiative to begin another project.

Even though we quadrupled the initial sum, I suspect the master would not be terribly happy with our stewardship. We could have done so much more. We could have made 10 times that amount if we had really tried, though we might have needed a Health Department inspection and occupancy license to continue selling food.

This whole project was a metaphor for life, as is the parable in Luke 19 in the first place. And I'm sure Rev. Killoran knew it when he issued his challenge. It showed me how relatively easy it is to raise money for good causes if you have the commitment. Even people with limited "talents" – monetary or otherwise – can make a difference, as this kitchen-challenged male proved by selling rave-producing muffins.

It was a graphic lesson in how quickly a group of people, say a church body, could raise enough money to feed and clothe the homeless.

So why don't we do more of that? My conservative friends will love this answer: Because we've found it too easy to let government programs take care of society's needs. And here we're all guilty, not just bleeding-heart liberals. We're too busy making a living, raising our kids, going to church and studying the Bible to make muffins or sandwiches so a hungry person might eat – and, in the process, possibly see the *true* message of Christ's teachings demonstrated in deed.

Great sermon, Pastor. It's a lesson I'll not soon forget. I'll be turning in the $16.66 next Sunday. All in all, a good investment of *your* talent, I would say.

CHAPTER THREE
ON DEADLINE

I was privileged to be part of a number of major news stories during my 45-year career as a journalist. Among them: the 1967 Detroit riots, the Mariel boatlift, the near-meltdown of the Three Mile Island Nuclear Plant, the assassination of President Kennedy, the collapse of the Skyway Bridge, and the biggest news event of all, the terrorist attacks of Sept. 11, 2001. For some of these, I became both reporter and commentator, as the following examples reveal. If I were on the scene of a breaking news story, I was expected to first report it for the news pages and later opine about it for the opinion pages. That was the case for the Mariel Boatlift and Three Mile Island stories.

News-wise, 1980 was a big year for the Bradenton Herald *– and for me as a journalist. Just two years into my career as an editorialist, I was honing my skills at opinion-writing and absorbing knowledge of the history of Florida and my new hometown, Bradenton. In spring of that year, I persuaded my boss, Executive Editor Wayne Poston, to send me to Tallahassee to see the Florida Legislature in session, so I could comment on our legislators' actions from an authoritative perspective, that is, with personal knowledge of the chambers, the process and the behind-the-curtain venue where it was said the real action took place out of public view. That would be the rotunda that divided the House and Senate chambers. It was pejoratively known by Capitol insiders as Gucci Gulch, because of all the lobbyists wearing Gucci loafers who congregated there waiting for their bought-and-paid-for legislators to emerge from chambers.*

Poston agreed that I should experience that, so I began what would become a routine exercise anytime I planned to go out of town, whether on a work-related trip like this or a personal vacation. I wrote three or four editorials ahead of departure, for publication on the days that I was gone. Big-city Editorial Page editors with staffs of 10 or more writers would blanch at such a prodigious production rate. Accustomed to turning out perhaps three or four pieces a week, they assumed the results couldn't help but be shallow, poorly written and mere repetition of already-known facts, not meaningful, in-depth commentary. But that was the lot of the one-person editorial shop on most small newspapers. If you didn't produce, there would be a blank hole on the Opinion Page. And that never, ever happened. By now I felt the quality of my work measured up to that of my better-resourced fellow editorialists – at least most of the time. That was one reason for the Tallahassee trip: To help me write with authority and personal knowledge about state government.

Except the trip never happened. For weeks we had been reading news reports about Cuban dissidents seeking refuge at the Peruvian Embassy in Havana, by international rules of diplomacy safe from interference by Fidel Castro's goons. Early in the week of April 21, the dictator blinked. He said that an unspecified number of "misfits" and "scum" seeking refuge at the embassy would be allowed to emigrate from the port of Mariel, not far from Havana.

That was the signal the Cuban-American community in South Florida had been waiting for. Thousands raced to Key West to arrange for boats to pick up family members. Near week's end, a flotilla of private boats was being assembled to make the crossing of the Florida Straits to rescue those refugees. I sensed history in the making, and told my wife, "We're going to Key West, not Tallahassee." (I called my editor to ask permission before heading south, and he agreed.) Since she could speak and understand basic Spanish, Jo Anne would serve as my interpreter. We arrived in Key West near the end of the day on April 26, and immediately went to work. Here is the news report I filed the following day, **Sunday, April 27, 1980.**

Cuban-Americans Seeking Relatives Crowd Key West

KEY WEST – Suspense clings as heavily as the dirt and heat in the humid air outside the weather-beaten Southernmost Chamber of Commerce here.

Hundreds of Cuban-Americans mill about under the trees in the dusty, littered front yard of the old clapboard building, the site of a refugee-processing center operated by volunteers from the Committee of Cuban Refugees of Key West and Miami.

It takes two policemen to direct traffic as carload after carload of Cuban-Americans joins the throngs waiting for word of relatives making the journey across the Florida Straits from Cuba.

Every time a yellow school bus bearing another load of newly arrived refugees from the nearby docks rounds the corner, a cheer goes up from the crowd. Then they run toward the bus, searching the sunburned faces for one they recognize, grasping at hands stretched from the bus windows, shouting *"Bien venidos"* (Welcome).

The refugees, their faces streaked with sunscreen, emerge from the bus and walk a human gauntlet into the chamber building, just as many did when they left the Peruvian Embassy in Havana. But this gauntlet is cheering and hugging and crying, not cursing, spitting and hitting.

They are hustled inside the chamber building, where volunteers are waiting with hot meals and cold drinks, medical care and forms to fill out.

Ida Amima, her sister Bertha Gasca and niece Lourdes Hernandez, all of Miami, are typical of those outside the chamber. They or a member of their family have been waiting since Wednesday for word of Ida's brother, his wife and two children who have been at the embassy for six days.

"It really is strange waiting here; you don't know when they are coming or if they are coming," said Miss Hernandez, 21. Chimed in Mrs. Gasca, 48, "We were calling him all week. He was there for six days without sleeping or eating. Finally, the government gave him the papers he needed to get out, and finally we got in touch by telephone. We didn't talk to them too long. They are afraid to talk."

After her brother got the papers to leave, he was allowed to go home. There he found the authorities had taken everything from him: his food, books, his job and furnishings. His neighbors threw stones at him as he arrived.

Inside the chamber building, exhausted volunteers maintain a cheerful, almost festive attitude, as busload after busload of refugees rolls up.

"We've been working so hard we don't know what day this is," says Roberto Garcia, director of the Refugee Committee.

Garcia estimated that 4,000 refugees have been processed since last Monday, when the Freedom Flotilla, as the boatlift is now called, began. "We are exhausted – we have been here since 5 a.m.," said Mary Castillo as she sorted clothing in a room that looks like a branch of Goodwill. Piles of slacks, shirts, blouses, skirts and sweaters line the shelves. Huge piles of trash bags filled with more clothing wait to be sorted, and outside a steady stream of cars, vans and pickups drop off more to aid those who arrive with only the clothes on their backs.

Food is arriving the same way – in cardboard boxes, grocery and garbage bags, crammed into the private vehicles of Cuban-Americans from South Florida who have left jobs and businesses to help and to wait.

Boxes of food and commodities stacked six feet high fill one corner: Canned milk, salmon, tuna, fruit and meat, cookies, baby food, diapers. In a steamy, cramped kitchen, women prepare hot meals of rice, chicken and beans. At a makeshift lunch counter, baloney sandwiches are being wrapped by another brigade.

At a counter marked "Information and Processing," volunteers await with tablets and forms to record the names of the new arrivals, and in a makeshift clinic, doctors and nurses check their physical condition.

Any seriously ill refugees will be flown by jet or driven by ambulance to one of five Miami hospitals set up to treat the refugees – all arranged by the volunteer committee.

A lucky few will join family members pressed against the doors and windows outside. For them, the wait is over.

A Mercy Mission of Staggering Proportions

*I am forced to stop as I type these articles into my computer to wipe tears from my eyes. Even after 40 years the memories stirred by reading my accounts of that historic exodus is that emotional. And I can't help but think of it in the context of the Latin-American refugees crowding our southern border at this moment, seeking exactly the same things that the Cubans were in 1980: Freedom from oppression. Economic opportunity. A better life for their children. Except for most of today's refugees, there is no equivalent of the Committee for Cuban Refugees that sprang up in response to the Freedom Flotilla. Today in Texas, Arizona and New Mexico, many languish in prison-like "shelters" for weeks, often separated from their children, unable to contact relatives in this country to come to their rescue. It is striking how similar to Fidel Castro's response to the 1980 exodus is the Trump administration's response to today's caravans of Guatemalans, El Salvadorans, Hondurans and Mexicans: Merciless, cruel, vengeful, inhumane. Even the labels the leaders attach to them are similar. **Fidel:** Scum. Misfits. Trash. Homosexuals. **Trump:** Murderers. Rapists. Vicious. Criminals from "shithole" countries.*

I am spending considerable space on this topic because it was so historic, so emotional, and so massive. As I wrote the article below describing the logistics of the Freedom Flotilla on Sunday, April 27, 400 boats had left Key West for Mariel. They were joining an estimated 2,000 boats standing by at Mariel for Cuban authorities to process the Peruvian Embassy refugees plus other Cubans who wished to leave as well. On that day, a Refugee Committee official estimated that 200 tons of food and 100 tons of clothing has been donated to the refugee center established at the Southernmost Chamber of Commerce, and more was arriving by the hour. Ten boats carrying about 800 refugees had arrived in Key West that day. It was at that point that Gov. Bob Graham called out the National Guard. He ordered not just military troops but medical teams, buses, ambulances, trucks and medical supplies be dispatched to Key West to assist the beleaguered volunteers who had been filling the gap for more than a week.

Ah, those volunteers. The Cuban-Americans who lived in Key West were the first responders, and their homes became unofficial hostels when the hotels and motels filled up. One family had 50 persons camped out in their three-bedroom home. One of the couples leading the volunteer effort, Arturo and Aleida Cobo, had 10 different families, some from as far away as New York and California, crashing at their home, even as both worked 72 hours straight to maintain order at the refugee center they had helped set up.

*So how did this flotilla happen? How did it operate? I attempted to provide some answers in the following article, written on that Monday and published next day, **April 29**.*

When Cuba Opens Door: Run Fast

KEY WEST – Maria Rodriguez was giving a test to one of her classes at an upstate New York university last Tuesday when she got the phone call from a friend in Key West:

"Come now. It might be your last chance to get your brother out of Cuba," she was told.

Maria dropped everything and went. A substitute was called to finish her class, and she went home to pack a bag. She was in Key West by

Wednesday afternoon, and on a boat bound for Cuba by Thursday evening.

(To protect Maria's brother and family from reprisals should they not get out this week, her real identity has been changed here. Her relatives, including some in Bradenton, would talk only on condition that their names not be revealed. Some members of her family have spent time in Cuban jails.)

Maria did what thousands of other Cuban-Americans did last week when it became evident that neither the Cuban nor U.S. government was stopping the "Freedom Flotilla" ferrying refugees from Mariel to Key West. They left jobs, businesses and homes, took savings out of the bank and headed for Key West to charter a boat.

"When the door to freedom opens for our families, we go!" explained Aleida Cobo, 30, of Key West, emphasizing her last word with a wave of the palm toward Cuba. "Everyone wants to get their family out. Wouldn't you?"

Maria was luckier than most of the Cuban-Americans who jammed into Key West looking for boats to take them to Cuba. She had friends in Key West to help her make arrangements for chartering a boat and stayed in their home while that was being done.

Many others know no one here, and either cannot find or can't afford motel rooms for what may be a long wait. They can be seen all over Key West, eating and sleeping in cars and vans, standing on street corners, lined up at McDonald's and Burger King for yet another fast food meal while they wait for the boats to return.

Maria's friend in Key West muffed her first chance to get a boat. "I know someone who had a boat and offered to take five people over," said the friend, the wife of a doctor. "But I couldn't think of anyone just then. Later, I remembered Maria's brother, but by then the boat was already spoken for."

When Maria arrived last Wednesday, the two started trying to find another boat. A patient at the doctor's clinic told him of a small boat for hire, about a 24-footer. A friend who knew something about boats went to look at it. It was rejected as unseaworthy.

Maria and her friends quickly realized they would need a bigger boat to be safe. And she met another woman like herself, trying to get out five family members. A neighbor of her Key West friends had six people staying with her who wanted to go. That made eight persons, and with each paying $2,500, they could afford the $20,000 being asked for a 65-foot shrimp boat capable of holding 200 persons. A captain and two crewmen would operate the vessel.

Fidel Castro's "four-for-one" rule (four refugees from the embassy for every family member allowed to leave) meant that a boat of at least that size would be necessary for the eight families to get five or six relatives each.

The deal was struck on Thursday. Then two of the eight partners backed out. The anxiety and frustration were too much for Maria. She broke down and started crying, said her friend.

But then, just as suddenly, two more people were found who wanted to go, and the deal was on again. Maria and seven other people she had never seen before Thursday were off to Mariel on a mission of mercy that none was sure would succeed. Her relatives in Bradenton do not know when she will return. It may be three or four days, it may be a week or more.

A relative of Maria's in Venezuela had contacted her brother in Havana last week to be sure he wanted to flee, the Key West friend related. "After all, he has a wife and three children under 8, and that is quite an ordeal to put them through. The brother answered his relative in Venezuela, 'If someone doesn't come for us, we are going to go on a rubber tire'."

To get approval to leave, Cubans first must be on an official list, qualification for which is having relatives in the United States. Then they must stay in their homes until the authorities tell them it is time to go.

When it is, they are given 10 minutes to leave, taking nothing with them except what they wear. Maria's brother, her friend said, was sleeping on the floor beside the door for fear he would miss the knock when the authorities came.

A refugee lifts her hands in prayerful thanks as she steps onto American soil in Mariel boatlift. | Courtesy Jo Anne Klement

There is no assurance that Maria will be able to bring back all five members of her brother's family, however. In recent days, Cuban officials have started splitting families up at Mariel, allowing a mother to go but keeping back her son, a husband but not the wife, and forcing the boats to take strangers instead. It is an apparent ploy to force the Cuban-Americans to make the trip more than once, so that Castro can get rid of more of the "undesirables" who are being forced to join the exodus.

Two of the eight chartering the boat with Maria are husband and wife, so the trip has cost their family $5,000. They both went so that if Cuban officials deny passage to the relatives of the wife, then the husband's might get on. Or some of both. They are hedging their bet any way they can.

Not everyone is fortunate enough to have these options. Boats, at least affordable boats, are in short supply now in Key West. "Everything that floats" is already in Cuba, said one sailor who returned over the weekend. A boat shopping guide with more than 100 pages of advertising produced not one lead for a frustrated Miamian trying to get to Cuba to bring back several uncles, aunts and cousins. All were already sold.

Sunday, an estimated 400 boats left Garrison Bight in Key West, some as small as 18 feet, even as the Coast Guard was warning of high seas and squalls in the Florida Straits. A storm with 78-mile-an-hour winds, in fact, raked the Keys Sunday afternoon, but it did not stop the exodus. Most of the Cuban-Americans in the small boats are landlubbers who know virtually nothing about deep-sea boating, but that doesn't deter them. They head off in tiny outboards, gas-filled plastic milk jugs and picnic coolers full of food and cold drinks stacked in the boat wells.

Rather than rent their boats and risk having them lost at sea or confiscated by Cuban or U.S. authorities, some boat owners are offering to sell them outright to the desperate Cuban-Americans. "A boat you could have sold for $1,500 two weeks ago is worth $7,000 now," said Julian Ibanez of Hialeah, a furniture salesman-turned-boat-broker. "A 36-foot fisherman worth $5,000 had an asking price of $22,000, but no one was desperate enough to pay that."

Boats with "For Sale" signs on them are parked all along U.S. 1 from Homestead to the Keys. Nearly every gas station and empty lot in Key West sports a boat for sale.

"Ready to go. 31-foot diesel. $25,000," read the hand-painted sign beside one. "For Sale. Ready. $5,800," said another on the side of a small outboard.

AND THEN, A BIG SCOOP

While I was reporting this, I also was pursuing another angle, one which, if verified, could have a huge potential impact. I was among only a handful of reporters on the scene in those early days of the exodus. Besides being given free rein to roam the refugee center in the Southernmost Chamber of Commerce, journalists also were allowed to go down to the docks at Garrison Bight, where the boats bearing refugees were landing. We saw many of them as they first stepped onto American soil, their faces streaked with sunscreen, their clothing disheveled and dirty. A few knelt and kissed the ground. Others raised their arms and flashed V for victory signs with their fingers. There were tears in the eyes of many. But there were some, all men, who showed no emotion as they walked off the boats, their faces blank and their eyes vacant. There was something not right with these men, and I began to inquire about them with the happier refugees as they waited to be processed. As they recounted their panicky escape from Cuba and the harrowing journey across the straits, they cast anxious glances at the silent men near the rear of the line. And what they told me about them raised my journalistic adrenalin sky-high. I knew I had a scoop! Here is how I reported it on Monday, April 28.

Refugees: Castro Is Emptying Jails

KEY WEST – Fidel Castro is opening the jails of Cuba and passing off criminals as political refugees to discredit the current exodus, a number of refugees report.

He is also allowing mobs to turn vicious dogs on refugees departing the for the U.S. via the "Freedom Flotilla" at the Cuban port of Mariel, say doctors who have treated a number of dog-bite victims among the newly arrived refugees.

The claims that criminals are entering as refugees could not be independently verified Sunday, but FBI, Immigration and Customs officials at the old naval air station entry point here admit there's little they could do to prevent it.

"We think it's a joke the way the government is letting anyone through," said Immigration Inspector J. H. Carroll. "Anyone can say, 'I'm a political prisoner,' even if he's murdered two people and raped three more."

A customs official who asked not to be identified admitted that "We've received some information that Castro is sending criminals with fake passports, but it's going to be hard to check it out." He said refugees are screened thoroughly after transfer to Miami, and their names and fingerprints run through FBI files and possibly those of Interpol, the worldwide police agency, to screen out known criminals.

An FBI official here said, "No one high-up seems to be concerned. We'd be derelict in our duty if we didn't try to check, but it's very hard to do. We can only process these people by name and occupation and send them on to Miami for further checking.

"This thing is still mushrooming. We're just trying to do our job here on the front lines and let the proper agencies worry about that. The State Department, Immigration and Customs are not on the same wavelength."

The inclusion of criminals, if true, could have a significant impact on the human exodus that is centered here. Castro charged two weeks ago that the more than 10,000 Cubans jammed into the Peruvian Embassy were delinquents, misfits, homosexuals and "trash." By putting precisely this kind of person on the boatlift, he would be able to say, "I told you so" to the rest of the world while cleaning the social misfits from his jails.

Leaders of the volunteer Committee of Cuban Refugees of Key West and Miami, who are coordinating a massive relief effort here, seem more concerned with the effect of such allegations on the exodus than whether the reports are true. They fear that if President Carter believes the charges, he will stop the exodus before their relatives can escape."

"Sure, and we have some potheads, too," one weary Cuban-American said in response to a question about the criminal issue. "But think about all the people who will suffer if the boats can't get through." It is certain that Castro is turning loose many political prisoners, whose only crime was to speak out against his regime, and it is possible that some of the refugees are mistaking them for criminals of the "common" variety.

Three refugees who escaped Saturday on an inner tube raft told how prisoners were taken from an east Havana jail to an area on Avenue 43 between 195th and 196th Streets and then bused to Mariel and represented to the boat captains as refugees from the Peruvian Embassy. Other reporters got similar reports from the refugees they interviewed.

A 15-year-old mother, cradling an infant in her arms, said Cuban authorities were taking passports of "big people" such as government officials, journalists and educated people and giving them to delinquents, common people and those with no education." She had no doubt of the purpose of this move: "To make Castro's words come true – that only the misfits and undesirables are fleeing."

As they left, many of the refugees had been "tortured and humiliated" by crowds apparently operating with Castro's approval, said Dr. Raul Reyes, a Miami physician who spent his weekend treating sick and injured refugees as they got off the boats. He said there have been seven cases of dog bites from German shepherds and Doberman pinschers turned on the refugees by angry Cubans who consider them turncoats.

Some have come in with cracked and broken ribs from having been hit by pipes and clubs as they boarded the boats. One man had an ear nearly torn off by a zealous Castro supporter trying to get in his licks.

Most of the refugees are suffering nothing worse than seasickness and dehydration from their voyage. Those who were in the Peruvian Embassy compound, however, suffer from stomach disorders and malnutrition Dr. Reyes said.

MEANWHILE, BACK AT THE RANCH. . .

To my knowledge, that was the first published report on Castro's jail-emptying strategy, but it didn't make many waves. The editor laying out the paper that day didn't even put it on the front page, where it ought to have been. Later I learned that Castro also was forcing patients from Cuba's mental institutions onto the boats, which probably accounts for the vacant stares of some of those male refugees I had noticed. As we now know, Castro's strategy worked. The criminals and mentally ill "refugees" he foisted off on the relatives of the genuine political refugees committed many crimes in the early months and years after the boatlift, giving all of the Marielitos a black eye. It was just one more sad chapter in the depressing history of Cuba under Castro.

*By the middle of that historic week, it was time for the adventure to end. I filed a few more sidebars detailing what daily life was like for ordinary Cubans, how one wealthy Miamian traded a diamond ring for a boat to rescue a relative from Mariel, and how three men made the crossing to Key West on a crude raft made from a tractor tire tube and canvas. On Wednesday, April 30, Jo Anne and I headed home. I quickly changed hats and became the editorialist again, and for the following Sunday's edition, **May 4**, I offered this personal reflection.*

Freedom: Ask Cuban Refugees What It Means

KEY WEST – Libertad. Libertad. Libertad.

It is the pat answer the Cubans give when asked why they left their homeland to start anew in the United States.

Freedom. Freedom. Freedom

The word is on the lips of every Cuban here, from the affluent Miami matrons who fled 20 years ago to the frightened peasant whose face is still covered with sunscreen from his 12-hour voyage to Key West.

Freedom. You hear it so much it starts to sound trite, especially if you're a comfortable American who's questioning whether he really likes all these poor, uneducated foreigners crowding into his already crowded, increasingly poor homeland.

Few Americans can relate to the "libertad" of which the Cubans speak, and few try because we are generations removed from the time when this might have happened in our family tree. Why, we feel persecuted if someone cuts in front of us in the checkout line.

Nowhere was the American apathy more evident than in laid-back Key West last week, where Bermuda-shorts-clad tourists, on-the-make singles and spaced-out druggies cruised the boutiques and bars of trendy Duval Street, oblivious to the modern-day Dunkirk being staged by the Cubans just two blocks away.

What a paradox of values it was: On Duval, jaded American society parading back and forth in search of artificial thrills from sex, drugs and expensive gewgaws, and around the corner on Simonton, the Cubans mortgaging their futures and risking their lives in tiny boats so their relatives might join this society.

For the Cubans, despite their anxiety over family members making the trip to Cuba, this was a festive occasion, to be savored to the fullest. They had waited 15 years for Castro to open the doors just this tiny crack, and though it might be slammed shut again at any moment, they were celebrating this chance at freedom.

It was like I imagine the Fourth of July used to be in this country before it got to be un-chic to wave the flag and talk about patriotism. Patriotism burned in the eyes of the Cubans – patriotism for *this* country, not theirs. It showed in the bumper stickers on their cars that said in Spanish, "When tyranny is the rule, revolution is in order," and in the T-shirts that some enterprising Key West capitalist had rushed onto the market with the legend, "Freedom Boatlift – Cuba to Key West 1980."

I have no doubt that if someone had been selling fireworks and miniature American flags, he could have done a land office business in those, too. From Miami I have heard that the streets of Little Havana – indeed, all of the city – are overflowing with joyous celebrations.

The Cubans can get excited about freedom because they know its price and have paid it. It is the substance of individuality, of personal integrity, of one's very human nature. For those denied it, freedom is as dear as life itself. For those who have it handed to them, it is taken for granted.

One who knows the ways of communism only from books and newspapers feels chills run up his spine hearing the stories of life in Cuba from the lips of those who have just left it. Orwell's Big Brother of *1984* was not fiction but a fact of everyday life to the Cubans. About all that was lacking to complete the Orwellian picture was a TV screen in their homes monitoring their activities and telling them what to do next. But the neighborhood committees worked about as well as a TV monitor.

"They watch you day and night," said a newly arrived refugee. "These people on the committees, they never sleep."

I'm thankful for the Cuban refugees and welcome them to America. They are the new patriots who will keep the spirit of liberty alive for another generation. Key West last week showed that that spirit certainly needs some new blood.

WHEN GALLOWS HUMOR BECOMES REALITY

May 1980 was a very busy month for journalists in Florida. Barely had I unpacked my bag from Key West when an even bigger news story, at least of local impact, broke. It was Friday, May 9, a typical crunch workday at the Bradenton Herald. *We were tasked with putting out that day's paper, which came out in the afternoon, and then turning right around to begin producing the Saturday and Sunday papers, which were morning editions. I, of course, had an editorial prepared for that day's edition and was polishing my offerings for Saturday and Sunday while also selecting and editing the letters to the editor, syndicated columns and cartoons that would be published on all three days.*

Journalists are famous for their gallows humor. Witness to so much tragedy, we often resort to wisecracks to ease the stress of a particularly gruesome news event. For as long as I had been working at the Herald, *an editor or reporter leaving the building would say, "I'm going to the dentist. Call me if the Skyway falls." Or, "I'm going home for the day. Don't call me unless the Skyway falls."*

The Skyway was the Sunshine Skyway, the 150-foot-high suspension bridge that spanned Tampa Bay between St. Petersburg in Pinellas County and Bradenton in Manatee County. Built in 1954, before the interstate highway system had drastically changed America's driving habits, it was a rickety structure of steel girders, terribly outdated for 1980s traffic. As a child, I had built Tinker Toy bridges that looked a good deal like the Skyway. As an adult, I always had white knuckles when crossing the bridge. The metallic hummm of the tires as they passed over the steel grate that formed the bridge's flooring at its peak was especially unnerving.

Early on the morning of May 9, the Skyway fell. A freighter drifted off course in a fierce thunderstorm, knocking down several piers of the southbound span, taking 35 people to a horrible death. Four hours before deadline.

The staff went into full disaster mode. All employees not already at work were called and directed to strategic locations. Boats were borrowed or rented to view the disaster by water. An airplane was leased for aerial surveillance. Every available body was marshalled to get the story. In those pre-internet, pre-cell phone days, photographers had to shoot film and get it to a darkroom for processing into useable photographs. Reporters had to relay details from two-way radios in their cars if they could get to them or from pay phones if they could find them, or else return to the office to type their stories.

This was not a day for editorializing. I was pressed into service working with reporters who were on the scene, taking dictation over the phone and editing copy as it began to appear from reporters who had come back to the office. But I knew that when Friday's paper was put to bed I would have to try to write about the tragedy, to somehow sum up the grief, anger, and horror of 35 innocent lives so tragically ended, and also of course try to answer the most pressing question: Why?

*The product of that effort, written post-adrenaline-rush Friday afternoon, lacks the immediacy and drama that I might have summoned up six hours earlier. But it offers a number of insights into the why – especially, why the disaster should not have happened. Here it is, published **May 11, 1980**, two days after the Skyway fell.*

A Tragedy That Shouldn't Have Happened

Just over two years ago, the Tampa Bay area had a warning of the prospects for disaster on the Sunshine Skyway. On a clear, calm afternoon, an 851-foot ore carrier called the Phosphate Conveyor lost power and steering in the shipping channel a half mile from the bridge. It regained power and its anchor held just 40 feet from the piers of the main northbound span.

Department of Transportation engineers admitted at the time that a direct hit on one of the main supporting piers would have toppled the pier, and the bridge with it.

But like the busy executive who ignores warning signs of heart disease until the massive attack that kills him, the DOT ignored the warning from the May 2, 1978, near-miss by the Phosphate Conveyor. Friday morning, the disaster that was averted by 40 feet in 1978 happened.

The tragedy should not have happened. While it is easy and perhaps unfair to point fingers and find solutions in hindsight, it must be noted that the DOT and Coast Guard had warnings such a disaster could occur. The three relatively minor bridge bumpings earlier this year gave fresh reminders of the dangers presented by huge freighters negotiating the narrow channel under the bridge. And still, nothing was done.

Finding someone to blame for the disaster will not bring back the 35 victims, will not replace the $50 million bridge, will not make up for the millions of dollars' worth of extra driving and lost time for motorists unable to use the bridge. But it may ease the shock of Tampa Bay residents to know who and why something so horrible could happen. And ensure that it does not happen again.

And so the questions, which proper investigatory bodies must find answers for:

- Why was the ship traversing the narrow, tricky channel in so fierce a storm – one that the U.S. Weather Bureau had tracked across the Gulf the night before? If they hadn't the sense to stay in port, why didn't the pilot or captain wait out the storm in the channel, even if it meant turning around rather than risk the bridge passage?
- How did the ship get 800 feet south of the bridge opening? Was the pilot asleep? Why didn't radar prevent the crash? In light of the fact that there have been four collisions in the channel in the last four months, are the pilots qualified to guide ships through Tampa Bay?
- Why is there no fender system around the main piers at the bridge? The fenders that protected the bridge when it was built rusted away by 1970 and were replaced with clusters of wooden poles bound with rusty cable – so inadequate as to be worthless,

as Friday's disaster proved. With the clear warning of potential disaster in 1978, why was nothing done?

Obviously, the same old casual navigation practices cannot prevail in Tampa Bay after this. If the Blackthorn tragedy on Jan. 26 wasn't enough to shock officials into action, the Skyway should be. Perhaps the Skyway wasn't designed to safely accommodate huge new freighters of the Summit Venture's size – certainly not during heavy storms. New navigation rules will have to be written limiting ship movements.

Precautions for vehicular traffic also will need to be taken. Barriers to halt traffic when ships are passing beneath the bridge would be one solution. They would be unpopular traffic bottlenecks, but they would keep others from meeting the same horrible deaths as the 35 who drove off the edge of the bridge Friday.

TWENTY YEARS LATER

*While I didn't manage to capture the adrenalin-fueled passion with which we all wrote on the day of the bridge collapse, I got another shot at it two decades later. On the 20th anniversary of the Skyway's collapse, I was asked to write the lead article summarizing that unforgettable day. As I read through the clips of that day, it all came rushing back, and I believe I managed to capture the emotion and drama fairly well. Here, in quite lengthy detail, as gleaned from clips and my own memory, is a retrospective on the Skyway that was published on **May 7, 2000**.*

A Span Fell, and 35 Died

'This is Mayday. Stop the traffic on that Skyway Bridge!'

The early morning of May 9, 1980, felt like a day without a dawn. Going outside to fetch something from the car at about 7:30 a.m., I was struck by the pitch darkness of the sky, as if the night hadn't ended at its normal time. That inky blackness, I would come to learn, would be the cause of – and fitting backdrop for – the horror that was to come.

It was so dark, my wife and I discussed the wisdom of letting the kids walk to the bus stop, all of 200 feet from our front door. As we scurried to get their lunches packed and backpacks organized, we volleyed over who was in the better position to drive them to school. She had an early appointment outside the office; I had my usual Friday morning crunch of preparing Opinion Page content for the weekend editions of the *Herald*.

As I scanned the black sky for some sign of the oncoming storm's direction, little did I know that, within a few minutes, my routine would be turned upside down and I would be facing one of the most incredible news events of my career.

My immediate thoughts were on tornadoes. Twenty-two years of living in the flat expanses of Texas had taught me that this was the kind of sky from which tornado funnels dipped. I didn't mention that thought later when I got to the newsroom, though. We'd been through enough Florida thunderstorms to know better than get excited every time the sky turned black. Why, this could all blow over in a few minutes. The rain would be good for the lawn, the school bus would be along shortly and, once safely on it, the kids were in good hands.

That was the kind of ambivalence with which we began our day, not knowing that about 15 miles away a 609-foot freighter named Summit Venture, buffeted by 60-mph winds and steering through this very storm's blinding rain and darkness in near-zero visibility, was headed for disaster at the mouth of Tampa Bay.

With empty cargo holds and empty bilge tanks, the giant freighter, longer than two football fields, was a 19,735-ton floating cigar box, pushed by the storm's howling gales some 800 feet out of the shipping channel designated to take it safely beneath the Sunshine Skyway Bridge. At about the moment our children boarded the school bus and we drove to work that Friday morning, the Summit Venture smashed into the second support column south of the bridge's highest span, crumbling the column and taking out 1,297 feet of roadway and superstructure at the bridge's pinnacle, 150 feet in the air.

In the next few sickening moments, 35 people on the road above – ordinary people like us on their way to work, appointments, family reunions – met death in one of the most horrible ways imaginable: driving off the shattered end of the bridge into thin air and falling, falling, falling into a spaghetti-like tangle of steel girders, broken concrete and roiling water below.

As day-shift employees arrived at the *Herald* on 13th Street West in downtown Bradenton around 8 a.m., a handful of editors and reporters from the City Desk, News Desk and Sports Desk had already been at work for several hours, preparing copy for the first edition. An afternoon newspaper then, the *Herald* had to be in news racks and stores by 11:30 a.m. and on the way to customers' homes by 1 p.m.

The newsroom's first word of the Skyway disaster came from the Pressroom. A printer had heard a bulletin on the radio. The first reaction of many in the newsroom was disbelief. Surely this was someone's idea of a sick joke. But it merited checking out. A reporter called the Skyway tollgate office on the north end. A toll collector confirmed that something terrible had happened on the bridge but didn't know what.

The staff mobilization quickly started. Someone began calling off-duty reporters to come in immediately, and every warm body was drafted for an assignment. Our Tallahassee reporter, Joe Parham – back from covering the Legislature only a few hours before – and a photographer headed for the bridge. Chief photographer Carson Baldwin was authorized to charter a plane to get aerial shots of the scene. Outdoors writer Jerry Hill began calling fishing buddies looking for boats to borrow. Then-Publisher Bill LaMee volunteered his own boat, and a marine team set off.

Reporters were dispatched as they arrived: one more to the Skyway, another to the bus station in Sarasota where a Greyhound was overdue; another to Mullet Key in Fort De Soto Park in Pinellas County, where victims' bodies would be taken for transport to a morgue in Tampa.

Others were on the telephone to the Coast Guard, to the Journal of Commerce in New York for background on the ship, to the engineering firm that designed the bridge, to witnesses or relatives of potential victims.

. . .There was no hysteria and very little emotion as we worked to cover the story of a lifetime. Professional instincts – and adrenaline – kicked in to overcome the shock of the event; the atmosphere in the newsroom was business-like. Later, though, pent-up emotions would give way to shock. One former copy editor admits today that, after finishing her shift, she went home and wept, thinking about the victims: "It was one of the few stories I ever cried over."

Throughout the Tampa Bay area, others were rocked by similar emotions. So many could identify with this bridge, a truly breath-taking landmark in Manatee and Pinellas counties. Yet those of us with fears of great heights always had a vaguely unsettling feeling about the Skyway. Its spider-web-like steel superstructure perched on skinny concrete piers seemed a rather fragile connection to Earth. From a distance it looked more like a child's Erector Set project than a feat of modern engineering that connected two peninsulas across 15 miles of Tampa Bay.

Up close, its narrow lanes, built for the small cars of the post-war '40s and '50s, afforded no room for error. You gripped the steering wheel with both hands and shut out all distractions when crossing the Skyway, trying to block mental images of losing control and going off the edge or, God forbid, a freighter crashing into the bridge as you crossed.

On this day, that vision became reality for several dozen people, 35 of whom died and a handful of whom lived to tell about it. Many people were imagining their horror as they waited for news of the crash.

The details that are now indelibly imprinted in the memories of all who were here at the time were slow to trickle in that morning. Vehicles had driven off the shattered end of the bridge at its highest span during what some called a mini-hurricane; no one knew how many. A loaded Greyhound bus was believed to have been among them, and possibly a bus full of farm workers.

Then word came that the driver of one of those cars was alive. Somehow Wesley MacIntire had escaped from his little Ford pickup truck after it plunged off the bridge, ricocheted off the Summit Venture and began to sink in the bay. His rescue sparked hope that perhaps others would be saved, that this would not be the human disaster we feared. Around mid-morning, with the clock ticking toward a late deadline of 11:30 a.m., the *Herald* got a big break. Advertising sales representative Don Albritton arrived for work, pale and shaken. A resident of St. Petersburg, he had been on the bridge when the ship struck it. Albritton's dramatic, eye-witness account of the nightmarish scene put into words the visions readers had of what it must have been like on the bridge that morning.

"The superstructure started to come down," Albritton said. "I slammed on my brakes, threw my car into reverse and started to blow my horn and yell at other passing cars. . .It was raining heavily, and the bridge began to shake just like an earthquake. Large girders began to crash down. . .I think I was the second to last car to go over the bridge before it happened."

And, he confirmed, a bus "went roaring by" despite his efforts to warn the driver to stop.

But others were luckier. Richard Hornbuckle and three co-workers from a St. Petersburg auto dealership, en route to Avon Park to pick up vehicles, were near the top of the span with the wind "blowing like a hurricane" when traffic ahead came to a stop. He jammed on the brakes to avoid a rear-end crash just as the roadway ahead – including the cars in front of him and a bus that came flying by on his left – disappeared. His panic stop put his car into a skid on the bridge's slick metal grating. It came to a halt a heart-stopping two feet from the edge. The sight of

Hornbuckle's yellow Buick on the lip of a precariously dangling section of bridge became an iconic image of the Skyway story.

In those days before cell phones, editors communicated with reporters and photographers in the field via two-way radios in their cars. But all the photographers and reporters had been forced to leave their cars near the bottom of the intact but now-closed northbound Skyway span, so they had to walk up the bridge to view the scene and interview public safety officials directing rescue and recovery efforts. With the clock ticking away, we had to get film back and begin processing it to have pictures in time for the first edition.

A copy editor was delegated to drive a company van to retrieve the film. But first he stopped at his home in Palmetto, loaded up a bike belonging to one of his sons, and drove to the foot of the Skyway. He rode the bike up the steep grade of the bridge, met our photographer, got his film and headed back. For an out-of-shape, 30-something father of three, the ride down was as terrifying as the ride up was hard, but he returned with the film in time to make deadline.

Amid the heartbreaking stories of loss in that first day's report were heartwarming stories of good fortune. One was about Manatee County schoolteacher Terry Butterfield, who normally would have been crossing the bridge just about the time the ship struck it but was running late because he stopped to iron a pair of trousers after noticing a stain on the pair he was wearing. Frustrated because he was late for work and stuck behind slow-moving traffic on the rain-swept bridge, Butterfield was about to pull to the left to pass when he saw a car pulled off in the emergency lane with the driver waving frantically. Thinking the driver had run out of gas, Butterfield recalled a sermon he had heard in church Sunday on the theme: We are our brother's keeper. He pulled over in front of the stalled car and got out to see how he could help the driver. It was Don Albritton, and his greeting was chilling: "The bridge is out."

Friday's first edition, which came off the presses around 12:30 p.m., contained many of those details in its three pages of Skyway-related content. We were the first paper on the street in Manatee County with

151

coverage of the tragedy, and pressmen recall we upped the press run by as many as 1,000 additional copies to meet demand. The edition, published barely five hours after the tragedy occurred, contained a lead story with a surprisingly accurate account of the fatalities, 32 – just three fewer than the ultimate death toll would prove to be. Dramatic aerial shots showed a shattered bridge, rescue efforts on the water, and a haunting image of the Summit Venture at anchor to the west of the broken bridge, shards of girders and highway asphalt dangling from its enormous bow like broken pieces of a child's toy.

Stories included an interview with Albritton . . .and the search for bodies. Inside was a review of the bridge's history and its accident record, which included four mishaps in a 19-day span three months earlier.

One of the more vivid memories in the hours that followed was the recovery of the Greyhound bus, which carried the driver and 22 passengers to their deaths. At times as the tide receded, its outline could be seen below the surface of the water, trapped in the tangle of girders and concrete beneath one of the shattered pilings. From the top of the north span, 150 feet in the air, it looked like a smashed Matchbox car, said one witness, its top flattened to window level by fallen girders as it plummeted into the bay.

Mayor Wayne Poston, who was then the *Herald's* editor, walked up to the north bridge Friday afternoon after the paper was out to see the scene for himself. He called it "a chilling thing. It was an incredible vision. I just couldn't imagine this happening." Watching a crane lift the crumpled bus from the water and dump in on a nearby barge, he said, "was horrible. I imagined the people on the bus and how the fall must have seemed like an hour to them."

Saturday was no day off for most of us. There was still a great deal of reporting to do as more bodies were recovered, victims were identified, and analysis of what went wrong began to emerge. Many of us helped produce a 12-page section that went into the Sunday edition, a compilation of the highlights of our previous coverage.

Sunday also brought the first attempts at assessing blame, and here the real shock of the tragedy began to take on new dimensions. The Skyway, it turned out, had been an accident waiting to happen – had indeed happened many times before in less dramatic ways. But the warnings had been ignored. In our Sunday editorial headlined "A Tragedy That Shouldn't Have Happened," we recounted the startling series of accidents in the two previous years, including one just the previous Feb. 16 involving the same pilot in what in retrospect seemed an eerie dress rehearsal for the Summit Venture disaster.

Like an accursed Captain Ahab, John E. Lerro, piloting the 720-foot Janna Dan into Tampa Ban on Feb. 16, tried to maneuver around the wreckage of the Coast Guard cutter Blackthorn, misjudged his detour and put the huge freighter into the path of the Skyway. The bow stopped short of the bridge but the stern – its holds empty and riding high in the water just as the Summit Venture's would – was pushed by the current and strong winds toward a bridge piling. It sheared off a protective wooden fender like a toothpick before crashing into the piling. Fortunately for the motorists who foolishly stopped to gawk, Lerro's error left only a 10-foot-long, 2-inch-deep gash in the piling, and no structural damage.

Coming so soon after the Jan. 28 sinking of the Blackthorn, which cost 25 lives in a collision with a tanker, this accident should have sounded alarm bells about the Skyway, but it did not.

The real precursor to the Summit Venture had occurred two years earlier on May 2, 1978, when the 851-foot Phosphate Conveyor ore carrier lost power about a half-mile from the Skyway. As the crew frantically worked to stop the ship, the engines restarted, and the anchor held. The ship stopped just 40 feet from the bridge.

Florida Department of Transportation engineers said at the time that a direct hit on one of the main supporting piers would have toppled the pier and the bridge with it. But nothing was done to strengthen the wooden fender system that was supposed to repel stray vessels.

No state-of-the-art navigation system was installed to guide ships more precisely along Tampa Bay's winding 40-mile shipping channel and through the "800-foot hole" between the bridge's concrete columns.

No rules against traversing the Skyway during heavy weather were implemented.

And no vehicular traffic barriers were installed on the roadway to stop drivers when a ship was passing under the bridge, as some suggested.

In retrospect, the tragedy that occurred May 8, 1980, seemed entirely preventable, adding unfathomably to the sorrow for the 35 victims' grieving relatives and to the shock throughout the Tampa Bay community.

Those of us who drive the bridge regularly watched the tragedy unfold in stunned fascination, as if we had somehow expected it to happen someday. Now we no longer had to wonder what it would be like to go off the edge. We had seen it.

A LUCKY BREAK ON BREAKING NEWS

It seems my early years as an editorialist were blessed by lucky breaks. Just a year prior to the Mariel Boatlift adventure described above, I was in the right place at the right time for another major news event, one that would give me my first national scoop. It happened because I decided that, if I were going to make editorial writing my career, which seemed like a good idea, I ought to learn a bit more about how to do it.

So roughly two years into my stint as the Herald's *opinion editor, I persuaded my boss, Wayne Poston, to finance a week of training at the American Press Institute in Reston, Va. API is the newspaper industry's trade organization, funded by all of the major news organizations in the country. Back then, it regularly conducted week-long seminars on various specialties of news gathering and writing, from investigative reporting to copy editing/headline writing to crime reporting to . . . editorial writing. In late March*

1979, I was sitting in an API classroom with about 25 other journalists who specialized in opinion writing, being taught by some of the best writers in the business. It was the first time I had been among my own kind, and it felt good. Laboring in a one-person shop for month after month, always under the gun to produce more and better copy with virtually no resources other than your own brain capacity and physical stamina, is a lonely existence. Here, rubbing elbows with editors who had shops of eight, 10 or more writers, I was able to hold my own in discussions of style, tone and structure. I felt like I belonged.

I knew that one of the highlights of an API seminar for opinion writers was a private briefing at the White House with the President. I had met Jimmy Carter the previous year on the campaign trail, but of course was awed at the prospect of a personal visit with the President of the United States. The White House visit was traditionally the last event of the seminar, held on Friday afternoon, just before a brief graduation and farewell ceremony. However, this was no ordinary Friday afternoon at the White House. For this had been the week of Three Mile Island – the nuclear generating plant in Pennsylvania that had undergone a near-meltdown a couple of days earlier. Nevertheless, President Carter took time to fulfill his commitment to the API opinion writers' seminar and made the meeting an official press conference on Three Mile Island – his first official comments about the near disaster. No outside reporters were invited – it was just the 25 API opinion writers. Afterward, Carter's Press Secretary Jody Powell led us to a newsroom equipped with typewriters and telephones and assured us no statement would be made about what the President had said until we had time to file our stories.

A national scoop! When we had finished and were escorted from the West Wing, we were besieged by the White House Press Corps. "What did the President say?" they begged. "Come on, guys, give us a break!" I had had no greater pleasure up until that moment than to be able to tell none other than Sam Donaldson, the acerbic ABC TV reporter who was known for baiting the president: "No comment."

*Here is the story I filed on that press conference, published **March 31, 1979***:

Carter Vows Stricter Nuclear Safety

WASHINGTON – The White House is reassessing safety precautions at the nation's nuclear power plants as a result of the accident at Pennsylvania's Three Mile Island Plant, President Carter said Friday.

At a White House press conference with editorial-page writers and editors attending an American Press Institute seminar, the president said he has been in touch with Gov. Dick Thornburg of Pennsylvania and is "very closely monitoring" the situation.

He defended the "remarkable safety records" of nuclear plants but said the accident "will make all of us reassess precautions on safety" and "will lead inexorably to tighter regulation" of nuclear power plants.

Carter opened the press conference by promising to reveal his new energy policies next week. The energy act passed by Congress last year "encompassed only 50 percent of what I asked" almost two years ago, Carter said, and since then the energy problem has become "much worse."

While he did not reveal specifics of his new plan, voluntary conservation will be a "crucial element," he emphasized. This was a contradiction of the position taken by his economic adviser, Alfred E. Kahn, who on Friday morning had told the editors that voluntary conservation measures are "for the birds."

Taken aback by the statement, the president said the energy crisis "obviously requires a broad interrelated program," including voluntary controls, authority to institute gas rationing and price increases, which he called "inevitable."

Carter said the convening of a constitutional convention to insert a deficit-spending prohibition "would be one of the most ill-advised moves I can imagine." To cover all the possible dangerous ramifications of such an amendment would require a document larger than the Constitution itself, he said. He said it would be more advisable to voluntarily rule out deficit financing by cutting spending and balancing the budget.

Carter called the immigration commission headed by former Florida Gov. Reubin Askew one answer to the growing problem of illegal immigration but said "no one has discovered an adequate answer to the problem. An immigration proposal he made 18 months ago has not been acted on by Congress, he said. Mexico's "rapidly improving economic prospects," as a result of its new-found oil reserves, should do more than anything else to solve the problem of aliens.

On the domestic economic front, the president expressed satisfaction with compliance with his 7 percent wage guideline. "In general, the American people have complied very well, and I hope it continues," he said.

Meeting President Carter at the White House during Three Mile Island crisis | Courtesy of White House

He was not asked specifically whether he considered the Teamsters Union's wage demand, which totals about 35 percent over three years, in line with his guideline, but said the Teamsters "are negotiating in good faith."

Friday morning, Kahn had defended the Teamsters demands as "an equitable interpretation of the standards." That interpretation has been justified by calling a high percentage of the Teamsters' demands "catch-up" gains on cost-of-living boosts since the last Teamster contract three years ago, rather than outright wage increases.

Disputing a view commonly held among Americans that the United States' position in world affairs is declining, the president said the country's influence has been substantially enhanced" in the last 10 to 15 years. He cited the talks with Russia, the opening of relations with China, the Egypt-Israel peace agreement, and improved relations with Eastern European and NATO nations as proof of his contentions.

"On balance, it's a record of progress," Carter said. In the past, the role of the U.S. has been one of dominance; "now, I look on Canada and Mexico more as equals," he said.

THE BIGGEST STORY OF ALL: 9/11

Well, no big breaking news there, but news nonetheless. New regulations to make nuclear plants safer. A clash of views with his economic adviser on the merits of voluntary energy controls. And new efforts to deal with the problem of illegal immigration. Once again, I am struck by the fact that so many issues we were grappling with four decades ago are still with us today, like immigrants at our southern border. And a call for wage restraint! Who can imagine a time when a union demand for a 7 percent wage increase was considered "restraint"? And a 35 percent wage demand over three years was mostly considered "catch-up" for lost buying power? Those of us who lived through those times can. That was the norm in the '60s and '70s, before conservatives succeeded in emasculating the unions.

But that's another story. Time to move on to another major national news story on which I was involved as an editorialist/reporter. That would be Sept. 11, 2001, when Islamic terrorists hijacked four passenger airliners and flew them into the World Trade Center, the Pentagon and, thanks to the heroics of doomed passengers, the ground at Shanksville, Pa., instead of the White House or Capitol. I was in the weekly meeting of the Publisher's Executive Committee at the Bradenton Herald, *going over the usual run-down of circulation figures, ad revenue, upcoming special news sections and other routine business. The routine was shattered by the publisher's executive assistant interrupting to report that a plane had struck one of the towers of the World Trade Center in Lower Manhattan.*

Executives scattered to tune in television sets in their various offices, and I joined reporters in the newsroom glued to the set mounted over the copy desk. Though we were in a different newsroom in a far different building than that of May 9, 1980, the feeling was exactly the same as that of the morning of the Skyway collapse. Shock gave way to dread as details of mass casualties began to filter in. When the second plane struck the other tower just after 9 a.m., the tension was broken by the adrenalin rush of the need to respond to a breaking news story of huge proportions. The Executive Committee quickly re-assembled, and after a brief discussion of logistics, it was decided that we would publish a special edition – an Extra. This was an act so rare that, despite multiple decades of cumulative newspaper experience among the executive team, no one in the room had ever worked on one. The press deadline would be 1 p.m. It was now roughly 9:30 a.m.

Unlike 21 years earlier, there were plenty of editors to handle copy and design pages. My job was – what else? – just to write an editorial. Just. To sum up the grief, anger, fear and resolve of a nation under attack and perhaps to suggest ways our leaders ought to respond. And have it ready in roughly two hours, as deadlines for inside pages were earlier than for the front page. The pressure was intense. My heart was pounding, my brain reeling. I forced myself to calm down, begin to assemble the known facts, focus my thoughts, and started typing. Here is what I came up with on that unforgettable morning.

This Is War

Sept. 11, 2001 – a day that will live in infamy as surely as does the one 60 years ago when American military bases at Pearl Harbor were savagely attacked and this nation went to war.

A horrified nation watched this morning as cowardly terrorists brought death and destruction to New York City and Washington on an unprecedented scale. There are no words adequate to describe the shock and revulsion felt by millions of Americans as they watched the dense plumes of smoke billow up from the World Trade Center and the Pentagon after hijacked planes crashed kamikaze-style into the buildings.

Awaiting even sketchy estimates on the extent of casualties, stunned TV viewers could only imagine the horror that thousands of people on the planes and in the buildings were facing. Then watching the collapse of the tops of both World Trade Center towers just minutes apart, as if in a surreal slow-motion movie, the scope of this national calamity became all too clear to most of us. We saw the Murrah Federal Building in Oklahoma City – we understood what happens when high-rise buildings fall into themselves like a stack of pancakes.

It is too early to suggest what course the country should take in reacting to this devastating attack. But the cowards responsible should know this: They will not escape retribution. America does not tolerate unprovoked attacks on its territory or citizens. The Japanese learned to their great sorrow the price of their sneak attack on Pearl Harbor. So will the organization behind Tuesday's attacks, obviously the work of a well-organized and extensive conspiracy.

As did Pearl Harbor, Tuesday's massive terrorist attack doubtless will put this country on a war footing. Exactly how that will play out in the days ahead remains to be seen. But it is clear that we face a formidable enemy, and we must be prepared to battle that enemy, whoever it turns out to be.

Make no mistake: This is war.

One Day Later

Nineteen years later, I am relieved to see that I managed to come up with these few coherent thoughts on that terrible morning. The piece was appropriately brief. I believe I succeeded in summing up the shock and grief called for by the attacks. But I also managed a call to arms – literally – being among the first to do so. But there was no resting on laurels. With the Extra selling out on the streets, we still had a newspaper to put out the next day, Wednesday. So, pausing for a quick lunch at my desk while I read the Extra and the latest news updates, I once again forced myself to focus and take a somewhat longer-range look at the meaning of the terrorist attacks. As you will see, I took the key points from the Extra piece and added context and background for a more definitive call to unity and action. Here is my offering for **Sept. 12, 2001.**

A Time to Grieve – and to Unite

Sixty years ago, after a day that still lives in infamy, America girded its loins and went to war. In an outpouring of national unity unprecedented in our nation's history, an America stripped of its innocence by the Japanese attack on Pearl Harbor aroused itself from its internationalist lethargy and virtually overnight mobilized to defeat the Nazism, Fascism and Imperialism that the Axis powers wished to impose on the rest of the world.

On this morning after another day that will live in infamy, America faces another test of its national resolve. Can it muster the spirit of selflessness and unity needed to defeat the forces of evil that struck at three of its

161

most visible symbols of power on Tuesday: the World Trade Center, the State Department and the Pentagon? The answer must be: Yes. America must and will come together to deal with this threat to its security that is as shattering, if not more-so, as Pearl Harbor in 1941.

After the divisiveness of Vietnam and 25 years of relative peace – or at least nothing more than small wars largely fought with smart bombs that required little national sacrifice – we have so often asked ourselves if we as a nation had it in us to respond as did the "Greatest Generation" in 1941. Now we have a chance to find out. The children and grandchildren of that generation must be willing to step forward and make the sacrifices needed to defeat the enemies who would destroy us from within.

Make no mistake. This is war. The cowards responsible must know that they will not escape retribution. America does not tolerate unprovoked attacks on its territory or citizens, as the Japanese learned to their great sorrow.

The horror of Tuesday's terrorist attacks unfolding minute by minute with a stunned nation watching on TV represents a shared traumatic experience that should bind us together as one people. Few will ever forget the shock and revulsion they felt as they watched the dense plumes of smoke billow up from the World Trade Center and the Pentagon after hijacked planes crashed kamikaze-style into the buildings. We could only imagine the horror that thousands of people in the buildings and on the planes were facing. Then watching the collapse of both World Trade Center towers just minutes apart as if in a surreal slow-motion movie, the scale of this calamity became all too real to most of us. The death toll will be horrible, for we remember all too well the Murrah Federal Building in Oklahoma City in the worst terrorist attack on U.S. soil before Tuesday.

The shock and horror we felt Tuesday gives way to grief today, and to anger. But even as we strategize on finding and punishing those responsible, we must not lose sight of the basic values that have guided our nation for all of its history. Let us not jump to conclusions about who might have done it and let us not demonize all who might resemble them. Blind hatred that panics us into acting against our basic principles will further demean us as a nation and make the terrorist attack a success.

Certainly, this attack calls for assistance from all who call themselves allies in identifying and bringing to justice the attackers. They cannot have succeeded without help or at least acceptance by one or more governments. Many of our allies have friendly relations with those governments. We should not be shy in demanding help from them to investigate and apprehend those suspected of involvement.

In that regard the view of Chris Yates, an aviation expert at Jane's Transport in London, is instructive. Calling it perhaps the most malicious terrorist attack that has ever taken place in the world, Yates told reporters that it takes a logistics operation from the terror group involved that is second to none. Only a very small handful of terror groups is on that list.

Certainly, the attacks will have a profound impact on this nation's sense of security. It introduces a new weapon into the terrorist arsenal: the fully loaded commercial airliner. All previous precautions imposed to protect against truck bombs and suicide bombers are rendered moot by this new tactic.

This raises obvious questions about airline security. How did this many hijackers get by the airport security checkpoints? What weapons could have been successfully smuggled aboard to force a pilot to crash into a building? It all suggests a reordering of military priorities. While we spend billions on missile shields to ward off missile attacks, a fanatic with a hand weapon manages to do as much damage as one of Saddam Hussein's Scuds.

The nation will look to President Bush and his advisers for leadership in this crisis with an intensity unmatched since World War II. The president must pour all federal resources into investigating the attacks and in aiding the wounded and survivors of the dead. And in that effort may the words of Japanese Adm. Isoroku Yamamoto after the attack on

Pearl Harbor be the inspiration for us all: "I fear all we have done is to awaken a sleeping giant and fill him with a terrible resolve."

Twelve Days Later

I'm proud of this perspective, all these years later. I acknowledged the grief and anger as the shock wore off, I called for national unity to find the perpetrators, and warned against selling out our values in that effort. I foresaw new airport security measures (though perhaps no one had any idea how drastic those measures would become), new military priorities, and federal support for the victims and survivors.

The week that followed was hectic for all of us in news-gathering. We continued to report and comment on the attacks as more details emerged. But in Southwest Florida we also had Mother Nature to contend with. While the terrorists turned airliners into deadly missiles headed for America's seat of government, Tropical Depression Gabrielle was gathering strength in the Atlantic and heading for our coast. Hurricane Gabrielle made landfall near Venice, just 30 miles south of Bradenton, as a Category 1 storm on Friday, Sept. 14, causing two deaths, $230 million in damage, minor flooding and power outages affecting 570,000 people. While not a crippling storm to the degree many would be a few years in the future, it caused quite a bit of damage in my neighborhood, toppling ancient oaks onto roadways and ripping roofs off mobile homes and sheds. For me, dealing with 9/11 and a load of personal grief, it was almost the straw that broke the camel's back, as the following column, published on Sept. 23, attests.

Since Sept. 11, Real Men DO Cry

I had been back home from burying my mother two days when the World Trade Center and Pentagon were struck by hijacked airliners on Sept. 11. Suddenly my personal grief was greatly diminished, and a universal grief for the senseless slaughter I had watched unfold on TV took over. Along with millions of Americans, I dealt with a profound sadness for the loss of so many people in Washington and New York, all strangers yet connected by our national heritage and shared values.

Besides dealing with the loss at a personal level, my job required me to interpret it for thousands of readers – to attempt to give meaning and insight into the deaths of so many innocent people. Never have I felt so inadequate. Sorting through hundreds of editorials, columns and emails from news sources around the world, I had to try each day to distill the most relevant elements of this unbelievable story into cohesive editorials that might in some way help readers deal with their emotions over this worst single day's loss of life in modern U.S. history.

Exhausting as it was, the pace of work kept me from thinking too much about my own emotions. Most of the time.

Occasionally, though, despite my best efforts, they would seep out, to my utter surprise. Watching tearful interviews with family members of missing World Trade Center employees, I would find involuntary tears running down my cheeks. Talking to my family in Texas, I would be unable to speak at times, overcome with emotion. And several times, at unexpected moments, I simply broke down.

Men aren't supposed to cry. At least not real men. Boys grow up hearing that from a tender age. It's not just in *our* culture, either. It's almost universally accepted that men should keep their emotions inside.

But since the World Trade Center and Pentagon disasters, lots of men – including me – are crying quite openly. CBS newscaster Dan Rather broke down twice Monday night during an interview with David Letterman. Tough New York City firefighters were shown crying on each other's shoulders. Even President Bush was close to tears on the day after the terrorist disaster at an Oval Office press conference.

Crying is cathartic. It provides relief from bottled up emotions that must be vented. Tears "humanize the soul," said 19th century clergyman Edward Thomson. They are "the safety valves of the heart when too much pressure is laid on it," said 19th century British Author Albert Smith. Sir Walter Scott, the Scottish writer, was even more eloquent. "Tears are the softening showers which cause the seed of heaven to spring up in the human heart."

I suspect many other Americans have shared this emotional roller coaster with me over the last 12 days, but we are still too new at this "we-are-family" business to admit it to each other. With the added grief of losing three family members in four months, I had more experience at it than most.

Everyone took their own experiences into the terrorist attacks. Along with a familiarity with death, I had vivid flashes of "There, but for the grace of God, go I." My new daughter-in-law had flown to Boston, site of two of the hijackings, on business just two weeks before. My daughter and son-in -law had flown to New York for a weekend getaway just three weeks earlier, staying in a friend's apartment near the World Trade Center. The subway entrance they used was at the foot of the WTC. My wife and I had been to Washington just a month before and remembered driving by the Pentagon on the way to the airport. What if any of those trips had been a few weeks later? What if the hijackers had launched their plans a few weeks sooner?

Thus it was at church last Sunday, torn by grief, relief and anger, I was pretty much an emotional wreck. The first point in the message from visiting minister the Rev. Ed Moss, pastor of Countryside Community Fellowship in East Manatee, was apt: It's OK to cry. "Weep for those who weep," he said. "Care enough to cry." No problem, Rev. Moss, I thought. I've got it covered.

But his main point wasn't as easy: Forgive. "Love your enemy and pray for those who persecute you. It is always wrong to carry out vengeance on your enemies," he said.

I didn't want to hear it. No, not these mass-murderers – they don't deserve forgiveness. But even as I resisted, I knew deep down that Rev. Moss was right. If my Christian faith means anything, it means letting go the hate for even these terrorists and reflecting God's love for every human being. Our government will deal with their crimes to bring justice to the victims and their families. But it is not up to us to condemn or judge these people trapped in the darkness of their ignorance of God's love and mercy. We are only to show them love and to share the good news of God's son Jesus with them.

I prayed silently for the grace to do that, hard though it would be. And at that moment a huge wave of relief came over me – and a flood of tears.

ONE MONTH LATER

It was inevitable, I suppose. After an event like 9/11, the Herald's letter box began filling with hate mail – and crazy mail. It got so ridiculous that a week or so in I felt the need to tell our readers: Get a grip. That, in fact, was the headline on the column I wrote for **Sunday, Sept. 30.**

Nation Needs to Get A Grip

Get a grip.

That's what I want to say to certain people who have shared their ideas with me in emails, phone calls and letters since the terrorist attacks on Sept. 11. As cynical as I ought to be after 39 years in the newspaper business, I continue to be amazed at the ways different people react to the attacks.

Take the suggestion from a Bradenton woman that we should cancel Halloween trick-or-treating because we don't know "how many kids are subjected to getting killed in ways we hadn't thought possible" before Sept. 11. How? Well, take superhero costumes like Spiderman, Superman and the like, she said. Hypothetically, "Say you have 5,000 people dressed as such a 'hero.' Out of that 5,000, say 2,000 are potential terrorists. OK, they come in our small town, they start shooting, we call law enforcement and they ask, 'What did the shooter look like?'

"We say, 'Well, he had a Batman suit on,' or something of that heroic nature. The law enforcers go there and 300 of them have the same costume on. The enforcers ask which one did it. We answer, 'I don't know, they all look alike.' "

I try logic with her. Are we talking about terrorist kids here, or adults? It's mostly the kids who dress up as Superman on Halloween. If adults dressed as the superhero start firing at kids, they'll stand out right away. What is the likelihood that 2,000 terrorists would come to this town? And if there were 5,000 people in Manatee County dressed in similar costumes they would be scattered all over town. So how could the terrorists do more than random shootings? And if they wanted to do that, they could do it from concealment without a costume, any day.

Get a grip.

From a Palmetto man, there's this suggestion for dealing with an anti-war protester.

"Approach student talking about 'peace' and saying there should be 'no retaliation.' Engage in brief conversation; ask if military force is appropriate. When he says 'No,' ask 'Why not?' Wait until he says something to the effect of, 'Because that would just cause more innocent deaths, which would be awful and we should not cause more violence.'

"When he's in mid-sentence, punch him in the face as hard as you can. When he gets back up to punch you, point out that it would be a mistake and contrary to his values to strike you, because that would 'be awful and he should not cause more violence.' Wait until he agrees and he has pledged not to commit additional violence. Punch him in the face again, harder this time. Repeat steps 5 through 8 until he understands that sometimes it is necessary to punch back."

That kind of assault and battery should be good for at least a year in jail.

Get a grip.

People are overreacting in many ways. At newspapers in Texas and Oregon, journalists have been fired for writing columns questioning President Bush's circuitous route back to the White House on Sept. 11. In Longboat Key, a Brit who owns a Mexican restaurant has his storefront vandalized and sees his business dry up because years ago he borrowed the money to buy it from a member of the royal family of the United Arab Emirates. This, according to a Longboat Key weekly, equated to an "FBI probe into terrorist financing."

Get a grip.

One caller to the *Herald* metro desk this week told of seeing a man bent over a local supermarket meat cooler with a small brush, dusting the meat. By the time police arrived the man had disappeared. A *Herald* editor had a call from a friend in Jacksonville who said someone reported birds were falling from the sky, dead.

In Toronto, the *Globe and Mail* newspaper reported that the Canadian military has given orders for its members not to be seen in uniform, except when they're actually on the base working. The paper also reported a reader inquiring whether she should buy bottled water, in fear that Lake Ontario could be poisoned by terrorists. Another wanted to know whether her mutual funds might collapse into worthlessness.

Get a grip, everyone.

Mental health experts call this "hypervigilance" and say it is a useful mechanism for regaining control of a situation that seems out of control. But it's also just what the terrorists want: To create such fear that it brings a country to its knees.

I admit it's hard to know just how far you need to go to protect yourself and your family from random terrorist acts. I worry about more airplane hijackings. I worry about suicide bombers in trucks or on foot.

But I also worry about getting hit by a drunken driver on my way home from the movies. I worry about my house catching fire from its old wiring. Sometimes I worry about having a heart attack. Does any of that worrying help? Of course not. No, I'm not buying a gas mask. I'm not searching the Web for vaccines. I'm not cashing in my 401K investments. I'm not going to stop driving or flying.

And I'll be at the door with a full candy bowl for trick-or-treaters on Halloween.

THREE MONTHS LATER

In December of 2001, just three months after 9/11, I again headed for Washington on official business. I was among a group of 25 journalists from around the country invited to attend a seminar on terrorism in Washington, D.C., sponsored by the Knight Center for Specialized Journalism at the University of Maryland. Because the Herald was part of the Knight-Ridder chain (now operating as McClatchy News), I was given preference in the selection process and thus found myself sitting beside journalists from some of the largest newspapers in the country. I was eager to learn all I could about our government's efforts to deal with the new global terrorism threat. The following two columns came from my experiences on that field trip, published around **mid-December 2001.**

Pentagon Wounds Healing Quickly – Except in the Mind

WASHINGTON – It is business as usual at the Pentagon these days. That's natural since war *is* the usual business of this unique office complex, and people here are just too busy to let a terrorist attack shut them down. Busy making war against terrorism, of course.

At least that is my impression after a tour of the Pentagon "Ground Zero" and a visit with Defense Secretary Donald Rumsfeld as part of a "Fighting Terrorism" seminar sponsored by the Knight Center at the University of Maryland. No doubt there are deep psychic scars in the minds of many Pentagon workers from the Sept. 11 terrorist attack, but they aren't visible in the maze of offices one passes en-route to the Secretary's office. The only reminders of Sept. 11 are in the dozens of drawings and cards from school children that line the corridor walls.

As for the physical evidence on the building's exterior, well, if you had been on Mars for the last three months and saw the west side of the Pentagon today you would think only that it is being remodeled. Essentially, it is a construction project. Any evidence of sheared-off walls and charred, collapsed roofs has been gone since Nov. 19. What one sees today is a plywood- and scaffold-enclosed U-shape cut into 300 feet of the 900-foot-wide western façade of the Pentagon, three of its five rings deep. Some 700 construction workers clamber through the building site in a 24-7 operation, repairing damaged offices in the 1.2 million square feet of the building that suffered damage and preparing the site for the 400,000 square feet that must be rebuilt.

Already concrete has been poured for some of the footers, and soon new walls of Indiana limestone will start to rise. The goal of holding the rededication ceremony in just nine months seems entirely realistic, given the building's symbolism and the determination one senses throughout the vast complex. Of course, there's deep symbolism in the scheduled date for the rededication: Sept. 11, 2002. Exactly 12 months from hell on earth to complete restoration. Take that, Osama bin Laden.

As for the Secretary of Defense, you can't help liking him. He is the same self-assured, easy-going man in person as he comes across during briefings on television. Void of pretension, he puts journalists at ease with his informal manner and dry wit. He laughs easily and reduces complex questions to simple, easily understood answers.

The first question from our group is one that most Americans want to ask. What is the end point of this war? When will it be over, and how will we know? It may never be completely over, Rumsfeld answers. "Terrorism has always been there and will always be there. . .It will be more like the Cold War than World War II. We'll know it's over when we can go out of the house and look up without fear, when fewer people are willing to strap on explosives and blow themselves up."

Rumsfeld fields questions from our group on a variety of subjects – unfortunately, breaking no news that would give us scoops on the Pentagon press corps. Though he certainly has urgent business elsewhere – Kandahar is about to fall on this day – he seems reluctant to end the session with the visiting journalists, perhaps because we're not the same ones he deals with day in and day out. In fact, after almost 40 minutes – 10 more than scheduled – an admiral dripping with gold braid interrupts to tell him he is late for an appointment with the Secretary of the Navy.

We kept the SecNav waiting! A heady thought as we are escorted from the secretary's richly paneled corridor to the plain, institutional gray of the correspondents' corridor. Here we see where the Pentagon reporters sit for those daily briefings, the front row self-assigned to the network correspondents to facilitate cutaway shots of the reporters asking their questions. Then there are two hours of briefings by Pentagon security and press officers.

Finally, we are escorted out of the vast building through the Potomac entrance, emerging into the late afternoon light just in time to see a jet airliner climb into the sky, probably from nearby Reagan National Airport. Several in our group look at the plane and then at each other, and the unspoken message is clear: Imagine that fateful day, when a plane just like this, taking off from nearby Dulles International, made a wide arc over western Virginia and came back, aimed at the virtual spot on which we are standing. Then Rumsfeld's answer to the question about knowing when the war is over is fully grasped: Not as long as you look up into the sky and imagine what it's like to have a plane coming down on you.

Mosque Visit Gives Profound Insights into Terrorism

F alls Church, VA. – Dusk is falling on a warm December day at the Dar al-Hijra Mosque here – a signal that it is time to break the Ramadan fast. In the foyer of the modern, two-story building, trays of dates are placed on tables and men dip their fingers in for a handful of the sweet fruit, the first nourishment these devout Muslims have had since dawn. At sunset, an elder calls prayers, and they hurry to the prayer hall. Evening prayers concluded, the congregation adjourns to a large dining hall where a sumptuous feast awaits: a variety of soups and salads, several rice dishes and meats and a groaning tableful of desserts.

This is the introduction for 24 journalists to a typical Muslim service during the holy month of Ramadan. The journalists, attending a seminar on "Fighting Terrorism" at the University of Maryland's Knight Center for Specialized Journalism, show by body language and muted talk that they are out of their element and uncharacteristically ill at ease.

I know I am. Though our hosts could not be nicer, I feel like an intruder, a non-believer in a sacred place. I guiltily realize that I am afraid of these men, especially those wearing strange shirts and caps and speaking in unfamiliar languages. With Sept. 11 images fresh in my mind, I am mentally profiling them as potential terrorists.

It is exactly what I have railed against since the terrorist attacks – the extension of the crimes of a few fanatics onto an entire population of law-abiding people, even American citizens. It is this irrational fear of "the other" that has prompted many attacks on Muslim-Americans since Sept. 11 by bigoted, hate-filled individuals. Yet the feeling of "otherness" is palpable here, amid the unfamiliar rituals, dress, foods and language.

It is this feeling that Americans, perhaps led by media commentators like us, must get past if we are to be a truly united country committed to equal rights and religious freedom, say the mosque leaders in a panel discussion following the dinner.

"It has come through strongly in your coverage since 9/11, the idea that Islam is different and foreign and 'other'," says Ayesha Ahmad, a member of the mosque and a graduate student at the University of Maryland. "As Muslims, we have a lot to do to get our side of the story out."

Yet the media focus has had positive elements, says Dr. Sulayman S. Nyang, chairman of African Studies at Howard University. "Sept. 11, a tragic event, showed America that we are part of a globalizing world. A hundred years from now, historians will write that you woke up to the rest of the world" on that date.

And, despite the isolated attacks on Muslims, America has taken a moral step forward in comparison to its treatment of resident ethnic groups in past conflicts: German-Americans in World War I and Japanese-Americans in World War II. Nyang praised President Bush for having "built a firewall against that kind of hate" with statements of support for Muslims.

The panelists pleaded against identifying all Muslims with the "extremist fringe" whose radical interpretations of the Quran justify terrorism. "They are like the militia in Idaho" who justify crimes by their interpretation of the Constitution. "The only way they (Muslim extremists) can get support to advance their agenda is to wrap themselves in the flag of Islam," Nyang said.

For almost an hour there was a positive exchange of views as panelists defended mainstream Muslim views and journalists asked questions. But then a question triggered a hot-button word: Israel. In the heated debate that followed, it became clear that the conflicts between Israel and Palestine drive Muslim feelings toward the United States, both here and abroad. One journalist read an excerpt from a press release by the Muslim American Society issued on Sept. 18 that, while condemning the terrorist attacks, also suggested that the United States undertake "an objective study to examine the possible relationship between our foreign policies and the anti-American sentiment that has engulfed many nations."

Such code words linking the terrorist attacks to U.S. support of Israel is simply unacceptable, said the journalist. Nothing justifies the flying of passenger planes into office skyscrapers filled with civilians.

After that, all neutral ground for reasoned debate vanished, and the panel discussion broke up soon thereafter. But our hosts remained ever pleasant, presenting each departing visitor with an English-language copy of the Quran and a color poster. The poster consisted of a tree showing the branches of Christianity and Islam coming from a trunk formed by Adam, Noah and Abraham. At the tip of one branch was Jesus; at the other, Muhammad. The trunk branched at Isaac and Ishmael.

The implication was profound. Can this be what this whole conflict is about – from suicide bombings of Manhattan towers to suicide bombers in Jerusalem marketplaces to the '67 and '73 Middle Eastern wars, down through history to the Crusades and countless wars before that? To two jealous women and two sons competing for the same man's love over 4,000 years ago?

Everything I have learned thus far indicates it is, which offers little hope for resolutions anytime soon. No wonder I still feel uneasy as our bus pulls away from the mosque.

THE POISONING OF PUBLIC DISCOURSE

Almost two decades after the 9/11 attacks, it's easy to forget just how worried and scared Americans were during the early weeks post-attack – and for good reason. And it wasn't just out of fear of hijacked planes crashing into your home or school or workplace. For just seven days after 9/11, a new terrorist threat emerged that affected the country almost as profoundly as the airliner hijackings. Anthrax-laced letters began arriving at the offices of media companies and members of Congress. These weren't typical fake-poison envelopes containing flour or dusted with rat poison or the like. These anonymous letters contained deadly anthrax spores. They continued to arrive at various locations well into October: first to the National Inquirer *in Boca Raton, later to ABC News, CBS*

News, NBC News, the New York Post *and the offices of Democratic Senators Patrick Leahy and Tom Daschle. Five people died, and 17 were treated for anthrax poisoning.*

The poison mailings touched off one of the largest investigations in FBI history, and for months thereafter changed the way American business handled mail. Remember, in 2001 the internet was still in its infancy, and emails had not yet overtaken the U.S. Postal Service as the main medium of written communication. At the Herald, *Publisher Mac Tully ordered a portable building installed outside our main offices on Manatee Avenue. All incoming mail was processed there by employees wearing protective hazmat suits and gloves before being distributed to the various departments. Many other companies instituted similar precautionary measures. As the recipient of letters to the editor, I was concerned about my safety and appreciated Mr. Tully's concern for employee welfare. And, of course, the anthrax scare forced me to take an entirely new view of hate mail. It was reflected in this column, published in* **mid-November, 2001.**

Hate Mail Takes Scary New Aspect

I have been receiving poisonous mail for years.

Fortunately, it has not been of the white-powder variety that has been landing in news media and government offices for the last few weeks. Mine has followed the traditional lines of insults, warnings and wishes for evil that hate-letter writers have always used – until now. Since anthrax-laced letters have turned up at several newspaper offices, three TV networks and the offices of two members of the U.S. Senate, hate mail has taken on a frightening new dimension.

Never again will I joke about the rantings of some of my readers who express their disagreement with *Herald* editorials and columns in particularly colorful ways. Now, you never know what else the letter might contain besides profane aspersions on my intelligence or ancestry.

There's nothing even remotely funny about anonymous threats through the mail whether genuine or hoaxes.

I'm not alone. *St. Petersburg Times* columnist Elijah Gosier, who used to shrug off hate mail, especially from one prolific hate mailer, was quoted as saying recently, "I'm not opening the envelopes anymore."

In Tucson, Ariz., the *Daily Star* went further. It announced in a column by the editor and publisher that it would no longer accept letters to the editor sent by mail because of the anthrax scare. Instead of mailing letters, the paper invited readers to fax, email or hand-deliver letters to the editor as well as announcements of upcoming events for its feature section and community calendar.

I know we have to be careful about the handling of mail in light of the anthrax contamination of the Postal Service in recent weeks. At the *Herald* we have made several changes as a safety precaution. All mail is being screened and opened in a separate facility, before it enters our main office building, to prevent any suspect mail from contaminating our work space. Hopefully that's just a temporary measure until postal authorities can assure us the mail is once again safe.

However, I certainly hope we never find it necessary to stop accepting letters mailed to and delivered by the Postal Service as the *Tucson Daily Star* has. That would be a terrible inconvenience to many and the breaking of an almost sacred link between us and our readers. As one of my fellow editorial writers observed in a recent online discussion of the *Daily Star's* action, "There's something about the U.S. Mail that is too closely intertwined with our roots to be so casually abandoned."

Letters to the editor represent a microcosm of the community, a reflection of the public mood and of our success or failure at reflecting it. Reading letters to the editor is generally the high point of my day, for the mail brings positive affirmation of my efforts to stimulate thought about as often as it brings criticism of them.

I have dozens of relationships with people I've never met except through their letters to the editor. I know their addresses and plenty about their private lives, accumulated in bits and pieces of personal information dropped into letters over the years. I recognize the handwriting and even the typewriter style of many. Quite a few come in jerky longhand that is barely legible, generally with apologies about hands made shaky by strokes or old age. Many come filled with misspelled words and grammar mistakes.

I try to imagine the laborious efforts that went into these letters – the people sitting down and taking pen in hand to share their views about what they're reading in the *Herald* – finding paper, an envelope, a stamp and return address label. These letters, obviously, are important to the writers, and they are to us. I try also to imagine these same people going to a fax machine or computer to deliver that letter to us. Most won't be able to do that. So, without the Postal Service, their views would not get into the newspaper.

For those who do have access to faxes or email servers, however, I urge you to use one of those systems to deliver your letters to the editor. It will ensure my getting them much faster, as our new mail-handling procedures will inevitably create some delay in the mail reaching me. (The same holds true for news releases and news items to other departments as well.)

Regarding potential anthrax-laced mail, my peer at the *Arkansas Democrat-Gazette* in Little Rock, Paul Greenberg, observed wryly in a recent online discussion, "These times do indeed make some of us nostalgic about the bad old days, when the weapon of choice was the tire iron rather than the anthrax bacillus."

Greenberg said that his department has equipped its two mail clerks with face masks and latex gloves to be used at their discretion. And, he said, "I threw a few of the gloves in my bottom left-hand drawer next to the bourbon should an unusually suspicious envelope arrive (as opposed to the usually suspicious kind). I'm confident this precaution will be needed. The bourbon, I mean."

My sentiments exactly. Please don't stop writing.

ALMOST 60 YEARS EARLIER

Looking back from the perspective of the Twitter world, how innocent and naïve that last column sounds. While the occasional hate-letter came through, most of the mail I received as editor was civil, reasonable – and signed. That was a basic requirement. Compare that with the trolls who haunt public discourse today, routinely posting hateful messages and even death threats to anyone who criticizes their candidate or cause. I seldom even bother reading the letters on today's Opinion Pages. They mostly seem polarized and predictable – and pointless. At a time when many people refuse to accept basic factual information, there seems no point in engaging them in debating the nuances of a complex issue like immigration reform, gun safety, or deficit spending. Back in the day, letter-writers carried on impassioned debates on such issues, taking up one another's points and arguing for or against – always without personal invective. If any tried that, I used my editor's pen to delete such language. The letters, as stated above, were sacrosanct.

But that was another era. Going back to the earliest beginnings of my career takes me to November 1963. The assassination of President John F. Kennedy occurred precisely one year into my first job at the Daily Oklahoman *in Oklahoma City. I have no clips from that day, as my role was relatively minor given my lowly status as a cub reporter. But I did reminisce about it many years later, on the 40th anniversary of JFK's assassination. Here is that column, from* **fall 2003.**

What I Was Doing When I Heard
JFK Had Been Shot

I was a young general assignment reporter in November 1963, writing features, suburban news and occasional police stories for the *Daily Oklahoman* in Oklahoma City. Twenty-three and single, I had no friends outside the newspaper, and my family was 150 miles away in Texas.

On Nov. 22, I was driving to the bank to deposit my paycheck when I heard the news bulletin: President Kennedy had been shot in a motorcade in Dallas. I got a sick feeling in my stomach but continued driving, parked and hurried into the bank. Knowing I had to get to the newspaper fast, I don't remember what I said to the teller who handled my transaction. I do remember that her face was pale and her expression wooden.

At the newspaper the staff was huddled around the teletype machines spitting out bulletins on the shooting. A cluster of editors met in the Managing Editor's office on one side of the newsroom. There was an eerie hush in that vast space, in contrast to the usual clatter of typewriters, ringing phones and cross-desk conversations.

When the bulletin came across that the president was dead, some people cursed, some turned away in tears, some returned to their desks, stunned. Soon the editors came out and gathered the staff into a cluster in the center of the newsroom. It was the first really big story I'd ever been witness to, and I watched in awe as the newsroom sprang into action.

The managing editor made a short speech, acknowledging the tragedy and exhorting us to rise to the challenge of producing a newspaper that did justice to the subject – one that many readers would save for generations. Then he began to give out assignments. Every staffer would be involved. The main story would be handled by our star rewrite man, supplemented by the wire services. The political writer would do a backgrounder on the nasty partisan politics in Texas, the court reporter would look into the issue of succession. The police reporter would get law enforcement reaction. The education writer went to the schools to talk to teachers and students. The arts writer, whose coverage of cultural events had regularly taken him to Dallas, 200 miles away, was dispatched there with a photographer and instructions to get sidebars. Sports writers were sent into the streets to get reaction from ordinary folks.

I ached to be sent to Dallas. I knew the city, having gone to college just 30 miles north in Denton, and worked nights downtown for a few months. But as one of the greenest reporters on staff, I knew I would be one of the last considered for this assignment. The one I got was not exactly a Page One contender: Recap LBJ's recent visit to Oklahoma City; call those with whom he spent time for reaction and insights.

But at least I had something to do. I felt good being part of a great story, despite its tragedy. It was my first awareness that, in pursuit of a story, journalists must stifle their emotions and just focus on getting the facts. You can consider your own feelings later, when your job is done.

I had plenty of opportunity for that in the weeks ahead. By coincidence I was scheduled to take a week's vacation the week after the assassination. My plans included a trip to Washington to visit friends. The city was still deep in mourning for the fallen president. Flags were at half-staff, and few tourists were visible. I went to Arlington National Cemetery to visit JFK's grave. From the Senate gallery I saw his youngest brother Teddy on the floor and was surprised to see him back in public so soon after the tragedy.

I flew back via Love Field in Dallas to visit family, and we drove to the scene of the shooting. It was all there, just as seen in countless replays on TV: The Texas School Book Depository, the grassy knoll in Dealey Plaza, the street JFK's limousine traveled when he was shot. I myself had driven this street many times on the way out of downtown Dallas.

I don't know why I felt compelled to visit these places, so anchored in grief. I suppose I wanted to try to absorb the meaning of it, to be able to tell my grandchildren: I was there. Though I didn't see these historic events in person, I felt the spirit of the places where they occurred. It felt sad and lonely there, as I tried to put myself in the place of the witnesses. Perhaps it was akin to visiting a Civil War battlefield and imagining what it must have been like for the combatants.

When they're old enough, I'll try to tell my grandchildren about that day and explain what it meant to this country. I want to be sure they're not among the generations that grow up knowing little or nothing about this president and how hard his death hit us. If my memory holds up, I'll try to describe the sense of loss and sadness, especially for the president's family, that Americans felt. I'll keep a clipping of this article, so I can remember exactly what I was doing when I heard President Kennedy had been shot.

ONE YEAR EARLIER

Recalling the JFK story really takes me back to my early years in journalism. But I came close to not having that career – or the fulfilling life that followed over the next six decades. That's because I was satisfying my military obligation, serving my required six months of active duty as a member of the U.S. Naval Air Reserve. In October 1962, I was one month from completing that active duty and beginning my journalism career in Oklahoma City, where a job awaited me as a reporter for the Daily Oklahoman/Oklahoma City Times. *I wasn't yet credentialed to have a role in covering this news story, but I wrote a column about my recollection of that period 38 years later. Here it is, from **Dec. 31, 2000.***

13 Days When World – and a Scared Sailor – Held Their Breaths

I will be among the first in line for the Jan. 12 opening of "13 Days," the Kevin Costner movie that covers the drama of the Cuban missile crisis. Watching the previews in recent weeks has dredged up memories and emotions that I had long forgotten – or suppressed – for I had a close personal relationship with those events.

In October 1962 I was a Seaman Third Class in the U.S. Navy Reserve, on active duty and a prime candidate for the front lines of the Navy blockade that President Kennedy ordered to stop shipment of Russian missiles to Cuba. In other words, where the shooting would start, if there was to be a war.

At the outbreak of the crisis I was at my home base at Naval Air Station Dallas, counting the days to my return to civilian life. In less than one month, my active duty tour would be completed and I would head to my first real job, as a cub reporter for the *Daily Oklahoman/Oklahoma City Times*. My future lay ahead of me, clear and promising, and I could hardly wait to shuck my bell-bottomed dungarees and Donald Duck dress blues for regular clothes.

My world was changed abruptly on Oct. 22, when President Kennedy in a nationally televised address watched by 50 million Americans revealed that Russia had ballistic missiles with a range of 1,000 miles, capable of holding nuclear warheads, installed in Cuba and aimed at our shores 90 miles away. The president declared a "quarantine" of Cuba by ordering the Navy to blockade shipping lanes to the island, boarding and searching them for offensive weapons and sinking those that failed to comply.

His concluding statement sent a chill through the backbones of me and my fellow swabbies watching it in the Enlisted Men's Club that night: "My fellow citizens, let no one doubt that this is a difficult and dangerous effort on which we have set out. No one can foresee precisely what course it will take or what costs or casualties will be incurred. . .The cost of freedom is always high, but Americans have always paid it."

The casualties could well be *us*, we knew; the price could be *our* blood. And with my newly learned skills I was red meat for this mission. I had recently completed photo intelligence school, where I learned how to interpret aerial photos. I was painfully aware that it was this very specialty that had alerted the Pentagon to the missile build-up on Cuba in the first place; that's just what we were trained to do.

Kennedy's speech put the armed forces on alert: Discharges of Navy and Marine personnel were halted, all leaves were canceled, those on leave were recalled, and military bases went into high security mode. Reserve units like ours most likely would be sent to Key West to fill in for units deployed aboard ship and, if necessary, become replacements if there were casualties.

But that didn't happen immediately. While the logistics of such a move were being arranged and while the crisis was negotiated on the diplomatic front, we waited in high suspense for our orders.

The airborne squadrons had plenty to do to get their aircraft and reconnaissance equipment ready. But photointelligencemen didn't need much – some maps, a few documents, pens, measuring tools and the trusty stereoscopic glasses that turned flat photo images into three-dimensional panoramas. Under the eyes of a skilled photo analyst, camouflaged anti-aircraft guns, tanks or ballistic missiles popped out of an aerial photo for quick identification.

So we waited – and guarded the base. My most vivid memory of that time is walking sentry duty on the base flight line in the pitch-black Texas night, half a mile from any buildings, a scared 22-year-old with live ammunition in his rifle and doubts about his need to use it. At NAS Dallas, our ships challenging Russian ships on the high seas seemed a million miles away. Yet who knew whether the Russians might attack American bases to divert U.S. military forces from the Caribbean? Who knew whether enemy troops might sneak up from the boondocks and try to blow up our planes? Who knew how close we were to "thermonuclear world war," as Russian President Khrushchev had ominously warned?

I had lots to time to think on those long, post-midnight sentry tours. I thought about the possibility I might die. If it was in a nuclear blast, well, there wasn't much I could do about that. And certainly everyone else around me would be dead, too. If it was aboard a ship in the Caribbean, or defending a land-locked base in Texas, I hoped that I would do what I was supposed to do. I didn't question the fairness or the rightness of it. This was, after all, *our* country being threatened, *our* security at risk. Mine was just one generation removed from World War II – the children of those who fought it. And Vietnam had not yet occurred.

For 13 days we faced that possibility, our futures on hold, the world holding its breath while international leaders played chicken with nuclear missiles. And then, Khrushchev backed down. He called the ships carrying long-range missiles back home and agreed to dismantle the missiles already deployed in Cuba. The freeze on discharges was lifted, and I was mustered out within three weeks.

I took the reporter's job in Oklahoma City, launching a 36-year career in newspapering, and pretty much forgot those 13 days in October when we were so close to an apocalyptic war. Now, that time and those events seem so far away.

ANOTHER WAR, AND A COVER-UP

Before 9/11 there was the Gulf War. This was the label given the American-led 1991 campaign to drive Iraq's military forces from Kuwait, which they had invaded the previous year. Code-named Operation Desert Storm, this war engaged a coalition force from 35 nations allied against Iraq's President Saddam Hussein after he launched a pre-emptive strike against neighboring Kuwait in a dispute over oil prices and access to the Persian Gulf. The U.S. eventually poured more than 700,000 troops into the war, which the allies quickly won by forcing the Iraqis from Kuwait and wiping out many of them in savage aerial attacks as they retreated back into Iraq on what came to be known as "the Highway of Death."

But about five years later, American veterans of that war began complaining of health issues which they blamed on exposure to an array of chemical agents during the fighting. These included antidotes to nerve gas that they were forced to take while in country (recall Saddam Hussein was notorious for having used sarin gas against his own people a few years earlier) as well as claimed exposure to sarin and to depleted uranium used in U.S. anti-tank ammunition. Veterans complained of chronic fatigue, skin rashes, memory loss and birth defects among their children, a condition that became known as Gulf War Syndrome. Their complaints largely were ignored by the Pentagon and White House. I met often with local veterans and researched the issue independently to come up with the following article, labeled Gulf War Syndrome: A Special Editorial, published as a full-page article on **July 28, 1996.**

Did Pentagon Put Troops at Risk?

Our Gulf War Soldiers May Have Been Unwitting Agents in Their Own Chemical Poisoning

How far does the cover-up go on the Gulf War Syndrome? That should be the question on the lips of every member of Congress and presidential candidate as the Pentagon's five-year denial of a mystery ailment among veterans of the 1991 Kuwait-Iraq war begins to fall apart.

The first solid proof of a Pentagon cover-up came with the admission the week of July 8th that American service men and women may, indeed, have been exposed to nerve gas when they destroyed an Iraqi chemical weapons bunker in the days immediately following the cease-fire. The bunker contained weapons tipped with sarin, the deadly nerve gas spread in Tokyo subways two years ago by Japanese terrorists, as well as several forms of mustard gas.

This is the first time the Pentagon has admitted even the possibility that GIs were exposed to nerve gas, a possible explanation for the complaints by some of the veterans of Operation Desert Storm and Desert Shield of chronic fatigue, skin rashes, memory loss and birth defects among their children – the ailment that has been labeled Gulf War Syndrome. Reports of nerve gas exposure to U.S. troops were made by U.N. observers inspecting Iraqi operations in 1991, but Pentagon officials consistently maintained that Iraq did not use any chemical or biological weapons in the war.

Gross Level of Negligence

The suppressed reports of chemical weapons exposure may be only the tip of the iceberg of Pentagon complicity in covering up evidence of the massive chemical poisoning of America's armed forces during the Gulf War. At best the evidence indicates a gross level of negligence by military leaders in preparing their troops to deal with the chemical warfare threat by Iraqi President Saddam Hussein. At worst it suggests use of American troops as guinea pigs to test various methods of dealing with chemical warfare. Either conclusion would explain why the Pentagon has gone to such lengths to deny the existence of a large-scale ailment called Gulf War Syndrome, just as it did about Agent Orange following the Vietnam War.

The latest denial came in early April, when the Pentagon released results of a two-year study of 18,929 veterans – the largest of the kind undertaken. The study found "no clinical evidence for a previously unknown, serious illness or 'syndrome' among Persian Gulf veterans," said Dr. Stephen Joseph, assistant secretary of defense for health affairs. The study concluded that 18 percent of the symptoms were from psychological causes, 18 percent from "musculoskeletal" causes, 18 percent from "ill-defined" causes, 10 percent were healthy, and smaller percentages involved problems of the nervous system, skin disease, digestive system or respiratory system.

The Pentagon spokesman called this "the definitive report" on Gulf War Syndrome.

Not quite.

Troops Forced to Take Drugs

The definitive report on the illness has yet to be written. For none of the stories published thus far reveals the depth of Pentagon culpability in administering antidotes to nerve gas exposure that had not been proven for their intended use and that researchers as long ago as 1978 had warned could lead to nerve and muscle damage.

Two medications, pyridostigmine bromide (taken orally) and botulinum toxoid (a vaccine) were administered to most of the more than 700,000 Desert Storm troops as a preventive to potential exposure to nerve gas. The drugs, from a class of chemicals known as cholinesterase inhibitors, short-circuit nerve signals that control muscles. If taken before exposure to nerve gas, the drugs – nerve agents themselves – are supposed to inhibit the reaction to the chemicals in nerve-gas weapons.

Individually, the chemicals may have reacted as intended. But when two or more chemicals are present, or when wrong doses are administered, the drugs can actually *create* the nerve-signal short-circuiting rather than *prevent* it. In addition, scientists believe that at least 4 percent of people have a genetic deficiency of a blood-cleansing enzyme that fights off nerve agents, making them more susceptible to damage from these chemicals than the rest of the population.

This alone could account for the symptoms of which 30,000 to 40,000 Gulf War vets complain. But that isn't all of the risk that our troops encountered in the administration of these drugs. Two insect repellents that soldiers sprayed on themselves or on uniforms during the war, Deet and Permethrin, also contain forms of the cholinesterase inhibitors.

Thus our troops may have been unwitting agents in their own chemical poisoning, with the help of their own commanding officers, who, like good soldiers must, followed orders from higher up to make sure every GI took his or her anti-nerve-gas medication. Most did so without complaint, trusting their officers' judgment. Individuals who balked were threatened with court martial.

Could the Pentagon brass have known of the dangers inherent in the chemical cocktails which they forced upon their troops? Should they have been aware of the potential for chemical poisoning in improper administration of the medicines and insect repellents?

Unequivocally, yes. Bradenton Realtor Thomas Tiedt, a former pharmaceutical researcher, and two colleagues did a study in the mid-1970s under grants from the U.S. Public Health Service and the Muscular Dystrophy Association of America that proved the disruption of nerve signals from improper dosage of these chemicals.

Their research on neostigminem, a close relative of pyridostigmine, was published in the Journal of Pharmacology and Experimental Therapeutics in 1978. It warned that the drug could cause "profound psychological, electrophysiological and electron microscopic disruption of nerve endings and muscles.

It was also cited in a devastating 1994 report by the Senate Committee on Veterans' Affairs chaired by Sen. Jay Rockefeller, D-W.Va., after a thorough investigation of Gulf War Syndrome complaints. That report, which was shelved after Rockefeller lost his committee chairmanship in the 1994 Republican sweep of Congress, in effect charges that the Pentagon either recklessly or knowingly poisoned its own troops in a panicky reaction to Saddam's threat to unleash chemical warfare.

The drugs had not been approved by the Food and Drug Administration "as safe and effective for repeated use by healthy persons under any circumstances," the committee reported. They had received FDA approval only for treating patients with a neurological disorder called myasthenia gravis under carefully controlled clinical conditions.

Pentagon Violated Consent Rule

Pentagon brass sought an FDA waiver to distribute the drug to GIs using the Investigational New Drug (IND) procedure allowed by federal law. IND provides that an unproven vaccine or drug can be administered but only if recipients give informed consent, that is, are told of the potential risks and benefits of the medicine, orally and in writing, and choose whether to take the medicine. IND also requires the distribution be under carefully controlled conditions where safety and effectiveness can be evaluated.

In a survey of 150 Gulf War vets, the Rockefeller committee found that 86 percent received no information on what they were taking or the potential risks. Many said they were ordered under threat of court martial not to discuss their vaccinations with anyone, not even with medical professionals treating their adverse reactions to the vaccine.

These findings, says the committee report, "indicate that . . .the Air Force totally ignored the requirements of informed consent that are a central provision of the Nuremberg Code, the Declaration of Helsinki and the Common Rule," three ethics codes to which the U.S. Government subscribes that require that all research efforts are done with the voluntary, competent, informed and understanding consent of the subject, *whether during war or peace.*

The shocking possibility that the Pentagon knew it was administering unproven, dangerous drugs to troops – in effect using them as guinea pigs – is revealed by the committee's report on a pre-war test of one of the two drugs.

In August 1990, shortly after Saddam had invaded Kuwait but before U.S. troops were sent en masse to the Persian Gulf, Defense Department scientists wanted to test the effects of pyridostigmine on vision. They received FCA approval to conduct a study using four volunteers under informed consent conditions. First, the test ruled out anyone who had asthma, sensitivity to this or related drugs. Volunteers were informed that possible side effects could include nausea, vomiting, slow heart rate, sweating, diarrhea, abdominal cramps, weakness or muscle cramps or twitches, increased salivation, increased bronchial secretions and pupil constriction. The Pentagon researchers said that, "because of these side effects, all subjects will be admitted to Lyster Army Hospital as in-patients so that they will be medically monitored during evening periods of non-testing. A drug will be available at the test site to counteract the possible adverse side effects."

As the committee notes, "A few months later 400,000 U.S. soldiers were ordered to take the same dosage of the drug for days, weeks or months, none of whom had been screened for any of the diseases mentioned in the informed consent form given to the four men, none of whom were warned about the risks associated with the drug, and none of whom were given a choice of whether or not to take it."

Where's the Public Clamor?

The Pentagon has a tradition of testing unproven methods and antidotes on troops dating back at least to the post-Hiroshima tests of exposure to nuclear radiation and continuing to the use of Agent Orange in Vietnam. And it has an equally long tradition of denial and cover-up of its deeds.

With that record in mind and with the findings of the Rockefeller Commission and other studies in hand, it is difficult to understand why there isn't a clamor among citizens and members of Congress to get to the bottom of Gulf War Syndrome. Don't the men and women who risked their lives in defense of this country deserve better? Will we turn our backs on another generation of maimed and crippled soldiers, as we did to the Vietnam vets for so long denying their pain and refusing even to treat their injuries?

God forgive us if we do. And God help us as a nation, too, for what parent would allow a son or daughter to train for war knowing that their own government might poison them – and then deny it?

POST SCRIPT

Once again, I was denied my scoop. The above expose' of the Pentagon's cover-up of what amounted to criminal behavior went nowhere. Who pays attention to an obscure small-town newspaper writing about military malfeasance when there's a war against terrorism going on and a stained blue dress in the White House? Eventually, as veteran's groups grew more vocal, Congress acted, ordering the VA to contract with the National Academy of Sciences to look into Gulf War Syndrome. NAS subsequently issued 10 reports in the early 2000s, all confirming what I reported in the article above in 1996. The studies found that as many as 250,000 Gulf War veterans were suffering from neurological illnesses traced to the toxic agents to which they had been exposed, both by their own commanders and by the side-effects of exposure to burning compounds in battle. Today the VA recognizes and provides treatment for "medically unexplained illnesses or 'Gulf War Syndrome' which encompasses certain diagnosable chronic disability patterns" that include forms of multiple sclerosis.

Perhaps it wasn't all for naught. Perhaps someone clipped the article and sent it to friends in the military, or to their congressperson. At least I tried. Now, it's time to move on to another chapter.

CHAPTER FOUR
MY BLEEDING HEART

I have always been a defender of the underdog – the poor, the homeless, the disenfranchised, the people denied social justice. Probably most journalists are, or at least most were during my career. It comes with the natural curiosity that directed us into the profession in the first place. By definition, we care. About government corruption, of course. Also about going to war, and passing sewer bond issues, cracking down on drunk driving, and a hundred other issues related to public policy.

But we care about people who are in dire circumstances, who need help in obtaining adequate food, shelter, education, health care, transportation, civil rights and human dignity. It is not for nothing that the unofficial motto of editorialists is "to comfort the afflicted and afflict the comfortable." At least it's one that I often boasted of in prideful self-deprecation, along with my self-imposed label, "the man people love to hate." It was true. In the early days of my tenure as the Herald's *opinion editor, I would be shunned at cocktail parties and receptions, conversation groups turning their backs when they saw me approaching. Thankfully, that changed after I met Jo Anne. She was tight with the leading social circles, so her friends and their husbands, whose pet projects or causes I likely had written negative editorials about, had to be nice to me when they spoke to her. But at times the niceness was decidedly icy.*

Much of what I wrote in my columns during those 30 years had to do with issues related to social justice. My heart bled for the poor and the downtrodden, the victims and the friendless, society's castoffs. Often, I didn't just write about them *– I got out of the office and off the couch and actually* did *something to help them. That was what happened during the winter of 1983-'84, when a rare, bitter freeze wiped out the winter crops in the groves and fields of central Florida, leaving thousands of migrant workers without work*

*– or resources. The following column, published **Feb. 15, 1984**, is one of the most memorable of my action-oriented bleeding-heart tales.*

On Bradenton's Doorstep, There Is Famine

WIMAUMA – Poverty stalks the land in the rural backwaters of southwest Florida – a deep, empty-bellied kind of poverty that evokes Depression-era scenes of hunger and despair.

Here, in the freeze-ruined fields of southern Hillsborough County and northern Manatee County, hundreds of families huddle in shabby trailer camps like the pitiful Okies in "Grapes of Wrath," stranded in the vegetable basket of America with no way to feed themselves.

Here, five minutes from the neatly clipped lawns and swimming pools of the Sun City Center and King's Point retirement communities, hungry men and women, many carrying babies and toddlers, line up outside a makeshift soup kitchen four days a week for a plateful of beans, rice and tortillas.

Here, barely 30 minutes by interstate highway from the sleek Gulf-front condominiums of Anna Maria Island and Longboat Key, families of four, six, eight and more crowd into filthy, broken-down trailers unfit for human habitation that rent for $350 a month – many without electricity and most in fear of being evicted from even these squalid quarters because of overdue rent payments.

Rev. Bill Cruz calls it a famine – a stark, unequivocal word that we have never before heard used in reference to this land of plenty. They have famines in Chad or Pakistan or India. God sent famines upon the land in Old Testament times to punish iniquity. But famine in the United States in 1984?

Indeed, the word famine is not an exaggeration of the conditions that migrants face in this farming hamlet 35 miles northeast of Bradenton. Idled by the Christmas freeze that all but destroyed the source of their livelihood until April, hundreds of migrant families are almost entirely dependent upon handouts from Rev. Cruz's Good Samaritan Mission here or a similar relief center in Ruskin for their daily sustenance. Seventy-five to 100 families a day come to the mission's tiny frame house a block off S.R. 674 in Wimauma for rice, beans, flour, milk and canned goods.

And when the mission pantry's shelves are empty, or when they cannot buy gas for their pickups and cars or hitch a ride into town, the migrants scour the fields for snakes and armadillos, which they cook and eat. If there is no milk or infant formula, mothers boil rice and pour off some of the liquid to feed their babies. The rice water isn't very nutritious, but it is better than an empty stomach. Volunteer workers tell of visiting homes where children were being fed boiled onions – it was all they had to eat that day.

The migrants come here "so desperate, so frustrated," says Rev. Cruz. "They are idle, they have nothing to do. And they get nothing from the government." Few are eligible for the government "safety nets" that are supposed to keep people from having to eat snakes and rodents to stay alive. There were a few days' work last month laying plastic and staking the fields for the spring crop. The strawberries that didn't freeze provide perhaps one day of work a week, for a few. But the crop is sparse; a picker can fill only four or five flats a day, at $1.75 to $2.50 each. It is not enough for groceries, heat, electricity, gas to get to work, and the exorbitant rents of the tin ghettos in which they live.

All day long, a steady stream of men and women, desperation etched on their faces, files into Rev. Cruz's tiny office in the mission with slips of paper that reflect their tenuous existence. Here is Ventura Lemus, a young woman with an overdue bill from Tampa Electric Co. for $19.74 and a warning that the power will be turned off in two days if it isn't paid. Rev. Cruz sighs and adds Ventura's to a thick stack of such bills on his desk. He promises her he will call the utility on her behalf; TECO, he says later, has been good about carrying delinquent migrants' accounts if he speaks for them.

Here is Saul Serna, a tall man in his late 20s, with a bill for $43.67 for rent on his trailer lot that was due a week ago. Actually, the man owes $225 for three months' rent, but can avoid eviction if he comes up with the $43.67. Rev. Cruz sighs again, and repeats a phrase heard often when the mission's resources are exhausted: "Para manana" – which translates to "Come back tomorrow and maybe I can do something for you." Saul is too late for help today, the mission's treasury was drained that morning by a $700 payment to one landlord of several migrant families – who called later and said he needed more money or he would start evicting.

Here is Evodio Mendoza, a serious young man of about 22 with a wife and two children whose request is relatively simple: propane so his wife can cook. He had earned a few dollars the week before and had spent his last $2 on gasoline so he could look for work, he told Rev. Cruz. The minister sighs again, takes out his personal checkbook and writes a check to Evodio for $6.50.

There are many others this day who are turned away with "Para manana." Many days when the mission closes for the day, Rev. Cruz says, its shelves are empty, and it seems pointless to open up the next morning. "But I tell the volunteers, 'The Lord will provide,' and the next day a truck will drive up with $200 worth of food and we just say, 'Praise the Lord' and start passing it out."

That is basically the way Good Samaritan Mission survives – "waiting upon the Lord to provide" through the generosity of others. A non-denominational outreach of Rev. Cruz and his wife, Dora, Good Samaritan depends upon donations to supplement the $4,000 a month it receives from a Tampa relief fund, which he calls "a drop in the bucket."

Some federal disaster relief for the migrants may be available by March 1. That this is over two weeks off, and it is not known whether it will be enough to sustain the migrants until normal picking conditions return around April 1. The migrants need help now. They are desperate now.

Will you help? A relief effort called Friends of Migrants is underway in Manatee County to channel donations to Rev. Cruz's mission. We call upon everyone who reads this to reach out to these unfortunate people in their time of need with donations of food, clothing, blankets and money. Pastors and church leaders, surely there could be no better demonstration of your commitment to Christ's example of brotherly love than to join this effort. Specific food items needed are rice, pinto beans, shortening, flour, bread, sugar, dry noodles, canned goods, powdered milk and baby food. Church leaders, if you can, collect a van or pickup load and drive it up yourself. Take I-75 north to S.R. 674 East; Wimauma is just a few miles east of Sun City Center, and the mission is one block north of the highway at 12th and Center.

If you can't contribute through a church or other organization, we'll accept food contributions here at the *Herald*, 401 13th St. W. If you can give money, send checks made out to "Friends of Migrants" to First City Federal Savings and Loan Association, Attention: Annette Lee, P.O. Box 1969, Bradenton 33506.

Please, Manatee County, don't let these people down. Don't close your eyes to famine.

POST SCRIPT

That appeal generated an outpouring of food, clothing and blankets to the Herald's *lobby, so much that it took a caravan of vans, cars and station wagons to deliver it to Rev. Cruz a week later. I also made a personal appeal that Sunday at Church of the Cross, and a separate caravan embarked from there for Wimauma. I was unable to join either group, as they went on weekdays and I couldn't afford the time off from work.*

But later, I learned that there had been more than just brotherly love exchanged on those excursions into the fields of famine. Our church Youth Pastor had been part of the team from my church who delivered the supplies. In the course of conversation with Rev. Cruz, he learned of a Hispanic girl, no more than 15, who was pregnant out of wedlock, with no resources from her family. Over a period of weeks, the Youth Pastor and his wife gained the girl's trust and, seeing her increasingly desperate situation, offered to adopt the baby if she were willing to give it up. Arrangements were made through official channels, and shortly after her delivery they did add this baby to their family, which already consisted of two young boys. The baby also was a boy. They named him David, as a tribute to me for leading them to this precious new child.

Twenty years later, I came face to face with another kind of hunger, related to food and so much more. And it was much closer to home. I learned of it via a letter to the editor, surely the most touching of the thousands I had received in what by this time was a nearly 30-year career as Opinion Page editor. It once again prompted me to get up from behind my desk and do something to ease the heartache. The following was published as an editorial, not a personal column, around **mid-December 2004**. *It lays out in painful detail the plight of the mentally ill and homeless – and my effort to help one of those forgotten souls.*

'Alone and Broken'
It's Sad to Face Christmas with Dread

Where do I fit in?"

So began a letter to a *Herald* reporter last week from a local woman, facing the approach of Christmas with dread. Scraping by on a small disability check, with "my light bulbs unscrewed, my hot water turned off and my day-old bread from the soup kitchen starting to mold," the woman in her plaintive rhetorical query and plea for somebody simply to care seemed to sum up the very essence of what Christmas is *supposed* to be about: Love, sharing, family, hope, joy.

For her, however, it is merely a bitter but ubiquitous reminder of what it is *not*: The month of December, she wrote, "is just a never-ending assault on my spirit, one continuous lie. . ."

The further into the letter we read, the more painful it became for *us*: A veteran editor called it the most heart-breaking story he had heard in more than 40 years as a journalist, a tale worthy of Dickens.

Excerpts from the letter

The complete letter is more than 600 words long. Following are excerpts from it that capture the anguish and longing expressed in the full text:

"As the holidays approach, it seems so many people are touched with the Spirit of Christmas. I pray so hard to be touched by that Spirit, but all I feel is aloneness and pain. . .I am alone. I have no family or friends. None of the local community outreaches have any Angel Trees for people like me. . .

"Although I try not to focus on materialistic or negative things, I can't help but feel the pain that does not go away as the world celebrates the holidays. It has been years since I have gotten so much as a Christmas card. I hate to admit it, but it hurts. . .

"The month of December, to me, is just a never-ending assault on my spirit. One continuous lie, a never-ending fantasy of family, friends, food and giving, when year after year, I always wind up sitting alone, usually outside in the cold, watching families as they gather into churches or restaurants. I wonder what that feeling of 'Christmas Spirit and cheer' must be like. But no one ever sees me. I am invisible to the world. I am silent in my torments. I am broken within. Shattered pieces of a lost soul. A masterpiece with no canvas.

". . .Please pass this message on to anyone who might send me a card. I would give anything for just the bottom of the pot scraps of special holiday foods. . ."

A real person

Sadly, this is not a character from a Dickens novel but a real person in Manatee County. I called local mental health officials, who know her as well as hundreds more like her in our midst. This woman, who we'll refer to as Sally because she asked that her identity not be revealed, is an eloquent spokeswoman for an estimated 1,000 friendless people in Manatee County who are recovering from mental illness. The true number of those suffering from schizophrenia is closer to 3,000, but the smaller number represents those whose psychosis has cost them their homes, their careers and their families. In other words, those who are utterly alone.

Sally once had a husband, two children, a thriving business and a four-bedroom home in an upscale subdivision. Her schizophrenic episodes cost her everything, and she spent years living on the streets before being helped by Manatee Glens, Manatee County's primary mental health treatment center.

Sally for the past three years has had a relatively stable life. She lives alone in a tiny apartment off Cortez Road and dreams of being able to return to work to give meaning to her life and even supplement her desperately small disability check that forces her to forego air-conditioning in summer and to ration use of her hot water and lights. Disabled by a spinal problem and esophageal disorders as a result of childhood abuse and years of malnutrition, she feels she could do part-time work catering events or assisting in the kitchen, her former profession. She even longs just to do volunteer work to mingle with people, to be of value to someone.

But the stigma of mental illness never goes away, and she fears rejection – from painful experience. Her illness was graphically represented in the 2001 movie "A Brilliant Mind," with Russell Crowe playing math genius John Forbes Nash Jr., who sank into delusional schizophrenia for years but recovered to win a Nobel Prize in 1994. Sally, too, is described by one who knows her well as having a brilliant mind.

Resources available

There are resources for people like Sally. A drop-in center operated by Volunteers of America for mental patients who want social contact is within walking distance. And the Manatee chapter of the National Alliance for Mental Illness (NAMI) has an emergency fund to which she could apply for help with an electric bill or similar crisis.

The latter, in fact, is the most efficient way that readers moved by this editorial could do something to help Sally as well as others like her. Money, grocery or department store gift cards could enable NAMI's volunteer board to assure that needy clients don't have to beg for "pot scraps of special holiday foods" at Christmas. Send gift cards or checks made out to "NAMI-Manatee" to: National Alliance on Mental Illness, Manatee Chapter, P.O. Box 855, Anna Maria, FL 34216, or phone the group's help line at 758-3562 for more information. Of course, Manatee Glens, a United Way agency, also seeks to provide for special needs of the mentally ill, including offering a full Thanksgiving dinner for those with no place to go.

As for the isolation and depression that Sally described, only arms extended in friendship can heal this ache in a broken heart. Sally now has at least one friend who has made sure she will not be without a Christmas card, a small tree and a special meal this Christmas. There are hundreds more who may not be as fortunate. In the spirit of Christmas, reach out to them; help them "fit in."

POST SCRIPT

I was that friend for Sally, personally delivering the card, tree, food basket and gift card to her apartment in a shabby building barely three miles from my church. But I wasn't alone. Readers responded to this appeal by contributing more than $1,000 to NAMI, and a half-dozen sent me gift cards that I delivered to Sally, assuring her more than one nutritious meal that holiday season. Though I didn't write about it, that Christmas dinner in my home included a special *prayer for Sally and all of the friendless people who were living similar lives.*

BEFORE FAMINE – GENOCIDE

My very first case of bleeding heart compassion as Opinion Editor at the Bradenton Herald *came just two years into my career there. And it was by far the most ambitious act of mercy I have ever undertaken, before or since. One day in August 1979, I acquired a second family, members of which spoke no English and owned nothing except the clothes they were wearing. I blame – or credit, depending on my mood – my friend Ed Dick for this state of affairs. Ed walks out Christ's admonition to care for "the least of these" better than anyone I know in Manatee County. It would take chapters to enumerate the good deeds this saintly man and his late wife, Joanne, have performed in eight decades here.*

In 1979 he was the local spearhead for Refugee Inc., a group of volunteers formed to sponsor those fleeing the killing fields of Cambodia, where Pol Pot had launched a genocidal campaign that killed at least 2 million people and caused hundreds of thousands more to flee into neighboring Thailand, where makeshift jungle refugee camps had been established by the United Nations. Ed personally lobbied local church leaders to sponsor at least one family per church by appealing to the Opinion Page editor of the local newspaper – me. I agreed to publish an editorial about the initiative and to take the appeal to Church of the Cross leaders. The following Sunday I was given a slot during service to ask that we sponsor a Cambodian family. Almost before I knew it I found myself headed for Tampa International Airport to meet the family we had been assigned to sponsor. The details were vague – several families were arriving on the same flight, and leaders of Refugee Inc. would be there to connect sponsors with refugee families. Ours would perhaps be a family of four or five. The editorial that follows, published in **mid-August 1979,** *and the two columns after that provide snapshots of that experience – and adds a relevant commentary to the immigration debate raging in this country as I write.*

Why Help the Refugees?

A lump rises in the throat and the eyes moisten as they step into the plush terminal at Tampa International Airport – not because it's a typical airport scene with joyful hugs and squeals of delight. You have, after all, never seen them before; you cannot understand a word they say, nor they you; they are as foreign as space creatures emerging from a flying saucer.

No, the emotional choke is felt just because they are so pathetic, so absolutely defenseless and bewildered. And because you know why they are here and what they have gone through to get here. That's why you swallow hard as you greet the newest of the homeless and tempest-tossed from Southeast Asia's teeming shores and try to pronounce their tongue-twisting names: Ngov Kong Chek, Ngov Chea Ly Heang, Ngov Chung Huot, and on down the line of round Asian faces to tiny, precious little Ngov Ly Eang, who squirms in giggly embarrassment just like your own 6-year-old when called his name.

They seem so foreign, this Cambodian family in their drab, baggy trousers and shapeless cotton shirts, the women hunkered down on their haunches gently rocking sleeping children as they watch the tall Americans in whose hands rests their fate. But then, they also seem strangely familiar, and it takes a few minutes before you realize why: These are the faces you have seen in the newspapers and on TV for the 10 years that Americans fought over their far-away corner of the world.

That wrinkled grandmother – how many times did you see her sad face before burned-out villages, or stooped over a cooking pot beside a muddy road? And that gap-toothed young mother – how many like her have leaped out at you from Page One, grieving over a dead child or husband? The round face and narrow eyes of that ragged little girl – how many versions of her have greeted you over breakfast, begging from GIs or peddling goods in a marketplace?

You have seen these pitiful victims of senseless wars on the other side of the globe many times before, but never up close, within touching and speaking distance – never close enough to see the sadness in their eyes or to begin to sense the sorrow they must feel for their once-beautiful country, for the uprooted lives, for the family members who weren't strong or lucky enough to make it to Tampa International Airport, who will never make it.

You watch them stare at the thick carpet of the terminal, the brightly upholstered furniture, the soft recessed lighting, the seabird sculptures, the glittering gift stores and restaurants, and you actually feel guilty. You want to say proudly, "Look at all the fantastic things that we have here in America. Isn't this a great country?"

But instead you look guiltily away, because you realize just how extravagant, how sumptuous your life is compared to theirs. You remember the things that worried you and your family this morning before you left home – your jammed garbage disposal, your wife's balky auto, your son's pouting because his TV privileges were cut off, your soaring electrical bill; the lawn that needs mowing. How small! How meaningless!

And later, when a reader calls or writes to ask why – why take in these people who are so alien to our ways, and who will burden our welfare system and unbalance our job market, you have no trouble answering:

Because this is what America is all about. This is what made it so precious two, three, five, 10 generations ago to the huddled masses of Europe who yearned to breathe free – your own ancestors. Here, today, you are seeing Miss Liberty's promise fulfilled, just as it was for your grandparents, as the wretched refuse from another teeming shore step onto American soil.

They have found the lamp beside the golden door. They are free!

And the lump in your throat returns.

ONE MONTH LATER

Ten! We were responsible for a family of 10, not four or five as promised. A man and his wife, his elderly mother and adult sister, and the couple's six children ranging in age from 16 to 6. Ten strangers who have never before heard a Western language spoken, who understand only Cambodian and Mandarin Chinese. Ed Dick was there to assist in making introductions, and he brought with him a Vietnamese-American man who had fled the fall of Saigon four years earlier and who spoke enough Cambodian to get by.

What were we going to do with 10 people with whom we couldn't communicate? We couldn't accommodate four extra visitors in our home, let alone 10. In his calm and reassuring way, Ed told us not to worry, they could spend a few days with him until we found an apartment. He was used to unexpected guests, having hosted many refugees from the Vietnam exodus and also having taken in various homeless people from time to time. At one point during this rescue mission, he had as many as 14 refugees sleeping in his Bayshore Gardens home – that's how selfless he and his wife were.

A small but dedicated cohort of volunteers from Church of the Cross helped us get the family settled. The church provided funding to rent a relatively inexpensive three-bedroom apartment in East Bradenton, and the volunteers helped get them registered for social services, language classes for the adults at Manatee Vocational-Technical School and the children in a special class for non-English-speakers set up by the Manatee School District. A month later, I gave readers this update in a column published **Sept. 16, 1979.**

Refugees After a Month: New Ways, Words, Shoes

The biggest difference is their smile. It comes more naturally now, reflecting a genuine happiness emanating from the heart, rather than the superficial politeness that is an Oriental tradition.

But smiling is probably the easiest lesson the Indochinese refugees have learned in their first month in Bradenton. Most are adjusting remarkably well as they struggle with foreign customs, foods, money, religions and language. They have learned to use modern appliances, to tell time, to take prescription drugs, to ride the bus, to go to the grocery store.

They are still learning to shop for clothing, to write checks, to ask for goods by name, to cook strange foods (and to eat them), to pay bills, and to speak English.

They have made the rounds of the social service agencies – the food stamp and welfare office, the Health Department, the employment service, and CETA, the government's special Indochinese Refugee Assistance Program, which qualifies them for temporary benefits.

The biggest obstacle has been the language barrier, which can be a formidable handicap in certain situations. A simple medical check-up, for example, is impossible without an interpreter. So are the applications for food stamps, since regulations require that all facets of the program, including penalties for cheating, be explained in a language the recipient understands.

Most of the 45 refugees who have arrived in the past six weeks have been Cambodians of Chinese extraction. There is only a handful of English-speaking citizens in this area who also speak Cambodian or Chinese, and most of these hold down full-time jobs and some attend school part-time, too. While they have been for the most part cooperative in offering their services, interpreting has been a major problem for refugee sponsors.

Learning English has been made more difficult by the fact that the Cambodians, unlike the Vietnam refugees who came in 1975, have never been exposed to *any* western language, let alone English.

The situation has forced local sponsors to vie among themselves for the services of Chinese- or Cambodian-speaking Americans, and it has led to some almost comic interpreting arrangements. Say a sponsor wants to say something to a new Cambodian refugee. He gives the message to a Vietnamese who understands English, but not Cambodian. The Vietnamese gives the message to a Cambodian who understands Vietnamese but not English. The Cambodian gives the message to the refugee who understands Cambodian, but not English or Vietnamese.

The sponsor prays that the message was not too badly twisted in the process.

The best way around the problem, of course, is to teach the refugees English as rapidly as possible. This is being done through special English classes for the school-age children at Palmetto Elementary School, and for the adults at Manatee Vocational-Technical School.

At Palmetto, in a room set aside for the 11 Cambodian and Vietnamese children, the teaching problems are monumental. The two teachers have to contend with an age range of 6 to 18 and an educational level that in the Cambodian children is four to six years behind normal for their age, because Cambodian schools were closed in 1973. So the teachers are faced with, say, a 10-year-old who has never been to school and can't add, subtract, read or write in *any* language. Once he learns the "survival skills" the class is designed to give him, at what academic level does he start to learn all the rest – first grade?

Across the river at Vo-Tech, the children's parents are going through a similar learning experience. Some of the adults with minimal formal education in their homeland are having a harder time learning than their children, but they keep at it, for six hours a day in the classroom and lab and later at home with tapes and lessons.

The past month has been almost as educational for their sponsors as for the refugees themselves. More than one West Bradenton citizen who had never before been inside a welfare or food stamp office gained a new respect for the virtually thankless job the people there do. Many doubtless looked upon them as perpetrators of welfare chiselers, rather than overworked public servants trying to keep the poor and helpless alive and functioning, fighting a mountain of red tape and paperwork from one side and ignorance, apathy and hostility from the other. Almost without exception the social service workers have been cooperative, patient and understanding in helping the refugees get settled.

There have been many frustrations for the sponsors, but there have been compensations, too. Such as the spirit-lifting experience of first hearing

"Hello, how are you?" spoken in clear, understandable English by the young mother who just a month ago was virtually mute.

Watching three beaming little cherubs show off to a visitor by counting to 10, reciting their ABCs or saying, "Good morning" is enough to choke up one who remembers the thin, frightened little mice that got off a plane at Tampa International a month ago.

No Christmas-morning glow produced by the most generous Santa could compare with that left by the sight of an 11-year-old boy parading in the first pair of shoes and socks he has ever owned.

The past month has been full of beautiful experiences like that for the Manatee Countians who made a commitment to the refugees. They have learned a few things about smiling, too.

TWENTY-ONE YEARS LATER

I wish I had provided more details about the 11-year-old boy referenced above, getting his first pair of shoes. That was my experience with one of the children of the Ngov family we sponsored. It was in the first days of their arrival, and we had taken them to the neighborhood supermarket to acquaint them with American shopping ways and to purchase staples for their new home. Rounding the end of one aisle, we came upon a display of children's clothing and shoes. The 11-year-old, like everyone else in his family shod in rubber flip-flops, glommed onto a pair of cheap tennis shoes. He gingerly lifted them off the rack and looked pleading at first his mother, then me. I nodded affirmatively to the question asked by his eyes, and he sat in the middle of the aisle to put on the shoes. The fit seemed about right. He stood up, took a few steps, then stood on one foot and held the other out so he could better see his foot. The grin on his face and the sparkle in his eyes spoke volumes about how happy this had made him. And me.

I wrote a one-year update about the refugees' progress, but I didn't manage to maintain a close relationship with them. They were busy building new lives, and I was doing the same in a different context, *with my own new family and challenging new position. Life went on. More than two decades later, Ed Dick and the leaders of Refugee Inc. decided to hold a reunion of sponsors and the families they had helped. Here is my account of that event, published in **mid-July 2000.***

Former Refugee Family Validates the Truth of America's Promise

We'd grown apart over the years, as old friends sometimes do. But as I greeted the Ngov family on July 4 it was like old times, catching up on family doings and promising to do better at staying in touch.

They looked the same, yet they didn't. They were so . . . American-looking. Not that they shouldn't. After all, they've been American citizens for almost 15 years, and have long since achieved the American dream of a steady job, owning their home and cars, children healthy and launched into successful careers, taking vacations, spoiling grandchildren.

How different from 21 years ago, when I greeted them at Tampa International Airport, just off the plane from a refugee camp in Thailand where they had fled from the killing fields of their homeland, Cambodia. It was impossible not to be moved by their appearance as we were introduced. As I wrote at the time, they seemed "so pathetic, so absolutely defenseless and bewildered. . .so foreign. . .in their drab, baggy trousers and shapeless cotton shirts. . ."

Yet in 1979 I also saw them as strangely familiar because they conjured up images from news photos and TV from their war-torn land: Of a wrinkled grandmother weeping over her burned-out village, of an expressionless young mother stirring a cooking pot beside a muddy road, of sad-eyed children in threadbare clothing staring in wonderment at the tall Americans in whose hands their fate rested.

That would be me and my wife, along with a few others. As their sponsors we had primary responsibility for establishing them into a new life in Bradenton. We had the help of volunteers from our church and Refugee Inc., the task force of Manatee-Sarasota citizens formed to facilitate the resettlement of refugees from Cambodia and Laos in this area. But we had no idea what we were in for.

Looking back, I don't know how we did it: Finding housing for a family of 10, arranging for transportation to school, setting up visits to the Health Department, teaching them basic words, enrolling them in language classes – and all without understanding a single word of each other's language.

Yet compared to the challenges facing them, our burden was nothing. They had to learn a new language, new customs, new currency, new foods, new jobs – a new way of life. They adapted beautifully. Within a month I was able to report that they were learning to shop for their own groceries, to use American appliances, to ride county buses and to speak snatches of English, thanks to intensive classes at Manatee Vo-Tech. And they were smiling.

After one year I wrote that the refugees had "achieved a degree of self-sufficiency that makes close supervision by sponsors unnecessary. Many, in fact, are totally independent: working, driving cars, attending school, establishing credit – all the things any American citizen does." They were working at regular jobs, paying their own bills and handling most of their financial affairs on their own.

The children, I said, "so bashful and strange-looking in their Asian garb last year, now wear theme T-shirts, jeans and sneakers, read second- and third-grade level books in English, and sling American slang around like natives."

And 20 years later? Mr. and Mrs. Ngov own a small but comfortable west Bradenton home. They are fluent in English, wear typical American fashions, and are tuned in to the routine of American life. They have a satellite dish which enables them to watch programming from China

(Chinese is their native language.) Mr. Ngov has retired after 20 years in the maintenance department of the Manatee School District, and Mrs. Ngov works in a south Manatee electronics plant.

Five of their six children have college degrees. One daughter is a financial officer for an aerospace company in Alabama; another is a nurse in San Diego; one is a teacher in Okeechobee, and the fourth is a lawyer in Washington state. Of the two sons, the oldest works in a local electronics plant and the youngest is a computer engineer in Sarasota. All but one have been naturalized as American citizens.

Seeing them and their children settled so comfortably into the American culture and contributing so much to our economy was reassuring for me. There were times at first in '79 when I wondered whether they could ever adapt, whether it was a good idea to wrench people from their native land and plop them into a culture so foreign as ours was to them. Yet countless generations from other lands who preceded them – including my own grandparents from Germany – set an admirable example to follow. You pulled together as a family, you worked hard, you took advantage of every educational opportunity, you saved and helped the next generation climb a few rungs higher up the ladder.

I knew the story well – my oldest sister was the first in our family to go to college – but had taken it for granted as a second-generation American. The Ngov family's success helped remind me of just what this country means to freedom-lovers the world over. It is still the shining city on the hill, the beacon of hope for the oppressed and the dispossessed. I have witnessed it close-up and personal, and believe me, it gives you a good feeling.

PRESENT AT THE BIRTH OF THE CHRISTIAN RIGHT

Except in evangelical Christian circles, gay rights are now accepted across most of America. Openly gay athletes, actors, politicians and even ministers go about their business with little notice. They marry, they conceive and/or adopt children, engage in public displays of affection, and even run for president of the United States (South

Bend Mayor Pete Buttigieg). But it was not always so. Gays were still widely reviled and persecuted in the 1960s and '70s. But with the gay rights movement gaining momentum in the wake of the Stonewall Inn uprising in 1969, some bigger cities began stepping up to include gay rights language in anti-discrimination ordinances. Miami-Dade was one of them. On Jan. 18, 1977, by a 5-3 vote of the County Commission, Miami-Dade became the 40th municipality to formally ban discrimination on the basis of sexual orientation.

But an opposition movement called Save Our Children sprang up among Miami's evangelical Christian community. At its head was Florida's unofficial sweetheart, Anita Bryant, the nationally popular crooner who was the spokeswoman for the Florida Citrus Commission, hawking Florida orange juice in TV commercials with the oh, so wholesome message, "A day without orange juice is like a day without sunshine." She also did commercials for such iconic American brands as Coca-Cola, Tupperware and Holiday Inn. Many considered her America's sweetheart, not just Florida's.

Largely by demonizing gays as child molesters, the campaign succeeded in calling for a vote by the people on the gay rights ordinance. In a referendum held June 7, voters repealed the ordinance by a 2-1 majority. Though we had no idea at the time, this issue and this campaign would become the seed for the entry of conservative Christians into the political process – what came to be known as the Christian Right –a political force to be reckoned with. By the early '80s, nationally known evangelist Jerry Falwell made opposition to gay rights a major plank in his Moral Majority platform, helping usher in the Reagan conservative era. Opposition to gay rights continues to rank high on conservative agendas to this day.

*I could not remain silent. In my very first personal column since becoming Opinion Editor, I took on that icon of the Sunshine State, Anita Bryant, because I had a history with her. The following piece was printed **June 5, 1977**, just two days before Miamians went to the polls. It firmly established me as a bleeding-heart liberal.*

When Anita Was Still Beautiful. . . An Idol Crumbles with Time

It was the spring of 1963 when I met Anita Bryant. I was a 22-year-old cub reporter on the *Oklahoma City Times*. It was my first real newspaper job, and I was eager.

When my crusty city editor asked if I'd like to interview a Miss America runner-up, I leaped on the assignment. Would I? Wow! My first "celebrity" interview – with a beauty queen yet.

Miss Bryant, it seemed, fresh from her triumph at Atlantic City, was back in her native state and would be entertaining Sunday afternoon at a downtown convention. A furniture group, as I recall.

So, looking spiffy in my brand-new $29.95 suit from J.C. Penney, I showed up at an exhibit hall filled with sport-jacketed Oklahoma furniture salesmen and their evening-gowned wives (this was before leisure and pants suits). All eyes were turned to the stage where the most beautiful woman I had ever seen was singing, as I recall, "My Little Corner of the World" in the most beautiful voice I had ever heard.

I recall that she was wearing a white dress with a red floral pattern, a little red velvet cape, and high-heeled patent leather shoes. I was star-struck as she belted out her repertoire – songs like "Paper Rose," " 'Til There Was You," "Battle Hymn of the Republic," and a couple of gospel songs. She wound up, naturally, with a rousing rendition of "O-o-o-o-OK-lahoma," which brought the crowd to its feet in a standing ovation. That song *always* brings crowds to their feet in Oklahoma.

The author in his $29 suit, interviewing Anita Bryant | Courtesy Anita Bryant

Then it was time for my interview. The press agent handling the show's publicity brought Anita down from the stage and introduced me.

She was even more beautiful up close. Her skin was the smoothest, creamiest, most unblemished I had ever seen. Her voice could melt butter. Her face was angelic; her lips luscious; her waist miniscule.

I was speechless for a few seconds – her beauty was that dazzling to an unworldly farm boy used to women of less-perfect proportions. I managed to blurt out a few questions; I can't recall what they were. No doubt something about how she felt being a big-time beauty queen, her plans for the future, that sort of thing.

While we were talking, the press agent had his photographer take some pictures of us, no doubt figuring I'd be impressed with a picture of me interviewing Anita Bryant.

I was. I went back to the office and wrote a nice story of a local girl making good in the big time. My editor loved it, and it got prominent display in Monday's paper. The press agent sent me the picture of me interviewing Anita, and I was proud of it. I filed it away with other memorabilia one collects, and over the years followed her budding career

214

with a secret pride – as if I'd had something to do with it, though of course I hadn't.

I secretly cheered as she made it on the "Arthur Godfrey Show" and Don McNeil's "Breakfast Club." I watched her songs become gold records and the records become hot albums. I didn't even mind when she went into commercials and became the spokeswoman for some of the things that America loves most: orange juice, Coca-Cola, air-conditioning, orchids, patriotism, and God.

Now it's 14 years later, and the years have taken their toll on the naïve cub reporter. Now I'd resent having to go out on my day off – without extra pay – to interview a third-runner-up beauty contest winner for a trite feature story.

So, this spring, when Anita Bryant came to Bradenton, I didn't interview her. I didn't have to. As the crusty city editor, I sent another bright, eager though not naïve young reporter. He came back with a story about an Anita Bryant I didn't know – an Anita Bryant who smiled very little, whose all-American image was under attack, whose career was in jeopardy, whose once-fresh beauty had faded.

It was a jolt to see the 1977 Anita in pictures and on television. I noticed the harsh lines in her once-smooth complexion, even through the makeup. But it was more disturbing to hear what Anita Bryant had to say. She was here selling fanaticism, not apple pie. Instead of crooning love songs and hymns, she was spouting a message of bigotry and hate.

Could this be the same Anita Bryant? The one who invited folks to "come along with me, to my little corner of the world?" Now, it seemed, there was no room in her little corner of the world for anyone who disagreed with her narrow view of things.

It's sad to see an idol crumble, to have a pleasant memory shattered. Time does that, though. Fourteen years is a pretty long time.

SEVENTEEN YEARS LATER

Did that column ever stir up a hornets' nest of protest among readers! Letters – and subscription cancellations – flooded into the Herald *in the weeks that followed. But the publisher stood firm against the complaints, never once suggesting I apologize or moderate my views. In retrospect, if I were writing it today, I would do less body-shaming of Anita and be more specific about her right-wing crusade against gays. Notice nowhere in that piece is there a mention of gays or gay rights. But in crafting that piece, in my amateur way, I was speaking out not so much for gays as against hate. Because that was what the campaign had become – much as today's anti-gay, anti-immigrant, anti-Muslim crusades are: hate-fueled tirades playing on people's fears and prejudices, in the name of God. While gays have realized great gains in 45 years, the Christian Right continues its homophobic crusade that began with Anita Bryant in Florida in 1977.*

This was the first time one of my pieces riled up readers. And it was the first but not the only time the Florida Citrus Commission figured into them. In 1994, that agency, responsible for promoting Florida's iconic agricultural product, made a major advertising buy on Rush Limbaugh's radio talk show. I promptly wrote an editorial critical of that move, citing Limbaugh's bombastic style of personal attacks and reckless disregard for facts. I don't have a copy of that editorial, but I do have my column written in response to the wave of angry mail, phone calls and subscription cancellations it produced. The editorial also prompted the publisher, Dot Ridings, to write her own column defending the newspaper's stand and bemoaning the uncivil tone of reader responses. "Why are we all so angry at each other?," she asked in the lead to that column., She noted that the newspaper had received "a few" cancellations and 15 letters to the editor disagreeing with the paper's position, and that a readers' poll published on Monday had received almost 400 replies by Friday. One reader whose call she answered "was so apoplectic over our editorial that he talked about burning all copies of the Herald *he could get his hands on," she wrote.*

*My response, published just below Dot's on the op-ed page on **Feb. 27, 1994**, gave me a chance to recall an event from my youth that perhaps was a precursor to my later liberal bent and certainly was a portent for the kind of hateful rhetoric, modeled by President Trump, that has become all too common today.*

Those Whom Some Label 'Commies' Are the People with Open Minds

I was 12 the first time someone called me a Communist. I was in the seventh grade, and a bully a year ahead of me and at least a foot taller caught me behind the grandstands at a high school football game. "You're a Communist," he said, "and a commie-lover," and then threatened to beat me up.

Fortunately, there were too many people milling about for him to make good on the threat, but the names stung, just the same. I was too young to know much about geopolitics, but I knew that "commies" were godless people who wanted to overthrow our government and make us all slaves of their system.

At the time of the incident, my hometown was engaged in internecine religious warfare involving parochial versus public school education. My parents believed they should be able to decide which high school their children would attend; the bully's parents believed they had to send them to the school that the church leadership designated, the parochial one. If you didn't agree, you were a Communist.

Some things never change. More than 30 years later, I'm still being called a Communist. This past week several readers of this newspaper have called its editors Communists because we dared question the wisdom of the Florida Citrus Commission's selection of Rush Limbaugh as a spokesman for Florida orange juice. And I thought communism died three years ago when the Soviet Union fell apart. Just goes to show you how durable this form of slander is, surviving even the demise of its inventors in the Kremlin.

I don't understand this name-calling much better today than I did as a kid in 1952. Why do some folks always feel it necessary to cast aspersions on the patriotism of anyone who dares to disagree with their opinions? Are their ideas so weak, their arguments so feeble, that their only recourse is to attack their opponent's character?

It always seems that the folks with the least appreciation for the things that America stands for are the first to accuse another of being anti-American. They cloak themselves in the flag and the Constitution and then rush to silence anyone who claims the First Amendment right to speak out against a demagogic policy. Anyone who doesn't agree with *their* narrow point of view is a traitor.

The same people like to use the word "liberal" as if it were a four-letter word, an epithet that should make its targets recoil in shame and embarrassment. To me it has always been an honorable label that signified one's mind was open to new ideas, unbound by authoritarian rules that forced everyone into the same box. The latter is my understanding of communism. I guess that's why my parents became "Commies" in the eyes of some of their fellow townspeople – and I by association with them. They didn't want a bishop in a distant city telling them they must send their kids to an inferior school. Their hearts and minds told them it was wrong, and they obeyed those instead of the orthodoxy that said it had to be this way or no way.

Yet if anyone were to label my parents politically, it would have to be "conservative." They were God-fearing, church-going farmers who worked hard for everything they owned and expected everyone else to do the same. They would have starved before accepting welfare and disliked government programs that interfered with free-market forces for sale of their crops. They had rock-solid family values and tolerated no deviation from them by their children.

Yet some of their neighbors called them Communists because they dared to think for themselves – the very opposite of communism's central tenet of collective thought and collective policy dictated by a central authority. The paradox would be funny, were it not such a sad reflection of closed minds.

That same attitude comes through in much of the Rush Limbaugh mail. He is regarded as the fount of wisdom on all things political, moral and social, and if you disagree with him there must be something wrong with you.

Though the mounds of mail flooding in on this issue are overwhelmingly pro-Limbaugh, I don't think it represents the majority of Americans. I know there are too many people like my parents who recognize demagoguery when they see it and respect America's liberal traditions too much to turn the country over to a bigoted clown like him. He is a flash in the pan who will soon be forgotten, though a few die-hards will try to keep his fame alive.

The anti-"Communist" mentality hung on a long time in my hometown. Only in the last five years have some of its proponents come forward to apologize for the offensive words and deeds of the past, which included vandalism, beatings and one bombing. A hard core remains, however, still struggling to keep the parochial school going (though its academic standards are even lower than in the '50s) and still stirring dissension whenever they can. Doubtless they are "ditto heads" who worship at Limbaugh's throne, too, and consider his critics Commie-lovers.

Today, if I still lived in my hometown, perhaps the bully's son would be calling my kid a Communist. Some things never change.

FORGIVE ME, FATHER, FOR I HAVE SINNED

Well, I sure missed the mark with my prediction that Limbaugh would be a flash in the pan. He's still maniacally raging 25 years later, and he still has his loyal army of true believers, which sadly now includes the President of the United States, who shamefully awarded him with the Presidential Medal of Freedom at his 2020 State of the Union address.

Re-reading the following column reminds me just how privileged I was to be doing what I was doing as my job. Not only was I allowed to tell people what I was thinking every single day, I also got to hear people's confessions. Not that I was able to absolve people of their sins, as priests are. But perhaps by opening up to me people felt a sense of relief from guilt and shame. And if I managed to apply such knowledge to my daily writing efforts, maybe the world would be a slightly better place. That at least was my intent on most days.

The #MeToo movement began in 2017 when a tweet about sexual abuse allegations against Hollywood movie mogul Harvey Weinstein went viral. But sexual harassment is hardly a new societal issue. It became a topic of national debate in 1991, when the appointment of Clarence Thomas to the U.S. Supreme Court was being debated in the Senate Judiciary Committee. A former associate of Thomas, Anita Hill, testified about alleged harassment by Thomas. The hearings prompted me to write the following column, published in **late September 1991.**

How Many Men Have Something to Confess?

Don't dismiss the Clarence Thomas hearings as a trashy soap opera, a nasty political duel or a shameless sideshow put on by a flock of Senator Foghorns, though the Senate Judiciary Committee's spellbinding drama last weekend had a bit of each.

It was also rage-venting time for women who have suffered silently the humiliation and stress of sexual harassment in the workplace. And it was conscience-examination time for an awful lot of men across America. The phone calls and letters I've received over the past 10 days have reflected a depth of emotion and interest I haven't seen in years.

220

So many people want to talk about the Thomas hearings; so many people have theories about what happened. And as the responses by our readers' issue on sexual harassment indicate, so many people – mostly women – know about sexual harassment through personal experience.

One call above all the others stands out, because of the insights on the Hill-Thomas affair and because of what it says about where men and women have been and how far they have to go to overcome the sexual stereotyping that exists. The caller, a Bradenton retiree from a northern city, had a dark secret from his past that Prof. Anita Hill's graphic testimony had brought back to his consciousness and compelled him to share with someone.

"I know what happened with Judge Thomas," he said. "I went through the same thing 30 years ago, only it never came out. But if it did, I would do exactly the same thing – deny it."

He had been a 31-year-old junior executive, separated from his wife. A young woman, about 20, came to work in his office, and "I became obsessed with her. She was beautiful – built like you know what, and I was all alone, living in a furnished room. The loneliness just took over. I asked her out, and she rejected me. So I retaliated with sexual language" – the kind of language Anita Hill said Clarence Thomas spoke to her.

It lasted a month, he said, and finally the woman left the office, presumably to go to college. He eventually got back with his wife and forgot his obsession. But a year later the young woman called and demanded a job. The man was fear-stricken. Her implication was that if he didn't give her a job she would reveal his indiscretion. So he complied. She worked the summer and went back to college.

The next summer she called and demanded a job again. And again he complied. But he could see a disturbing pattern developing that threatened his peace of mind. "She didn't realize just how much fear and guilt I had. Outwardly I covered it up, but inwardly I was dying. I was just like Judge Thomas – I lost weight and couldn't sleep."

He lived in fear of the young woman's exposing his shameful secret for seven years, until she married and moved to a distant city. He kept it to himself for another eight years before finally telling a close male friend.

"I thought it was so unique," the man said. "But my friend said he'd done a similar thing when he was younger. He helped me realize that I wasn't a pervert, but that I'd just made a mistake. Finally, I sat down and asked God to forgive me, and I forgave myself."

And he was finally able to put the incident behind him – until last weekend. Hill's account brought back the memories – and the realization that his harassment victim undoubtedly was reliving her memories, too. Which meant he was still vulnerable – 30 years later. "If she called up today it would start all over again – the fear would take over," he admitted. And if she accused him, he would "act the same way as Judge Thomas – swear up and down it never happened."

There have to be lots of these kinds of stories out there, unconfessed and unresolved. If there are millions of outraged women recounting their painful tales of sexual harassment, there have to be a lot of uneasy men guiltily reliving their harassment past. As the caller said, in attempting to explain why this incident had occurred, "Back in those days, we could get away with it."

That's it, in a nutshell. Men have been able to get away with exploiting women since the dawn of civilization. The social contract gave men power over women that they have abused. We men have, all of us, done it. No, not all with graphic descriptions of sexual acts or career-threatening pressure for sexual favors. But in dozens of smaller ways – in the terms of address we use for women, in what we pay them, in the job assignments we give them, in inter-office banter, in the division of household work, in relationships whose goal is sexual conquest rather than intimate sharing of love.

It seems to me the Hill-Thomas affair has shown a lot of men that we've made mistakes and that we need to ask forgiveness – of God, of the women we've offended, and finally, ourselves. We have to start over with a clean slate and a new attitude. For sure, after last weekend, we can't get away with it anymore.

TAKING ON CITY HALL

Once again, my crystal ball-gazing efforts were way off the mark. Sexual harassment didn't go away after the Thomas hearings, and plenty of men still got away with it, as the Harvey Weinstein case and #MeToo prove. There was movement, for sure, but plenty of men continued to use their power to harass and exploit women.

On the subject of abuse of power, I was not shy about calling people out for it. I regularly took on powerful county commissioners who bent rules and used their position to enrich themselves. And then there was Bill Evers. Evers was a former sheriff's deputy and Highway Patrol trooper who had won election to the City Council in 1974. He was a vocal critic of the incumbent mayor, Abby Leach, who would have fit right in with Andy Griffith in Mayberry – which Bradenton in those days somewhat resembled. Not much got done in the city, while growth was exploding all over the unincorporated area, and the new De Soto Square mall was sounding the death knell for downtown Bradenton, once the hub of commerce for the entire county. So, after serving two terms as a councilman, Evers decided to run for mayor in 1980 as a reform candidate, promising to end the reign of good-old-boy governance by preceding administrations. He won, and did well enough in his first term to earn re-election four years later.

*But there was turmoil in city government, much of which only came to light later. A union movement began at the Police Department. As Police Commissioner as well as Mayor, Evers bitterly opposed unionization. Just how bitterly is reflected in the following column, printed **Feb. 17, 1985**. It marked what would become a verbal sparring match between me as the* Herald's *Opinion Page editor and the Mayor's Office for the next 16 years.*

Whistle-Blower Takes Stock: Career Ruined, Nerves Shot, Integrity Intact

If you want to know what it's like to be a whistle-blower, ask Tom Fleming.

Tom Fleming's career is destroyed, his self-esteem shattered, his ambition undermined. Fleming, once No. 3 man in the Bradenton Police Department, now aspires to get into a job with physical, not mental, stress – perhaps a maintenance business cleaning banks, stores and doctors' offices after hours, when it's nice and quiet and no one's around to hassle him. Tom Fleming, career cop who once told dozens of other cops what to do and who some said had what it takes to be chief, now has difficulty making simple family decisions.

Tom Fleming, police captain turned whistle-blower against a city administration bent on breaking a police union, has been vindicated in every impartial court proceeding he's faced so far in his battle to restore his reputation and career. But Tom Fleming is beaten, anyhow. The humiliation of being publicly fired, the anguish of facing trial on criminal charges, the stress of returning, under court order, to a job with no real power and the stigma of "snitch" hanging over his head, finally became too much even for a macho guy like Tom Fleming. "Emotionally, I couldn't handle it anymore," he says. "If I had my strength, I think I'd have stuck with it. . .But I finally just ran out of gas."

And so last week Tom Fleming buried the hatchet with the City of Bradenton, agreeing to resign from the police force and drop his civil rights lawsuit against the city in exchange for $40,000 in damages plus accumulated sick leave and vacation time. The City Council accepted the out-of-court settlement Wednesday. Evers finally had won: the last of the "union trouble-makers" was off the force for good. The whistle-blower was gone.

But Tom Fleming's law enforcement career should not end without one last hurrah for a man who chose integrity over chicanery, and without a final review of one of the sorriest chapters in Bradenton's recent political history. That review should begin with the fact that, until the police union activity began in 1980, no one ever said Tom Fleming wasn't a good cop. Brother of a Long Island policeman and son of a New York City fireman, Fleming had law enforcement in his blood. When he heard about openings on the Bradenton force in 1967, "I couldn't get down there fast enough" to apply. He was accepted and rose steadily through the ranks from patrolman to sergeant to, in 1980, captain, the No. 3 slot on the force. He was on good terms with Mayor Evers and his pal Bobby Molter, the politician and the insurance man who together did most of the running of the Police Department from City Hall. Former associates say Fleming was "an excellent administrator," a "decent individual."

The trouble started in late 1980, when petitions for a union certification election circulated among city policemen. Fleming was uneasy with the attitude among the brass, led by Evers as police commissioner, that supervisors should "get" the union activists. As part of management, Fleming was expected to cooperate in harassing the men, yet his conscience told him it was wrong. In May '81, subpoenaed to testify at an officer's grievance hearing in connection with the harassment, Fleming confirmed that city and police administrators were harassing union members. After that, his fall from grace was swift. He started getting the cold shoulder and being left out of policy discussions. Eventually he found himself demoted to supervisor of the graveyard shift and put on a year's probation for allegedly refusing to enforce department regulations as ordered.

The storm broke in May '82 when Fleming filed a grievance over the disciplinary action, complaining that he had been told by his chief and Evers to enforce the regulations unevenly against union members. Eleven days later, Fleming was fired, based on a list of 13 charges, most of which were trumped up from statements Fleming supposedly made to Molter's son, Danny, another Police Department hanger-on and pal of Evers'.

Denied a hearing by the city's Merit Board, loaded with Evers cronies, Fleming filed an unfair labor practice suit against the city with the Public

Employee Relations Commission (PERC). The city, which would pay more than $100,000 in legal fees battling the union during '82, spent over $32,000 defending itself against that one suit alone. Yet never once in all the controversy did the Bradenton City Council vote for an investigation of Fleming's charges nor to condemn the waste of taxpayers' funds in persecuting him and union activists. Then-Councilman Patrick Guinan stood alone in demanding an accounting and condemning the harassment, but his colleagues sat on their hands.

PERC upheld Fleming's charge on Feb. 3, 1983, ruling in a landmark decision that the city had illegally fired him for refusing to do its dirty work of union-busting. PERC said the city could not "employ managerial (employees) as 'spears' to be unlawfully thrust against legitimate organizational activity by public employees. . .To require Capt. Fleming to violate police officers' rights as a condition of his continued employment demonstrates a blatant disregard of the rights of police officers. . ." It ordered him restored to his old job.

Despite the clarity of that ruling, the city appealed the case to the Second District Court of Appeals. Meanwhile, it harassed him with a trumped-up criminal charge, accusing him of soliciting for perjury in an unrelated case. He was found innocent of that charge in July '83; the Appeals Court upheld PERC's decision on Oct. 20. Fleming was put back to work the next day and handed $30,000 in back pay.

But the last 15 months on the force have not been pleasant for Fleming. The city mocked the spirit of the PERC ruling by creating two new job titles, Deputy Chief and Major, which subordinated his captain's title. He was no longer given responsibility for the police auxiliary, crossing guards and job applicant investigations. "I wasn't in charge of anything," he says. "Before, I had worked on the budget, narcotics and knew every case doing down. Now I had nothing. I was left out of everything." At first everyone disappeared when he looked for someone to drink coffee with, though some relationships improved in time. Nevertheless, the feeling of being unwanted built until he was close to a nervous breakdown. It was then that Fleming, guided by his doctor's recommendation, decided to quit.

Neither Fleming nor his wife, Clare, who stuck by him throughout his long ordeal, holds any grudges for what happened. It has strengthened their faith in God and brought them closer as a family. "As a Christian, I'd feel guilty for being bitter," she says. "I hurt for Tom, though, knowing what he's been through."

Now, as they try to rebuild their lives, Fleming is sure of two things: One, police work is out, for good. "I guarantee you'll never see me in a uniform again, not even private security." And two, yes, he'd do it all over again. For though he's worried about being able to make a living for his family, he isn't worried about being able to live with himself.

Good luck, Tom Fleming. If we had more public servants like you willing to stand up for what's right, perhaps politicians like Evers wouldn't feel so free to toy with people's lives.

EIGHTEEN YEARS LATER

Tom Fleming came back into my life almost two decades later, during a period of violence in East Bradenton, the "other-side-of-the-tracks" neighborhood where most poor blacks and Hispanics lived. There had been a number of shootings, mostly involving gangs and turf wars over drugs, but innocent bystanders often became victims in shoot-outs. In shooting incidents where there were dozens of witnesses, police were frustrated by a lack of cooperation from citizens. Nobody was willing to give information about the perpetrators; investigations were stymied.

I wrote editorials and columns about that dilemma, noting that it wasn't just fear of retaliation for snitching that kept citizens from giving police information they needed. It was fear – and hatred – of police, bred by decades of abuse by racist cops. I reminded city leaders of the fatal shooting in East Bradenton of an obviously mentally-disturbed Haitian immigrant by a city cop for refusing to drop a beer bottle he was holding. In those pre-Ferguson, pre-Black Lives

Matter days of the mid-'90s, such shootings were all too common, not just in Bradenton but in many cities around the country. In this case, the ire of African Americans was exacerbated by the fact that, six months after the shooting, the cop was named Officer of the Year and, two months later, promoted to sergeant with a $25 weekly raise.

Citizen reticence to cooperate with police was, I wrote on April 27, 2003, "an understandable result of decades of police abuse of black citizens – of searches and beatings and humiliating insults by 'the man' with the badge and the gun. And, in too many cases, of 'Bradenton's finest' shooting first and asking questions later." A new police chief had just come in, expressing regret for the abuses of the past and promising reforms. Well and good, I wrote, but "he cannot undo the department's ugly record of overt and covert racism and brutality. It is etched into the minds of citizens who lived through (recent) years (of police abuse), enduring the humiliation and sharing the grief of police victims' families."

Of course, it stirred up a hornet's nest of protest by West Bradenton folks, as well as police and city government officials. And one of the people I heard from personally was Tom Fleming. He called me in response to that column, and I arranged to meet with him for an in-depth interview about what it was like on the streets of Bradenton during his years as a police officer. The account of that interview is too long to print in its entirety here, but a few excerpts make the point. This is from a full-page report on police brutality that I created, published on **May 11, 2003:**

Racism in Law Enforcement: An Ex-Cop Weighs In

Question: *Was there racism on the Bradenton police force back (in the '60s and '70s)?*

228

Answer: Yes. Some cops do a lot of hitting. That's not me. I never carried a nightstick or slapjack. I got into some tussles, but I like to think all of them were reasonable. I did not hit people in the face. . .But there are some who are extremely aggressive. They should not be in police work. . .But it wasn't just in BPD. In the Manatee Sheriff's Office under Sheriff Dick Weitzenfeld, there was a protective mentality. Sometimes deputies would come into Bradenton to rile up the city a little bit and then go back into the county – just trouble-makers.

Q.: *Meaning what?*

A: Harassing blacks. I remember one time, a car sped off from the Courthouse very fast. I followed, not giving chase, but soon came up on the car stopped by a sheriff's deputy. It developed into a stand-off kind of scenario with all kinds of blue lights and people coming into the street. It was totally unnecessary for a routine traffic stop. I kind of stood back and watched and wound up being reprimanded by my major for "not doing my job". . .They just promoted that kind of standoff atmosphere. It just aggravated the situation. My attitude was, write your ticket, turn off your blue light and get out of there.

Another example: A Florida Highway Patrol trooper pulled over a black driver in East Bradenton, with me backing him up. He said to me, "Boy, those (expletives) are making me nervous." This is a situation that goes way back. . .It's the attitude that prevailed in the '60s and '70s, and judging by what I see it continues today.

Q.: *Were you aware of mistreatment of blacks by police officers, either BPD or MSO – beatings, name-calling, humiliation?*

A: Yes. It happened, but you couldn't prove it if you didn't see it. I remember a black suspect bleeding, and asking what happened to him, and was told he fell and bumped his head. Years later I learned through another officer that the arresting officer hit him a roundhouse blow with his Kell light. That really bothered me. It's part of the attitude some officers make more contact than others. . .I remember one takedown when three of us had this big guy who was struggling. I have him in a

229

chokehold and one of my partners just cold-cocked him – kept hitting him in the head and face with his slapjack. There was no doubt in my mind that we'd gone beyond the safety range and overreacted. . .When you slap suspects in the head, slam 'em around, call them names and mistreat them after you cuff them, what do you expect them to do?

Q.: *On a scale of 1 to 10, from lowest to highest, how would you rate the BPD today on racism?*

A.: I can't give you a specific number since I've been out of it so long. I would say it's over 5 but under 10. At the MSO under Weitzenfeld it was much worse. He had a very aggressive force, though it was not just anti-black. It was almost like an endorsement of violence. The leadership sets the tone for how a department operates. It's easy for violence to become a way of life.

POST SCRIPT

I knew Sheriff Weitzenfeld's reputation for brutality. Cops joked about taking a suspect to the jail on the third floor of the Manatee County Courthouse. The prisoner would be in perfect health when he was escorted onto the elevator. But for some reason, he was bloody and staggering when the elevator doors opened on the jail floor. "He must have banged his head on the walls," deputies joked.

I made a visit to that jail early in my career at the Herald, *before becoming Opinion Editor, to interview a Russian immigrant for a story. Today, 43 years later, I can't remember what that immigrant's story was about. But I vividly remember noticing a chain dangling from a hook-and-eye device mounted into the ceiling of a jail corridor. I asked what it was for. "That's where they used to dangle prisoners for beatings," a deputy told me, matter-of-factly. His slight smile at "used to" told me it wasn't necessarily a practice of past sheriff's administrations.*

And now I must recount my final encounter with Tom Fleming. It deeply pains me to write about it. On Oct. 1, 2012, Fleming inexplicably shot his wife, Clare, to death. Shot her in the head in *their West Bradenton home. He didn't give a reason. Arresting officers said he seemed dazed, that his conversation didn't make sense. While awaiting trial in jail, he threw himself off the upper tier of a two-tier rank of cells. He survived the fall but suffered a broken hip that confined him to a wheelchair at his trial for second-degree murder, which began on **Dec. 26, 2013.***

Trial testimony revealed that the years had not been kind to Fleming and his wife. At the time of the shooting, they were in the process of separating. Tom was contemplating suicide, he testified, but the plan went horribly wrong.

His court-appointed attorney, Benedict P. Kuehne, explained it this way: "In a moment of heated passion, he was overcome and impelled by a blind and unreasoning fury to redress his imagined injury, his wife's callous remark, and while being anxious, depressed and suicidal, he fired the fatal shots."

In his testimony, Tom put it more simply: "I decided I was going to blow myself up in front of her. I walked in the bedroom and pointed the gun at her head. She turned around and she saw what I was doing, and she said go ahead. So I just pushed her and fired."

He was convicted and sentenced to life in prison. His appeal a few months later was denied.

I attended the trial and offered myself as a character witness. It was such a sad case that I felt someone needed to be there to talk about the kind of man Tom Fleming had been. Former City Councilman Patrick Guinan also was there as a character witness. Guinan was the only member of the City Council who had spoken up about the anti-union activity under Evers, the only one who protested Fleming's firing and harassment. But he was outvoted 4-1 on every motion he offered at public meetings and was subjected to outrageous vilification by Evers' cronies in the community.

I regret that I did not save a copy of the remarks I made in defense of Fleming. But afterward, Guinan shared with me a copy of his prepared remarks. He wasn't allowed to deliver the full speech he had prepared – I think we were given only five minutes each. His testimony was so moving, indeed heartbreaking, that I offer key excerpts here as a form of closure for a once-good cop who was dealt a terrible hand as well as a testament to the cost of abuse of power by elected officials.

Transcript of Testimony Prepared by Patrick Guinan for the Murder Trial of Tom Fleming

May it please the Court,

Your Honor, there is a terrible irony that confronts us as we meet today. . . We are confronted with a very vivid and heartbreaking story of deep sadness, the story of a man who will forever suffer the constant pain of unbearable guilt, the story of a pathetic and defeated and very fragile man with no hope, no love, and only a future of agony and despair. . .

This was a tragedy that should not have been. My family lost two dear and close friends, life-long friends. Good, loving, kind, caring friends. They were almost like relatives. Over 35 years, half of our lives, we knew Clare and Tom Fleming and their children and their mothers and fathers and their relatives. I knew them as well as I have known anyone. It should not have happened. It should not have happened. I have a hard time still believing that it did happen. I will never believe Tom Fleming KNEW WHAT HE WAS DOING.

. . .I am not here in any way to defend his actions or to condone what he has done, but I am here to introduce this man to this court by giving facts with true and honest descriptions of the man that I knew as Captain and husband and father and friend. . . I believe with all my heart that Tom Fleming is a decent, kind and caring good person and I believe that good people sometimes do bad things. Tom Fleming did a terrible thing. He caused the death of someone

he loved very much. He caused a death, BUT HE IS NOT A MURDERER.

I . . . beg this court for compassion and mercy and ask you to bestow and restore the gift of hope to a sick and pathetic living human being who probably hasn't many more years to live. Please give the gift of hope to a defeated, broken, destroyed man.

I have known Tom for over 35 years. I never knew anyone more professional as a law enforcement officer. There was no one more caring, or more conscientious, or more honest. He sincerely cared about the people he served and was always making sure everyone was treated fairly and given justice. This was his overall concern. He had earned a reputation as a top administrator and an honest and very good cop. He was well thought of by other police departments, and his name was mentioned when considering future promotions such as Police Chief and equal positions in the Manatee County Sheriff's Department.

He had a bright future and a reputation of which he could be very proud, but because of his sense of fairness and honesty his future and career in law enforcement were ended. He saw what he knew to be unfair and wrong, and his conscience would not let him stand by and allow it to happen, nor could he play the game in order to save his career. . . . This was the essence of Thomas Patrick Fleming. He wanted to do the right thing even when it would cause him to be hurt and his career destroyed.

I was a city official at the time and I saw all the official records and read all the facts and learned everything that had been done to Tom and other police officers. And I saw what he and his wife Clare and their family went through. After a year of fighting in the court and unbelievable stress on the family, Tom was vindicated by the courts and given his job back. But the price for victory was too, too, much. He was never the same. He was a defeated and destroyed man. . .

I knew Tom Fleming. Our families ate and played together, we had family picnics and cookouts. We golfed and swam, laughed and partied, went to ballgames; we were there to help each other. We were there to cry with each other when our parents died. We were together to celebrate the good times. We had sad times and happy times. We . . . went to church and we prayed together.

I was with Tom and Clare hundreds of times. And I saw only a loving couple. I never heard Tom say anything but loving and kind things about Clare, and she was always supportive of Tom in front of me. I never recall her making a negative comment about him. Tom and Clare were both very sincere and devout Catholics. They never missed Mass. They believed in the sacrament of Matrimony. . .Tom was a faithful, devoted and loving husband and would have done nothing to hurt Claire had he been in his right mind.

We will never know why this terrible loss happened. If you knew Tom and the man that he was, you would have to say over and over that **IT DOESN'T MAKE SENSE.** *Tom Fleming is not a murderer and it doesn't make sense. He must have been out his mind. He must have been mentally ill. He must have been sick in his heart and soul and mind because he never lived a life that would make anyone believe he could ever cause the death of his beloved wife.*

. . .It doesn't make sense. It doesn't make sense. Tom is not an evil person. He is not depraved. He did not hate his wife of 45 years. He loved her. In a fit of passion, he did a terrible thing. He is guilty of causing her death, but not of second-degree murder. Twenty-five years is a death sentence **and that may be the law but it would not be just or fair or right.**

Tom is a self-destroyed man who has lost everything. He is a sick man that will be punished by his terrible guilt for rest of his life. I ask for him mercy and compassion, and I ask this court to allow him to have just a little hope before his days on this earth are over.

FAREWELL TO A BULLY POLITICIAN

As I type the above article into my computer, I can't help but think of the management style of our current president and wonder how many people like Tom Fleming might be out there – loyal employees who were exploited in their boss' unethical schemes and then horribly abused when they resisted. Former Ambassador to Ukraine Marie Yovanovich is one. There must be hundreds like her whom Donald Trump has cast aside like used tissues over the years, and only a few of them have had the courage to strike back with tell-all books. As one who also has been so treated in my last career (not the newspaper one), I know how they feel.

I would like to close this episode with my final word to the protagonist of it all, Mayor Bill Evers. He served five four-year terms but was defeated in the 1999 election by a reform candidate who promised to get rid of the do-nothing administration that had held Bradenton back for two decades. That candidate was none other than my former editor, Wayne Poston. Wayne had retired as Executive Editor the year before and needed something to do as he was not the type to sit around the house watching daytime TV. He knew Evers' history all too well and was well-known and mostly well-liked by the movers and shakers of the city. Just before he took office in January 2000, I wrote the following "tribute" to the man I had nicknamed "Bulldozer Bill" and "Mussolini Bill" in editorials over the years.

Farewell, Mayor Evers – Nothing Personal in our Turbulent Tenure

Tuesday will mark the official end of the administration of Bradenton Mayor Bill Evers.

It is hard for me to think of Bradenton without thinking of him. Indeed, he has dominated local politics for so long that a great many residents do not know of or cannot remember a Bradenton when Bill Evers was not in charge.

Coincidentally, his political career has closely paralleled mine as an editor for this newspaper. I arrived in town only a year after he assumed his first office as a city councilman in 1974 and have been commenting on his actions ever since.

We have been through a lot, Bill Evers and me. We have fought and made up more often than most married couples, and we have presided, in our respective roles, over Bradenton's growth from a sleepy small town to the hub of an urban area with a population of over a quarter of a million.

There are some who think my often-adversarial role with Evers was personal – that I would do anything to see him banished from public life. Perhaps the mayor himself had those thoughts from time to time as this newspaper opposed him editorially on numerous policy decisions.

But as I pointed out to him on Dec. 22 as he presided over his last City Council meeting, it was never personal. It was always about differing views of what was best for Bradenton. The newspaper's Editorial Board always tried to look at all sides of each issue and formulate its position based on what it perceived as the greater public good, rather than that of a special interest. It was my role to put that position in writing, so it was generally to me whom the mayor would direct his ire when our editorials took him to task.

But as I also reminded Evers the other day, if you went back and counted the editorials of the last 20 years you would probably find that we supported his position more often than we opposed him. Few remember that we endorsed him in every one of his runs for mayor except the last. There were times when the endorsements were decidedly lukewarm, but the fact is that from 1979 until 1999, Bill Evers was in our view the strongest candidate for mayor that this city produced. And so we recommended citizens vote for him – even as we noted reservations about some of his policies.

Evers seldom saw it that way. It was almost always a personal issue – if you agreed with him you were his friend, but if you disagreed with him you were his enemy. He suffered from two all-too-common flaws in people in leadership roles: a too-thin skin and an easily aroused temper. In the end, those proved to be his downfall.

I have many vivid memories of Evers. The first was in the late '70s, when as a councilman he led the effort to repair the unsafe roof of Municipal Auditorium because "our kids shouldn't have to go to Sarasota to hold their proms." That resonated with local residents and with the *Herald* and helped establish Evers as a leader.

Another memory of Evers is from the early '80s, when as mayor and police commissioner he led the effort to break a newly-formed police union. (Evers and unions go way back in this town.) This is where I first saw the mayor's less-diplomatic side. Union officers were subjected to policies that undermined their morale. Several resigned, and one high-ranking officer, who was part of management, refused to go along with the policies. For that he was disciplined on trumped-up charges, shunned, demoted and ultimately broken in spirit by the stress. The union soon was voted out.

Evers could be theatrical, too. I remember in the mid-'80s when Evers was feuding with the Manatee County Commission over taxes. During a County Commission budget hearing he strode in to make a presentation, preceded by an aide throwing play money into the audience to dramatize his contention that the commission was wasting taxpayers' money.

A more positive memory was the role Evers played in getting McKechnie Field rebuilt to keep the Pittsburgh Pirates from abandoning Bradenton as their spring training headquarters. He and County Commissioner Joe McClash teamed up to convince the Chamber of Commerce and influential civic leaders to put together a financing plan to turn McKechnie into one of the best and most intimate ball parks on the spring training circuit. A few years later he would do the same thing for Pirate City, the team's crumbling training center on the east side.

Evers had a lot of nicknames over the years, some of which he acquired because of references in *Herald* editorials, some of which others pinned on him. "Bulldozer Bill" was one I may have coined in reference to his penchant for running over opponents who got in his way. There was "Mussolini Bill," which arose from our 1985 re-election endorsement – yes, endorsement – in which we noted that, like the Italian dictator credited with getting Italy's trains to run on time in the '30s, Bill Evers had done a pretty good job of keeping garbage collected and streets repaired, the essential services citizens expect of local government.

Perhaps the nickname that best suited the mayor was "Boss Evers," after "Boss" Richard Daley, Chicago's colorful, give-'em-hell mayor during the '60s and '70s. Daley was best remembered for his angry denunciation of anti-war demonstrators during the 1968 Democratic National Convention, when he turned the brutal Chicago police on the "hippie" throng. Rotund, red-faced and bombastic in exchanges with opponents, often in words that made grammar sticklers wince and critics snicker, Daley was the stereotype of old-fashioned, ward-heeling politician who rose through the ranks to become the top dog in city politics – and the most effective mayor in the country.

To compare Evers to Daley is a compliment, not a slam. While he physically resembles Daley in many ways, he also has Daley's acerbic personality, a certain degree of which is needed to make a government work effectively. While bulldozing methods and heated exchanges may not be the most diplomatic way to run a city, it goes a long way toward getting the job done.

Which is basically what Evers did for 20 years. Now that form of governance is out of fashion. Today, we expect coalition-building, collaboration, diversity. Bill Evers was not that kind of mayor; it was basically his way or the highway.

Wayne Poston defeated Evers by promising to be an open, collaborative mayor. We'll find out in the next four years whether the change we asked for is the one we really wanted.

TAKING ON A CRIME WAVE

*Crime was very much on my mind in 1998, probably because it struck close to home. Fortunately, it wasn't major. But twice being victimized by petty criminals within six months got me riled up. And I wanted the world to know about it. This is from **Jan. 25, 1998.***

Purse-Snatchers Foiled, But Crime Creates Another Bigger Victim

Crime claimed another victim in Bradenton last weekend. Two young punks, barely out of adolescence, tried to grab the purse of a woman I know.

Fortunately, there were no injuries, and nothing of material value was taken.

But something important was stolen nevertheless: The woman's trust in her fellow human beings. More angered than shaken by the Saturday afternoon attack at Beachway Shopping Center, the woman raged at the violation of her trust more than the fact that she almost lost cash, credit cards, keys and driver's license to a couple of teen-age thug wanna-be's.

An outgoing, friendly woman, she returned the greeting of one of the youths hanging around near the front of a store she was about to enter. When she emerged from the store, his friend spoke to her, asking for the time. As she obligingly shifted her purse to look at her watch, the first young man rushed up and grabbed at the purse strap.

But something – perhaps a reflex, perhaps instinct – make her hang on to the purse and say, "I don't think so!"

The kids – both skinny guys who were shorter than their would-be victim – didn't argue. They darted out the back of the center and hopped into an accomplice's getaway car – a white Oldsmobile with big tailpipes idling in the parking lot – and escaped.

Recounting the ordeal to relatives later, the woman fumed at the first youth's approach of greeting her and then his friend later asking for the time. These, she believes, are little civilities in the "social contract" by which a civilized society interacts.

"He violated that contract," she said. "He betrayed that little bit of trust that we extend to strangers just to be civil."

Of course, she understood that he then went much further than that by violating the law and attempting to take her valuables. But the greater damage, as far as she was concerned, was her broken trust. "I won't ever look at strangers the same again," she said. "I'll never know if they're just trying to set me up to rob me."

Later that evening, she fulfilled her own prophecy as she waited in the car while her husband gassed up at a service station hear her home. A car approached her open window and the driver, obviously lost, asked, "Do you live around here?"

"No, I don't," she lied, unwilling to engage in the lightest or seemingly innocent conversation with a stranger.

"You're not going to prey on me again," she told herself.

Even later, over dinner, she confided to her husband, like a deep, dark secret, that she was considering getting a gun. Suddenly a weapon for self-protection didn't seem like a radical idea.

That, of course, is the saddest part of the broken social contract – that this former pacifist has been changed into an angry, fighting-back victim.

PAYBACKS CAN BE HELL

The victim was my wife, Jo Anne. I did not identify her at her request. But the anger this incident stirred in her scared me. A gun? That was the last thing I wanted in our home. Fortunately, she didn't pursue that quest. And in time she forgot about her distrust of strangers and now readily offers greetings, directions, and the time to strangers who ask.

That June, however, I was the victim, this time of a hit-run driver. It was a minor fender-bender; the driver behind me failed to see me slowing to turn into a shopping center and bumped the rear of my car fairly briskly. I pulled into the parking lot and assumed the driver would do the same, so we could exchange insurance info and get on with our Saturday. But the driver did not pull into the lot and stop; instead, she sped off. Angered, I gave chase, hitting 60 and 70 miles an hour on residential streets. My passenger was an out-of-town applicant for an editor's position at the Herald; *we were heading for breakfast so I could tell him about the job he was considering. Not wishing to put him or myself in any more danger, I eventually gave up the chase, but not before he had written down the license plate number of her car. A couple of weeks later, here is how I handled that incident, published* **July 5, 1998.**

Message to a Hit-Run Driver: Don't Think You Got Away with It

Dear Pam,

No, it isn't over.

You probably thought that the message you left on my answering machine would get you off the hook for the hit-run crime you committed against me on May 23.

Sorry, answering-machine "apologies" don't cut it.

I want to look you in the eye and tell you how devasted I was by your action.

I want to hear you explain exactly why you drove away instead of stopping to render aid when you crashed into the rear of my car as I turned into the Albertson's Center off 75th at Manatee Avenue that pleasant spring Saturday morning.

I want to tell you how shook up my passenger and I were afterward – about how that shock ruined a business breakfast with a colleague who had flown 1,800 miles to look into a job opportunity in Bradenton.

I want to share with you my views about responsibility to one's fellow human in distress – especially when the distress is caused by you.

I want to hear your views on the Golden Rule. You know, do unto others as you would have them do unto you. I want to understand what you think about another rule that's as inexorable as the Golden one: What goes around, comes around.

And I want to hear you explain what you told your boyfriend and his parents, whose black Nissan Maxima you were driving when you decided to leave the scene of the accident. They reassured me you would do the right thing. Did you think their check for the damages to my car would placate me? Did you think you could once again sucker them into believing you'd cleared up everything with me? Did you think you could get away with yet another deception – as if trying to cover up a hit-run weren't enough?

Sorry, Pam, it isn't over. As you no doubt know, the terms of my offer to drop the matter are that you personally apologize to me. Why is this so important? Because I want you to learn something constructive from this experience. I want you to learn from this relatively small incident that there are consequences to irresponsible actions, before you do something majorly stupid.

Not that this wasn't bad. Sure, the damage to my car wasn't a lot, and neither my passenger nor I was injured – except for this persistent, aggravating ache in our necks. Did I mention the neck pain, Pam?

But the point is, you didn't know that. You didn't know whether we needed an ambulance or not, and you didn't care. You didn't care whether you had ruined my car or not. You just drove off – and endangered more innocent people as you attempted to elude my pursuit to get your license number.

Pam, the world is too full of people with such irresponsible attitudes. I read about them and their deeds every day in the headlines of this newspaper – people facing trial for fatal DUIs, people robbing and shooting each other for crack money, people dying in shootouts with police for failure to stop, people headed for long stretches in prison for stupid crimes that netted them peanuts and caused their victims untold grief.

Which one are you, Pam? How far down that road are you headed? I don't want to see your name in one of those headlines one of these days. Your crime against me was relatively small. But I don't want you to think for a minute you've gotten away with it. I want you to take from it a lesson about responsibility, about integrity, about courage.

I want you to know the cleansing power of confession and forgiveness. That sort of thing is out of fashion these days. Nobody, from tainted TV evangelists to corrupt congressmen to philandering presidents seems to be willing to own up to his or her mistakes and ask forgiveness in a sincere, no-strings-attached way. But you would be amazed at the results of such an admission. It's quite astounding, believe me. I've been there.

I'm offering you one more chance to do the right thing. Don't blow it.

POST SCRIPT

I never heard back from Pam, but her family was likely humiliated by my column, and perhaps they dealt with her in an appropriate way.

THOUGHTS ON DISABILITIES

Wow, I was really on my soapbox there. But it was the age. Bill Clinton was parsing the meaning of the verb "is," and members of Congress were selling themselves to the highest bidder. Crime was rampant in New York, Chicago and many major cities. I just felt I had to say something about it, which I was wont to do. Not that it has changed much since then – in fact, it's only gotten worse.

*I got back on the soapbox 15 months later, this time defending folks with disabilities – which included myself. Nine years after passage of the Americans with Disabilities Act, the disabled were still mostly invisible, not a very high priority for the majority of Americans who didn't have one. Here was my effort to change that, published around **Oct. 5, 1999**.*

Disabled Just Want Shot at Normal life

October is National Disability Awareness Month. I was made aware of the observance by an old friend, Ed Lopacki, who visited my office the other day to have his picture taken as an advocate for the disabled in his role as spokesman for the Suncoast Center for Independent Living and a member of the Manatee County Citizens Accessibility Task Force.

Ed and I go way back – to 1977, when we co-coached our sons' soccer team at the birth of the Manatee Area Youth Soccer Organization

(MAYSO), now a thriving, multi-league outfit that reaches into all areas of Manatee County.

Ed was a superb coach and a fine athlete in his own right whose lithe, lean frame made him a natural for the long-distance running he preferred. Ed doesn't run much these days – except in the figurative sense. He still has the same high energy level and the same sunny, optimistic outlook I remember from our coaching days, when the wandering attention of 6-year-old would-be Peles was enough to try the patience of a saint. Ever the cheerful one, Ed would encourage the boys with positive statements when I wanted to throw my whistle across the field and yell at them.

Ed now gets around in a wheelchair – he quickly admonishes that he is not "confined" to a wheelchair but is liberated by it – because of multiple sclerosis that took away his muscle control about nine years ago.

A lawyer by profession, he continues his private practice while working to raise the consciousness of the rest of the world about obstacles that confront the handicapped.

As I talked to Ed about some of the challenges a disabled person faces, I began to appreciate what a gift those of us in the "able" world have in our total mobility. We take it for granted we will be able to go anywhere we want to when we want to, enter any building we wish to, go through any door or corridor and use the bathroom facilities available anywhere in that building. But people in wheelchairs have no such guarantees. One or two steps are enough to keep them in the parking lot; a hard-opening door or inclined ramp can keep them from entering, and narrow corridors or doors can keep them from getting where they want to go – such as to the bathroom. Ed's disability – and the memories of how agile he used to be – certainly raised my consciousness of the challenges that disabilities can bring and how unconcerned the rest of the world – the "normal" world – can be.

I like to think my own relatively minor handicap has already raised my awareness of disability a bit above the average. I live with a moderate hearing loss, a condition I assume to be genetic, inherited from my mother's paternal side of the family. In my hometown the Ottos were known for being hard of hearing, but back then that, like so many disabilities, was assumed to be something you just lived with.

I have for almost 10 years worn hearing aids, which help me function at near-normal levels most of the time. But I am continually surprised at how many people are oblivious to my hearing loss. My aids aren't huge megaphones that cover the ear, but they're not invisible microchips, either. Very few people seem to notice, as demonstrated by their mumbling, whispering and swallowed sentences that I must ask them to repeat. . .

My hearing loss has also made me aware of the inequities in our cultural reactions to disabilities. For example, people usually give deference to individuals with vision problems if they are aware of the disability. But let someone display difficulties with hearing and the reaction can just as easily turn hostile: "What's wrong with you? I repeated my question twice; why can't you understand?" Just trying to be difficult, I guess.

And I've never understood why eyeglasses are more important to job performance than hearing aids. Glasses are almost universally covered in any decent group health-care insurance policy – at least one new pair a year. But hearing aids are not – despite the fact that a good pair of hearing aids costs 15 to 20 times more than a good pair of glasses costs and, for those with the problem, are just as critical to one's ability to function in a "normal" workplace.

You hear no advocates for equal hearing access in movies, churches or auditoriums. We have to fend for ourselves, which means turning the volume up or down, straining to make out the meaning of a speaker's message, or smiling and pretending to agree even though we aren't sure what was said.

. . . I (hope) for a heightened awareness of hearing disabilities, including pressure to have hearing aids covered by health insurance. Meanwhile, I hope this serves to heighten every reader's awareness of disabilities, whether represented by a wheelchair or tiny buttons in the ears or any number of other devices that help the disabled operate "normally." For as my friend Ed Lopacki says, any of us is just a blink away from wearing – that is, *not walking in* – his shoes.

THE MIRACLE OF SOUND

*A year or so after that column appeared, I acquired a new set of hearing aids. The result was so profound that I felt compelled to share it with my readers, still in hope that hearing impairment would get more attention in the people-with-disabilities world. This was published **around 2000**, but I don't have an exact date.*

A Routine Sound Is a Small Miracle

I heard a leaf fall the other day. A yellow leaf dropped from a limb of the ficus tree in a corner of my office and landed on a pile of papers with a very faint "plop."

It was one of the most thrilling sounds I have heard in a long time.

I know what you're thinking: This guy seriously needs to get a life. Or stop ingesting illegal substances.

Don't worry. My life isn't *that* boring, and I'm not on drugs. The sound of a leaf falling was a big event *because of the fact that I could hear it.* My new hearing aids have made such a difference in my life that it is as if I am hearing routine sounds for the first time.

I have known for some time that I needed to replace my old aids. They had become so unreliable that they were an impediment to hearing as often as they were an aid. At seven years of age, they were long past their life expectancy. But I put off the decision primarily because of the cost. The new state-of-the-art units needed for my type of hearing loss run about $2,000 per ear, vs. $900 for each for my old '95 model.

So, like many hearing-impaired people, I learned to fake it – nodding and smiling while conversations swirled around me, without a clue about the point being made. Or kept out of conversations altogether – pretending to be far away mentally from the conversation at hand. Or, worse, joining in and mishearing a key point, then enduring stares for having made a ridiculous, irrelevant comment.

But I finally bit the bullet and decided to spend the money. I made up my mind one night while watching "West Wing" with my wife, seeing her chuckle at the clever repartee between Josh and Sam for several minutes of the opening scenes. I had no clue what they were talking about because I couldn't understand a word they said. (In my defense, this show is especially notorious for mumbling dialogue.)

I got my new hearing aids about 10 days ago, and the difference is exhilarating. To help explain the improvement, I tell people that it is comparable to the improvement in vision when one turns on a ceiling light in a room with a single window to the outdoors. You can see without the light, but not very well. So it is with a hearing aid to help overcome hearing impairment.

My hearing aids are incredible devices. They are, in effect, miniature computers with build-in electronic digital programming that automatically adjusts sounds for my specific hearing needs. Worn behind the ears, each has two sets of microphones, picking up sounds from front and back and funneling them into my ear canal. There's a button on the back of each that I can touch to adjust the reception for different situations: ordinary conversations, noisy gatherings like parties, or talking on the telephone.

My first few days of rejuvenated hearing were filled with discoveries of formerly unheard sounds: The clicking of my car turn signal, for example. How many times have I been cursed as an old fogey for driving with a blinking taillight because I couldn't hear it? Or the beeping of the kitchen timer. How many pots have burned and steaks overcooked because I didn't hear the beep, even with the timer pinned to my shirt lapel? And how about the words of the songs sung by the choir and soloists at church? How many times have I simply turned them out because I couldn't understand what they were singing?

My elation over the restoration of my hearing is tempered by the frustration that I share with millions of fellow hearing-impaired people over the unequal recognition our disability receives. No insurance plan recognizes hearing aids as a coverable health issue. Few accommodations are made for hearing enhancement in public facilities.

I wish there were a crusader to take up the cause of equal rights for the hearing-impaired. That may happen when members of the baby boom generation get a little older and their years of grooving in blaring rock concerts take their toll. As we know, for baby boomers nothing significant has ever happened until they have experienced it. I'm sure the pressure of 50 million hard-of-hearing boomers to get hearing impairment raised on the disability scale will have an effect. My next set of hearing aids no doubt will be covered by my insurance.

Meanwhile, I would encourage all fellow hearing-loss victims – and we *are* victims – to get tested and find a way to afford hearing aids. Pay for them in installment payments, as you would a new car or refrigerator, if you have to. I guarantee you won't believe the difference.

TWENTY YEARS LATER

Part of the wish expressed above was realized as the boomers aged into deafness. T-coils have become more common in public auditoriums and theaters. Lately movie theaters have even provided captioning devices that enable hearing-impaired people like me to see the dialogue captions on a tiny screen as it is spoken on the big screen. But I was wrong about insurance policies changing. About seven years after writing the above piece about my new set of aids, they, too, began to fail me. And it was again time to bite the bullet to acquire the latest technology in hearing enhancement devices. Only this time the cost was $7,000 – all of it out of pocket. But once again, I was restored to near-normal in hearing capacity.

Now, though, almost two decades since that column was published, my hearing loss has gone from "moderate" to "profound," at least on the right. In 2018 it had gotten so bad that I was faced with a major decision: Live with progressively declining hearing capacity – and fork over another $7,000 for the latest technology in hearing aids – or surrender what hearing you still have to a cochlear implant. As I learned from my audiology doctor, a cochlear implant is an electronic device that is inserted into the skull next to the brain to mechanically transmit sound waves for processing. An implant may improve one's ability to understand speech – it has about an 85 percent success rate – but if it fails, you have permanently and totally lost your hearing on that side. After test-driving the latest hearing devices and finding only marginal improvements in my hearing capacity, I decided to go for it. And what do you know? Because this is a durable medical device, the entire cost is covered by Medicare.

In November 2018 I had a cochlear device implanted on my right side. It was not an easy decision, but I felt I had little choice if I wanted to continue to function at my job and in the world at large. Understanding the relationship of brain stimulation to dementia also made the decision easier. Studies have shown that people with severe hearing loss that is not addressed are more likely to develop Alzheimer's disease or some other form of dementia. The fact that this surgery and the device itself would be totally covered by my employer's health insurance sealed the deal. But it is not easy to retrain the brain to understand what the sounds generated by an electronic device mean in terms of human speech. It is a six-to-12-month relearning process. Today, almost two years after the implant was inserted, I have made great progress in understanding one-on-one conversation – as long as I can see the speaker's face – but I struggle among groups and in noisy environments like restaurants. And I still cannot use the telephone in a normal way. I have captioning devices on my mobile phone as well as my land line, without which I would be unable to ~~unable to~~ communicate by telephone. It is, as they say, what it is.

The next column may not be considered a social issue in the strictest sense of the term, but it is a societal one – one that affects the visual ambiance of our community and the heritage we leave for our children and grandchildren. And it is connected to taxes, so that qualifies it as a social issue in my mind. I had been hearing complaints for years about the "waste" of tax dollars by our elected officials in capital improvement projects. Every time a new building was erected or, it seemed, a repair or a new coat of paint was applied to an existing one – cries of "Taj Mahal" came in through letters to the editor and in comments at public meetings. Given that many of the most vociferous probably had no idea what the Taj Mahal actually was, I got back up on my soapbox somewhere around 2005 to deliver a message about frugality vs. bad taste in public construction.

Our Public Buildings Don't Have to Be Ugly

Must public buildings, especially schools, be bare-bones structures to satisfy citizens' demands for frugality with their tax dollars?

I ask the question in response to recurring criticism from some of our letter-writers about the perceived extravagance of newer public buildings, especially schools and government offices. That came up frequently in the campaign for the half-cent school sales tax increase that passed Tuesday. The School Administration Building on Manatee Avenue, across from the *Herald*, is perhaps the most frequently criticized such building, although the County Administration Building nine blocks to the west in downtown has had its share of criticism. Both have been called "Taj Mahals;" the school building also was called a "mausoleum" by a reader.

People have also referred to Lakewood Ranch High School as a "palace," and there have been several criticisms of the columns on the addition to Manatee High School and of the crayon-shaped pillars at Manatee Elementary on Manatee Avenue East.

"Everything is too fancy," said one voter interviewed by a *Herald* reporter on Election Day. "They have to have everything so beautiful. We already have so many taxes, and I'm on Social Security. I can't afford all of this fancy stuff."

Wrote another on the same day: "Forget the Doric columns, skip the 'elite college campus' look, eliminate costly imitative contemporary facades. . . and jettison all other costly perks having little to do with education or physical fitness."

I am as frugal as the next person – just ask my wife – but I resist the notion that our public buildings must be stripped down to ugly functionality to save a few bucks. Public buildings, especially schools, are reflections of our collective identity. They tell outsiders what we as a community think of ourselves. To me the Doric columns, if that's what they are, at Manatee High are symbols of tradition and old-fashioned values. Certainly, the addition put up a couple of years ago didn't *have* to have a columned portico that repeated the façade of the original main MHS entrance. But the fact that it did sends a message to students that their school is an important place, a beautiful place, to which they come to learn.

The whimsical crayon-shaped columns at Manatee Elementary are perfect for an elementary school. They, too, send a message to students: What you do is important enough to us to symbolize it in your school's architecture. And lest anyone think they're useless frills: They're functional posts supporting the walkway roof. The addition of the crayon shapes and colors cost very little if any additional money.

The importance of a pleasant school environment is recognized by educators the world over. In an article in the March edition of *The Sun*, an alternative magazine, entitled "Thinking Outside the Classroom," San Francisco educator Venobia Barlow argues that the school environment is an important factor in fostering a sense of compassion and empathy among students that helps discourage violence.

The sealed, windowless schools built in recent years show "how little a sense of place has had to education," Barlow said. "Wouldn't it be wonderful if all kids had a collective experience that fostered empathy by evoking in them the capacity for reverence and awe?"

To the interviewer's observation that her old high school resembled a maximum-security prison in which she has taught, Barlow said, "We laugh, but it's a painful truth; the architecture of schools is neo-penal."

As to the School Administration Building, which many cite as a symbol of wasteful spending, I think it's time to give up the Taj Mahal imagery. It is a functional office building that was badly needed to replace a crumbling former administration building on the same site. Its architecture is unusual, granted, made to look somewhat pagoda-like by a balcony that runs around the upper floor.

Its scale is somewhat off-putting, with five stories instead of Manatee County's traditional one or two. But I well remember the terrible blight that it replaced: a falling-down old school and dilapidated shacks. The site, selected to help preserve the downtown core after much debate, would only accommodate the needed office and parking space if the building were vertical.

The building's exterior walls are comprised of precast concrete with embedded coquina shells and aluminum-framed windows, typical office building construction, with the exception of some ceramic tile panels on the first story designed to relieve the concrete monotony of the overall façade. Note: *Ceramic tile, not marble.* I do not find that offensive. I'm proud that a building of some distinction represents our public school system – just as I am proud of every marble-clad federal building in Washington, D.C. Funny, I don't hear the local school critics bashing the Supreme Court Building or the Pentagon or the White House, to mention just a few of our more prominent public buildings in the nation's capital that drip with marble.

But enemy terrorists try to fly planes into those buildings precisely because of what they are: Symbols of this country's greatness. May we please close the case on cheap, ugly public buildings in Manatee County?

PACK YOUR BAGS

There is no way to provide a precise breakdown of the topics I covered in my editorials over 30 years, but I venture to say that the majority of them were related to social justice issues. Now it may be time for some lighter fare.

CHAPTER FIVE
ON THE ROAD

I was a junior in college before I ever traveled farther than 50 miles from home. Dallas and Fort Worth were the only cities I had ever visited. Stuck on the farm, seven miles from town and 15 miles from the nearest city, Gainesville, I longed to see the world. As I got older I began to fulfill my dreams of visiting new places and experiencing different cultures. And I never went on vacation without taking a notebook and recording trip highlights, my impressions of the places I visited, and insights into their relationship to my own life experiences. From Orlando to Atlanta to New York to Vegas to London to Paris to Buenos Aires and as far away as Terra del Fuego – literally the end of the world – I wrote about the places I visited. What follows is a collection of columns written during and immediately following my travels.

Though I enjoy travel, I obsess about being late, missing a connection, losing luggage, forgetting vital items. I have done all of this at some point. Perhaps I developed such fears on my very first trip, the one mentioned above when I was 21. My fraternity selected me to represent the chapter at the General Assembly of Lambda Chi Alpha in Cincinnati, Ohio. Instead of train or plane, the mode of transportation selected by my frugal brothers was Greyhound. The trip took an exhausting two days and nights, sitting and sleeping in an upright seat. By the time I arrived in Cincy I was looking somewhat bedraggled. How I looked forward to a nice shower and change of clothing at the hotel. But when the bus driver unloaded passengers' luggage, there was no bag for me. Somewhere between Texas and Cincinnati my luggage disappeared, doubtless mistakenly removed as passengers got on and off the bus at the frequent stops along the way. I had one change of clothing, toothbrush/toothpaste and shaving gear in a small carry-on, and that was it. Don't worry, Greyhound agents assured me in the station. We'll find it and get it to your hotel in short order.

Except they didn't. Not for the entire trip. The luggage never showed up. I checked in at the conference registration table and shared my plight with one of the fraternity leaders whom I had met back at the chapter. He loaned me a sports coat and tie. I sent the clothes I had been wearing to the hotel laundry and changed into my one set of fresh clothes. Someone directed me around the corner to a department store where I purchased a few pairs of underwear. I got by like that and wound up having an enjoyable conference in my first big northern city. But the experience of arriving with no luggage made a deep impression on me. Hence the following experience, published in **early December 2002**.

Holiday Travel: Maybe Four Hours Is a Little Early

L eave plenty early, they warned. The roads are going to be jammed. The parking lots are going to be full. The lines are going to be long. The delays are going to be horrendous. After all, it is Thanksgiving weekend, the second-heaviest travel period of the year and the first big holiday since the return to "normal" after last year's Sept. 11 terrorist attacks.

And as a kicker: It's the first holiday travel period with the new Transportation Security Administration handling security screening at the nation's airports; expect the worst.

All of which warnings my wife and I dutifully heeded in heading out the day before Thanksgiving to spend the holiday with relatives in Atlanta. For a 12:30 p.m. flight from Tampa International we left the front door at – I am embarrassed to admit it – 8 a.m.

OK, maybe that was overdoing the get-there-early thing a bit, but we *did* have to run a few errands on the way out of town: return a couple of videos to Blockbuster, hit the bank, mail a letter, grab breakfast to go. These days, you can't expect even the simplest of errands to be simple. Who knows when the customer in front of you at the drive-up bank window will choose this minute to wire money to Greece, refinance his mortgage and buy three certificates of deposit?

But waddya' know? It was a stress-free errand day, and we were on the road to Tampa by 8:30 a.m. Which meant we were at the long-term parking garage at TIA, preparing to be turned away by "Sorry, Full" signs, by 9:30 a.m.

But waddya' know? The garage had plenty of parking spaces. Which meant we were headed for the ticketing counter, preparing for an interminably long line, by 9:45 a.m.

But waddya' know? No line snaking around the terminal like a ride at Disney World. There were maybe six passengers ahead of us at the Air Tran counter. The whole check-in process took less than 15 minutes. Which meant that, by 10 a.m., we were ready to head for Airside C.

But wait! There was still security to clear. We'd heard the horror stories about zealous new TSA professionals making you leap through hoops to be cleared to board an actual flight. Last year the security checkpoint lines at some airports were blocks long, causing some cut-it-close travelers to miss their flights. But waddya' know? No big hang-ups at security. It took but 10 minutes or so to clear the screening by polite, professional TSA staffers. Which means that, by 10:15 a.m., we were ready to board our plane.

Which wouldn't be starting for another two hours.

Waiting in airports has never been a problem for me. I always bring plenty of reading materials for just such contingencies. But it might be a different story if I were traveling with two squirmy toddlers. Or with an elderly parent. Watching the TV coverage of the holiday travel story the day before our trip, we were frightened into leaving home far earlier than we needed to.

Certainly, there were lots of unknowns about this holiday, especially not knowing how the TSA screeners were going to affect travel. But I would credit TSA with improving the process. There were enough stations to keep long lines from forming, and the queuing process was orderly. There were plenty of screeners, who were uniformly polite and efficient in directing the emptying of pockets and wanding of those who triggered the X-ray beeper.

The good news is that our experience wasn't unusual. Press follow-ups on Thanksgiving holiday travel around the nation showed no major problems. *The Los Angeles Times* reported "an impressively smooth flow of some 10 million people and many more carry-ons. . .More than 30,000 new screeners in their even newer white shirts offered reassuring hope for similarly smooth, safe travel during the lengthier holiday season to come. At peak times, long lines flowed faster than Starbucks' – under 10 minutes in most places."

And apparently the screeners were effective. Associated Press reported that nationwide they seized 15,932 knives, 98 boxcutters, six guns and a brick during the holiday weekend. You gotta' wonder about people who don't yet know that you can't take knives aboard airplanes. Or guns. Or bricks.

All in all, it contributed to a renewed sense of security about air travel missing since Sept. 11, 2001. It was the unpredictability of that process during a couple of post 9/11 flights I made last year that prompted me to head for the airport so early last week – that and the constant warnings by Katie, Matt and Al on the *Today* show. I have been in those block-long lines, and watching the clock tick away toward boarding time as surly, couldn't- care-less screeners pawed through carry-on bags was incredibly stressful. Here's hoping those days are past and the normal one-hour-early standard will be sufficient. Take a bow, TIA, TSA, Air Tran and even Hartsfield International and MARTA in Atlanta. On this weekend, even that typically zoo of an airport and mass transit system was a piece of cake.

THE ALMOST-$15,000 BREAKFAST

For our 26th wedding anniversary, my wife and I decided on a getaway to the theme park haven of Orlando. But it wasn't thrilling *rides or awesome movie special effects that prompted me to write about that trip. It was a narrow escape from a very costly situation. It was published in **late October 2004.***

Nobody Warns You to Steer Clear of This Tourist Trap

I t all started with a cheap breakfast.

As a man known for budget-watching – OK, tight-fistedness – I considered it a sincere contribution to family fiscal health to suggest a budget chain, with an all-you-can-eat breakfast on our second morning in Orlando. After the sticker shock of a $30 breakfast for two on the first day of our stay at a fancy hotel across the street from Disney World, I was eager to get in the car and drive a couple of miles to the strip of chain establishments on the main drag.

Big mistake. Oh, the breakfast was as billed – all you can eat for $5.95, with a grease level below maximum cholesterol blockage. But it was at the cash register on the way out that Martians from a UFO burst in and kidnapped my wife and me and transported us to . . .an alien planet. When we woke up, we were seated in a gigantic room filled with hundreds of tables at which sat groups of three, four or five people, one of whom was wearing a yellow polo shirt. The noise level of hundreds of conversations going on simultaneously was startling. Though I've never been there, I thought perhaps this is what the pork belly pit at the Chicago Board of Trade must be like.

Every few minutes a yellow-shirted person would spring up, seize a microphone, ask for attention and announce in tones worthy of the Nobel Prize ceremony: "Ladies and gentlemen, may I present the newest owners of unit number so-and-so for the week of such and such, Mr. and Mrs. . . ."

Time share! The Orlando tourist trap that no one warns you about. We were in the middle of a boiler room of a major time-share project on the edge of the Magic Kingdom, being asked to sign a mortgage for "ownership" of one week of a condominium in perpetuity.

Well of course we hadn't been kidnapped by aliens. It was a booth near the cashier's stand of the restaurant advertising Disney ticket discounts, free meals and/or $70 cash that got our attention. Then it was the saleswoman's low-key but persistent sales pitch that persuaded us to sign up for a no-obligation tour that afternoon. And it was the idea of a carefree annual vacation in a beautiful country-club-quality development less than two miles from Disney's main entrance that brought us to this room – a setting in which I never thought I'd find myself.

And in practically no time, I –who had balked at paying $15 for bacon and eggs a few hours earlier – was almost ready to sign on the dotted line for $15,000 *and* a $600 annual membership fee.

Almost. Fortunately, my conservative German genes kicked in and I hesitated. Oh, we wanted this deal. With grandkids just approaching the age of Disney awareness, we thought this was a great time to snag a comfortable, affordable base for years of future family bliss built around Mickey and Friends. Besides, if we tired of Disney, there was always the time-share exchange registry, which for only a small fee allows you to exchange your week in Orlando for any of hundreds of resorts all over the world. And with the pre-construction discounts offered for Phase II of this project, we would save $3,000 over the price of the units when completed next spring.

It was tempting. And I could see why so many families – especially those from out of state – were signing up. There is something magical about Disney, especially when experienced with children. The manicured landscaping, the postcard-scene streets, the strolling fantasy characters, the rides and exhibits all contribute to a flight from reality that you want to continue for more than one day – a day that usually ends with a grumpy, two-hour drive home after dark. To lock in a comfortable, two-bedroom condo at today's prices, compared to the ever-rising cost of a single hotel room, seemed like a good deal.

But we asked to sleep on it. Surprisingly, the yellow-shirted salesman was not high-pressure. He was smooth as silk but not pushy, not arm-twisting. We walked out with our $70 and a stack of literature to help us make our decision. In the middle of the night I awoke from sleep with numbers flipping through my mind like a calculator. Fifteen-thousand dollars for the buy-in fee? Probably not a bad deal, as in 15 years we likely would cumulatively spend that much on vacation trips, whether to Disney or wherever. But $600 a year for the membership or maintenance fee was an open-ended expense that went on forever. And it would rise with inflation. If I lived 30 more years – doubtful – I would have paid at least $18,000 in annual fees – probably much more figuring inflation, special assessments, etc.

Suddenly, removed from the boiler room and the fantasies, the investment made less sense. Besides, we hadn't even checked in with our adult children to see if they *wanted* to spend weeks at Disney. (Turned out they didn't.) In the end we called and canceled our follow-up visit. I used the $70 to pay for breakfast the next day at our hotel – outrageously priced, but free of sales spiels and fantasies of fairy-tale family vacations. Even at $30, it seemed like a bargain breakfast.

SIX MONTHS LATER

*For my 65th birthday, my wife gave me a trip to Las Vegas. That was one of the items on my bucket list – not because I'm a gambler, but simply because I was curious about this city that is so unlike any other in the United States. This was published **April 10, 2005**.*

What Goes on in Vegas Is Fantasy

LAS VEGAS – I know you're not supposed to tell "what goes on in Vegas." But nobody swore me to secrecy, so I'm gonna'. At least the clean stuff.

Which, of course, is all I know, since I have no intertest in the other. If I did, do you think I'd tell?

My first visit to Sin City was an eye-opening glimpse into a parallel universe, where night and day blend seamlessly in sprawling casinos that never shut down. The other-worldly beeping of thousands of slot machines seldom leaves you, even during breakfast in a hotel dining room.

In this universe, a cross-section of America comes together to sample the forbidden fruit that Vegas offers. Farmers in overalls and John Deere caps share slot tips with tattooed and pierced punk rockers with spiked red hair. Chain-smoking little old ladies rub elbows with partying yuppies in tuxes and gowns.

Hardly anyone looks twice at a bride in full regalia, drink in one hand and a cigarette in the other, wandering the casino floor at midnight on Saturday. I'm hoping she's looking for the groom, but probably it's a more-promising slot machine.

Vegas has more kitsch per square inch than a big fat Greek wedding. It's a place where a half-size replica of the Eiffel Tower challenges the Great Pyramid of Egypt for visitor drawing power. Where auditoriums the size of sports arenas pack in audiences at upwards of $100 a head to hear has-been pop stars rehash their old material. Where on a Sunday morning people praising the Lord momentarily drown out slot machine humming at the House of Blues gospel brunch.

It is the adult equivalent of spring break. People come here to do what they would not do at home, to break the rules without fear of tongue-clucking by nosy neighbors or the arched eyebrows of the pastor.

Not necessarily really sinful stuff, though there certainly is opportunity for that. But silly stuff, like a pack of young men I saw walking down the strip clutching a can of beer in each hand. Or like me playing penny slot machines for an hour without losing more than the price of a Big Mac and fries. Or like staying up 'til 4 a.m. eavesdropping on the obsessed gamblers as their stacks of chips dwindle.

Indeed, though Las Vegas was birthed on the twin evils of gambling and prostitution, it has evolved into the adult playground of middle America, a Disney World for the mature where ordinary folks go to play adult games without fear of disapproval. Its gaudy hotels and attractions contribute to the escapism mentality, the no-one's-watching theme we see played out on Florida beaches every year by the college crowd.

You don't have to drink or gamble to enjoy the spectacle. Or spend a ton of money. Many of the strip hotels – there are at least 24 – offer free outdoor shows, such as the Mirage's volcano eruption and Bellagio's light show several times a day.

Yes, you can pay $130 a person to hear Barry Manilow croon cheesy hits from the '70s. Or you can pay $8.25 (drink included) to hear lounge entertainer Robbie Howard do amazing impersonations of Barry Manilow and two dozen other oldies but goodies at the Westward Ho, a two-story relic from the '50s.

Indeed, that Old West-themed hotel and casino is a throwback to Vegas' early days as Sin City. Howard's matinee performance in the Western Ho's "showroom" is reminiscent of American Legion halls back home, with patrons seated communally at long tables, nursing their free drinks, the aroma of last night's beer and cigarette smoke still heavy in the air. Howard's dad runs the lights and mom takes the tickets. During an hour-long show Howard sprinkles in a bit of bawdy humor and plenty of corny commentary on Vegas and long-dead stars. It's a refreshing break from the high-priced hotel shows that promise "Las Vegas-style" dancers – meaning nudity.

The best part of the trip – OK, right after the life-size replica of King Tut's tomb at the Jaw-dropping Luxor Hotel – was the Grand Canyon. No, I don't mean a New Vegas creation; the real deal. *The* Grand Canyon is a day trip – a very l-o-n-g day trip – from Vegas.

Gazing at the awesome void from the canyon's south rim, I thought about the artificial glitz of the Vegas strip, with its pretentious recreations of man-made wonders: The Pyramid, Eiffel Tower, New York City,

Venice, ancient Rome, medieval England, even the West Indies. You could probably fit the whole frenzied, decadent production into one tiny corner of the Grand Canyon and never know it was there.

That's an impressive piece of architecture. The canyon – and the magnificent vistas en-route of Nevada's magically blooming desert -- helped put Vegas into perspective. After a day or two, it's easy to get mentally lost on the strip, to forget that there's a real world out there where people go to work or school, eat dinner at 6, watch TV and go to bed at 11. And never touch a slot machine.

The difference between the two worlds is almost as wide as the Grand Canyon.

THIS IS THE WAY TO TRAVEL

I traveled to Europe for the first time in 1976, the year before I met Jo Anne. It was one of those if-it's-Tuesday-this-must-be-Belgium tours, something like eight cities in 14 days by bus. It would be another 13 years before I went back across the pond, this time with my wife for our first major trip as empty-nesters. This was half guided tour and half do-it-yourself trip planning. We spent a week on a bus tour of the Scottish Highlands and the second week in an apartment in London's Chelsea neighborhood, booked by my ever-inventive wife who wanted an authentic experience off the typical tourist grid. My biggest insight from this trip was the transit system, and I wrote about it upon our return in **October 1999.**

Britain's Trains a Model for Florida

I am sipping afternoon tea and nibbling shortbread cakes served by a smartly dressed steward aboard a train bound for London from Edinburgh, gazing at the pastoral Yorkshire farmland outside my window and wondering, "Why don't we have anything like this at home?"

Why, indeed, can my wife and I not hop a cab to the downtown train station in Bradenton, toss our luggage onto a rack and enjoy a relaxing and speedy ride to a carefree getaway at Disney World or Miami South Beach, as we are doing on our vacation to Scotland and England, I wonder as hedgerows and quaint farmhouses flash by at 125 mph? The thought of construction-plagued, traffic-clogged I-4 is laughable as I compare this pleasant connection between Britain's two ancient capitals with a similar journey between, say, Tampa and Orlando. This is indeed a civilized way to travel, I decide as I recline my seat a bit further for a short nap to refuel my body for a big night on the town in London.

Ah, rail travel! Ah, the spotless (at least in first class), on-time trains of BritRail, relieving tourists like us of the burden of coping with strange highways, strange driving customs and strange road signs. Our recent vacation to the British Isles was greatly enhanced by the reliability and flexibility of the train service, which we used for our Edinburgh-London connection as well as several side trips into the English countryside. Knowing of the uphill battle to establish bullet train service between Tampa and Miami via Orlando, I couldn't help wondering why we cannot see the wisdom of such a rail service in tourist-oriented Florida.

OK, the price tag might be a bit daunting: $6.2 billion. And I know how personally Americans take their cars because of the mobility and social status they represent. But thinking as a tourist, a train is the answer for inter-city travel. You don't have to cope with long lines at rental car agencies, learn the intricacies of a foreign car, pore over maps planning your route, pump and pay for gas (about $4.30 a gallon in Scotland and England), then worry about parking the car when you reach your destination.

My BritRail flexible pass, secured in advance through a travel agent in Bradenton for $315, gave me a first-class seat on a spotless train for any four days during the month I selected. An eight-day pass would have been $459. On the main Edinburgh-London journey plus the later side trips – York, Windsor and Bath – the stations were close to the center of town, making it easy to hop a subway, bus or cab to our ultimate destination.

There's the main drawback to a successful rail system here: very limited mass transit choices in the cities on the route. To be really useful to a tourist, a train system needs convenient bus or rail service to the most popular destinations. Actually, Orlando has a fairly decent bus system between downtown and the theme parks, and Miami has the people mover through the downtown core. But there aren't many options for the car-less tourist bound for the beaches, the Keys, shopping centers or other top tourist destinations.

But if growth projections hold true, it seems an investment in a highspeed rail system might be the best decision Florida could make, even at $6 billion-plus up front. Transportation planners project that by 2050 the main interstates in Florida will need 15 lanes in each direction to handle traffic. In other words, we won't be able to build lanes fast enough to keep up with the demand – even if we are willing to pave over all that valuable land.

And with dwindling fossil fuel resources intersecting with global warming to pose the threat of disastrous climactic change, it may not be that long before we have no choice but to turn to the kind of rail service that many Europeans take for granted.

I know how difficult such a decision will be. After all, we are now at least three generations away from any reliance on trains for inter-city travel in this country, except in the Northeast corridor from Boston to Washington. Even after my thoroughly enjoyable BritRail excursions as a tourist, I felt like kissing the hood of my own car in the parking lot at Tampa International Airport upon my return, so eager was I to reassert control over my mobility.

What I concluded from the experience is this: When it becomes easier to take the train to certain destinations than fight traffic, we'll park the car and buy a rail ticket. But before we can do that, we have to build the tracks and stations, a costly, multi-year process. Which of our would-be leaders is far-sighted enough to make such a decision today?

Twenty Years Later

Now we know the answer to that question: None, at least in Florida.

Two decades later, there still is no passenger rail service from Bradenton to Tampa or Tampa to Orlando. But at least we tried – briefly. In 2000, Florida voters approved a constitutional amendment requiring the state to build a high-speed rail line between Tampa and Orlando and then from Orlando to Miami, with construction to begin within three years. But in 2004, with planning for such a transit system well underway, Gov. Jeb Bush called for repeal of the amendment, contending it was too costly and voters didn't understand what they were voting for. The repeal referendum passed that November, and high-speed rail was dead.

In 2011, Gov. Rick Scott rejected $2.4 billion the federal government offered Florida – nearly 2 ½ billion dollars of free federal money, turned down! – to build a high-speed rail line from Tampa to Orlando, saying it would be a costly boondoggle. But seven years later it was revealed that Scott had invested in a credit fund run by the parent company of All Aboard Florida, a private entity that is building the Brightline rail line from Miami to Orlando, and recently expressed interest in extending it to Tampa. The Miami-Orlando line began service in 2018, but I doubt I will live to see the day when my idle dream of a leisurely train ride from Bradenton to Orlando will become a reality.

*We ventured across the Atlantic again in 2002, this time headed for Paris. My wife planned a two-week stay, once again opting to go native by renting an apartment on the Left Bank with a side trip to Normandy with friends from Bradenton who also were going to be in Paris while we were there. The trip gave me insights about my workaholic ways as well as smart urban planning, which I was more than happy to share with readers in this column published in **mid-May 2002**.*

Paris Offers Model
for Reviving American Downtowns

PARIS – I was well into the second week of my two-week vacation before I started getting a clue: I was as obsessed with getting stuff done as I am in my workaday world.

"Hurry up," I would nag my wife. "We've gotta' get going. We're going to miss the guided walk we planned. The museum opens at 10, and the lines are shorter now. The market ends at noon. We're going to miss lunch at that place in the guidebook. Hurry, hurry."

My wife finally knocked some sense into me after a week of such craziness. "Slow down and stop with the schedules," she ordered. "You are so obsessed with cramming everything in that you're not enjoying what you're seeing."

I had to admit she was absolutely right. I was so consumed with lists, schedules and maps that I didn't have time to savor the moment. Each place we visited became just one more thing to check off my list, rather than a chance to truly appreciate the character and setting of the place.

The fact that our vacation site was Paris made my tourism obsession all the more inappropriate. Here we were in the City of Light, the heartthrob of romantics, the cultural capital of the world, and I couldn't stop multi-tasking long enough to soak up the extraordinary experience of everyday Paris life for which we had come.

Perhaps you who have been to Paris can appreciate how difficult it is to be a laid-back vacationer in this city. There is just so much to see and do that you realize you're going to miss a lot of it unless you rush-rush-rush to make the most of every minute. If you fear you will never return, you can't afford to miss seeing all the places you've read about for years.

My wife's rebuke was a much-needed call for sanity. Her logic was, as usual, sound. Who says you have to see it all in one trip? Who says you will never return? Is one more cathedral or one more museum worth wearing both of us out?

After that, I tried to slow the pace down. I threw away my lists and tried to focus on just one big site a day. If we got diverted by interesting little streets or shops or parks along the way, that was all right, too. I enjoyed myself a lot more, and I know my wife did. Sometimes we stopped in sidewalk cafes for coffee or a cold drink and a snack and watched the world go by. Only then did I start to appreciate the Parisian way of life.

And it is vastly different from ours. In much of Paris, the 35-hour work week is becoming the norm. Judging by our fellow passengers on the Metro and city buses, the workday for professionals runs from about 9:30 or 10 a.m. until 6:30 or 7 p.m. Long lunch hours are routine; some companies even maintain charge accounts at nearby restaurants and allow their employees to eat free, up to a given amount. Nobody thinks of going out to dinner until 9 p.m., and it's a leisurely, two-hour affair with multiple courses, aperitifs, wines, desserts, lively conversation and lots of smoking.

People aren't in a constant rush to do just one more thing. They aren't consumed with efficiency, which can be a maddening thing to a tourist stuck in a long line at the bank with just one teller's window open. Paris has modern supermarkets, but most people shop daily for their home cooking ingredients from small shops in their neighborhood. The choices are myriad, and the quality is superb. It is the freshness of the ingredients, as much as the complicated sauces, that makes French food so delicious, in my opinion.

Excellent French restaurants are everywhere. . .On our one-block-long street, I counted 16 eating and/or drinking establishments. Most were tiny hole-in -the-wall places with five or six tables. At most the food was better than anything I could remember having back home.

I thought a lot, during that second week of really living the Paris lifestyle, what it is that makes everyone gush over the city's "charm." Why have endless movies and books romanticized the uniqueness of Paris culture?

I concluded it's because Parisians – and the French in general – know how to live. It's these leisurely lunches and dinners. It's the afternoon coffee break in a cozy sidewalk café. It's the attention to detail in everything, from the freshness of vegetables to the daily scrubbing of the city's gutters. They actually have crews of workers in green uniforms who hose down the streets, walks and gutters.

And much of Paris' charm is the setting. Six- and seven-story buildings with charming 17th- and 18th-century facades – even if brand new – dominate the central city. Their mass does not overwhelm, but rather invites one to pause and admire, especially with the shops, brasseries, bistros and bookstores that occupy most first floors. They create an active street life that invites you to join in. When you tire of the hustle and bustle, there are pleasant green spaces everywhere -- magnificent parks flanked by stunning public buildings filled with priceless works of art and historic treasures. All of that contributes to a sense of being part of a small village within an urban setting that is not intimidating.

I tried to relate this setting to something back home, and I remembered a spring Saturday morning at the Farmer's Market on Old Main Street in downtown Bradenton. I had a similar feeling as I sipped coffee at Robin's, chatted with friends and watched people browse the vegetable stalls. The restored, old two-story buildings, narrow street, shaded sidewalk cafes and attractive landscaping invited one to slow down, to window-shop, to stop for a coffee or ice cream, to savor the moment.

I'm not suggesting that two blocks of Old Main Street are akin to the historic, culture-soaked streets of Paris. But I am suggesting that Paris offers an attractive model for reviving American downtowns like Bradenton. We could do worse than to emulate the streets of Paris.

BUT IS IT SUSTAINABLE?

*I followed up the above column the following week with more observations about French working conditions. Ironically, as I write in **September 2019**, labor unions are staging strikes across France to protest restructuring of France's labor policies, including generous* *pensions and relatively short tenures to qualify for them. Today it is transit workers; last week lawyers, nurses and airline pilots walked out, crippling French courts, medical facilities and air transport system. The French way, it seems, may not have been sustainable.*

Can Workaholic America Learn from France's 35-Hour Week?

PARIS – In my last column I wrote about how my workaholic ways had adversely affected the enjoyment of a vacation in Paris for me and my wife. So focused was I on checking things off my list of must-sees, we were not enjoying much of what we were seeing. Which led to an appreciation for the French way of life – long lunch hours, elaborately prepared foods, low-tech offices, pleasant street life and low-stress atmosphere in general.

Since returning in late July I've done a bit of research into what's behind this laid-back attitude. What I learned was shocking.

For most of the go-go '90s, France's economy was a joke among the developed nations. While employment soared to record levels in the United States, Britain and other European trading partners, France enjoyed little of the technology-fueled economic boom. Hampered by restrictive labor contracts and costly social service obligations, French industry wasn't inclined to expand or innovate. Unemployment stayed stuck in the double digits. The French, with plenty of welfare benefits for those out of work and typically protective of their lifestyle, seemed content to be left behind in the rat race.

But as the '90s drew to a close a strange thing happened. Unemployment began to fall – from 12.6 percent in June '97 to 8.5 percent in June 2001, the lowest rate in 18 years – as jobs opened up and productivity improved.

Much of the improved climate is being credited to a factor that is anathema to multi-tasking U.S. workers: A 35-hour work week. Adopted voluntarily by some companies over the last few years and made official national policy in January 2000 for firms with 20 or more employees, the 35-hour week now affects roughly half of the work force. And it will be expanded to cover smaller companies next year.

Scorned by globally minded U.S. and British economists as a throwback to discredited socialist practices, the 35-hour week is revolutionizing the French workplace. It has been credited with creating 285,000 jobs and is expected to produce at least another 215,000 when fully implemented in 2003.

Consumer confidence – and spending – is up. The pessimism about the French economy is gone, and foreign investment in France is soaring.

A 35-hour work week! For American workers to whom a 50-hour week is normal and 60 not unusual, that would be an incredible gift of time – time to put into family, hobbies, volunteering. In other words, to enjoy life.

That's exactly what the already laid-back French are discovering. Two-thirds of those affected say it has improved their lives, according to a survey cited by John Lichfield that I found on the Internet. This is especially true for working women. Benedicte Rifai, a junior financial analyst with Elecvtricite de France, the French electricity board, said the 35-hour week is "fantastic, incredible, a complete change in the way I live. I see my small daughter for an extra day each week and my wages are virtually the same."

Incredibly, productivity is up in the French workplace, helping offset some of the added costs of the reduced work week. That's because workers have agreed to more scheduling flexibility in exchange for the shorter week. This helps managers to better adapt to shifting marketplace demands. One example cited was a Samsonite plant where workers agreed to work 45 hours a week in the busy summer season in exchange for a 32-hour week in the slow winter season. Some workers agreed to come in on Saturdays, even to work during August, France's near-sacred vacation month.

America has trumpeted its productivity in the information age, justifiably so. We have outperformed the world in producing the longest sustained economic growth period in peacetime. But at what cost to our collective happiness? Our sanity? Could some of the road rage, air rage and office rage that seem to be rampant be prevented by a shorter work week? Would a happier work force compensate for fewer hours worked in more work accomplished?

I don't know the answers to my questions. But I suspect the French are onto something. If work weren't so pressing, so ever-present, people might not be so resentful of it. They might even look forward to it much as they now do those all-too-brief weekends and vacations. Most would quickly become bored with no work and unlimited free time. It's the ideal balance that we seek – a balance which seemed so ideal to this Paris visitor.

And lest anyone think this column is self-serving, France's 35-hour week exempts senior business executives, doctors, lawyers, soldiers – and journalists.

ONE YEAR LATER

*I waited a year to write about one other experience in that 2002 trip to France. That was a side trip we took to the D-Day beaches of Normandy. Here is my account of that visit, published **June 9, 2003**.*

Visit to Normandy Beaches
Brings New Meaning to War

The 58th anniversary of D-Day on Thursday didn't get special advance coverage in the *Herald*, as it has on most round-numbered anniversaries like 50th or 55th. A story inside the Front section Friday reported on ceremonies in Normandy on Thursday honoring the D-Day anniversary. Reader Ed Irwin of Bradenton took us to task for hot having anything in Thursday, reminding us that many gave their lives on that day and their courage should "never, never be forgotten."

I don't think we'll ever forget, though we may get so preoccupied with the current war that we don't take the time to think about that one. Having just observed Memorial Day less than two weeks earlier, perhaps we assumed that we had done justice to the D-Day troops who didn't come home from the beaches of Normandy.

But we didn't. We couldn't ever do enough justice to their courage and sacrifice. Just a year ago I stood on one of those beaches, Omaha, and tried to imagine what it must have been like on that hellish June 6 in 1944. Fitting the actual terrain into the accounts of the assault in books and old movies, I was profoundly moved. This had to have been one of the most incredible military feats in the history of warfare. The Omaha landing site is the roughest beach terrain I have ever seen. The land rises from water's edge into a wild, thickly overgrown escarpment at a fairly sharp angle. Just walking down the designated path from the hilltop cemetery at Colleville-sur-Mer on a hot June day left me wilted. I couldn't imagine trying it without a groomed path, let alone trying to climb up it carrying heavy equipment and facing intense gunfire from enemy bunkers at the top.

Yet thousands of brave men did, and then pushed on inland to face day after day of deadly battles with retreating German troops until France had been liberated and German forces pushed across the Rhine. And thousands didn't make it. The American cemetery at Colleville-Osur-

Mer is an awesome place. My first glimpse of the rows of crosses and Stars of David stretching almost as far as the eye could see literally took my breath away. *So many!* You have to be steel-nerved to walk among those graves without getting misty-eyed, reading the names of young men cut down in the prime of their youth. We talk abstractly on Memorial Day and Veterans Day about the price of freedom; here, in this cemetery, it is all too graphically represented in these endless, perfectly symmetrical rows of tombstones.

Later, reading the accounts of the various landings etched in huge marble tablets at the open-air monument, orienting myself on the beachheads sprawling below my feet, I think I grasped, as fully as a non-participant can, the enormity of what those troops did on D-Day. It was an amazing feat of military strategy and of human courage.

I also tried to imagine what the German defenders of Normandy must have felt, staring out at the armada of ships in the roiling sea below them on June 6, 1944, and the Allied troops heading toward them in endless waves of landing craft. They literally had a killing field at their feet, but they must have known they stood little chance of driving the invaders back into the sea, so numerous were they.

At the remains of one heavily fortified German bunker near the cemetery, I stood in depressions twice as deep as my almost six-feet height, the craters left by the huge shells fired from Allied battleships. The land around and far inland from the bunker was pockmarked with those craters, a graphic indication of the pounding the Germans took.

It is important to have memorials like these, as vivid reminders of what war means. Seeing them makes it difficult to be complacent about our country and its freedoms, for they are secured at a very high price. Today, more brave Americans are writing new chapters in America's book of selfless service, putting their lives on the line to guarantee that the values our country stands for will be preserved for future generations.

I think daily about them. My D-Day memories help me imagine what it might be like in the desolate mountains of Afghanistan. The terrain is doubtless much different, but the challenges quite similar to those of the Greatest Generation. Their job is to stare death in the face and fight harder and smarter than the enemy in order to come back home to their loved ones. Ed Irwin is correct: They must never be forgotten.

TO THE BOTTOM OF THE WORLD

In 2004, we headed south, to the very tip of the southern hemisphere in Argentina. The main feature of this two-week trip was a cruise aboard a small passenger vessel through the Straits of Magellan, starting in Puerto Arenas, Chile, and winding up in Ushuia, Argentina, the jumping-off point for the Antarctic. I wrote three columns from that trip, two of them focusing on an issue that is very much before us today: climate change. Or, as we were still able to phrase it in those days, global warming. That was 16 years ago, when very little attention was being paid to the threats posed to earth's delicate climate balance by greenhouse gases. But it was impossible to overlook in the glacier fields and forests of Patagonia, where we were allowed to walk on 20,000-year-old ice sheets that were shrinking before our eyes and through primeval forests whose narrow temperature tolerance leaves them vulnerable to rising temperatures.

*The first was published on **April 4, 2004**; the second **on April 11, 2004.***

At World's End, You Can See the Glaciers Melting

TIERRA DEL FUEGO, ARGENTINA – Perhaps it is the harmonic reverberations of the chant shouted by 75 "explorers" in our "expedition" to the foot of Pia Glacier.

Or maybe it is the impromptu saxophone serenade played by Francisco, one of our guides, as we shiver in our yellow slickers on a drizzly morning at a glacial lake here.

More likely it is the combined effects of global warming and the infinitesimal turning of the earth on its axis in a celestial waltz choreographed millions of years ago.

At any rate, as we stare in awe at the towering mass of ice perhaps 200 yards away, a roar like a Florida thunderstorm in August rumbles through the valley, its sound echoing off the rock cliffs of Pia Fjord. Then, as our mouths gape in awe, a chunk of ice the size of a two-story house begins to break away from the leading edge of the glacier. As if in slow motion, the slab of ice that has stood in frozen indifference to the puny efforts of humankind for around 20,000 years tilts forward and then collapses upon itself, not unlike an unwanted building being imploded. With another mighty roar, it splashes into the lake, sending a cloud of mist at least a hundred feet into the air. That triggers a mini tsunami, raising whitecaps that send visitors near the shore scampering for higher ground.

Yes, the glaciers are melting.

You can see it for yourself, as I did, on a recent cruise through the Straits of Magellan at the southernmost tip of the world. Denials by self-serving politicians notwithstanding, the rapid melting of the glaciers is a major concern of environmentalists and government officials in Chile and Argentina. As it should be to their peers in the United States, especially in waterfront states like Florida.

Nothing I have seen can match the experience of this awesome glacial spectacle. My fellow passengers, some of whom had been lucky enough to have their cameras in position to capture the glacier "calving," as these episodes are called, agreed. The crew of our ship, who make this voyage weekly, told us how lucky we had been to see such a phenomenon.

But we missed by only a few days and a few miles an even more spectacular show. On March 17, the Perito Moreno Glacier in El Calafate, Argentina, staged a long-anticipated move that attracted 10,000 spectators. The glacier had slid down the mountain in 1988 far enough to form an ice dam across Lake Argentina, cutting the lake in two. But after 16 years the heat of the Antarctic summer and the pressure of billions of gallons of upstream water finally weakened the ice dam enough that it began to give way. In a three-column article on the icy spectacle the next day, the *Buenos Aires Herald* described it like this: "Around noon, the Perito Moreno seemed to wake up. Large parts of the glacier walls began to crumble away from the ice sheet and into the water, pitching white sparks upward in an icy fireworks-like display. . .Every 10 minutes or so, a piece of the glacial wall dislodged itself, crashing into the lake in a thunderous explosion of ice and water that sent large waves across the lower channel. . .Each time a new part of the wall fell, the viewing platform erupted in a collective gasp, often followed by squeals of delight and even applause."

As the paper concluded, lucky spectators had just had "a glance of a history whose units and scale are beyond even the scope of man's imagination." It is truly mind-boggling to witness these massive mountains of ice move in obedience to the laws of nature. But, as my short course on glaciers would soon reveal, it would be wrong to blame all of the glacial melting on global warming. No question it plays a role in this dramatic show. But also playing a part is a little-known natural force involving an anomaly in the earth's rotation.

According to Miguel Angel Alonso, who has written a handbook about glaciers, ice ages are regularly recurring events caused by the earth's rotation around the sun. As the earth completes a loop roughly every 100,000 years, its orbit changes from a perfect circle to an ellipse, which causes the angle of the earth's axis relative to the sun to change from 21.5 to 24.5 degrees and back again. This is what creates the seasons and, the bigger the degree of inclination of the axis, the more extreme the season. About once every 41,000 years, the inclination reaches its farthest distance from the sun, and an ice age begins. That last began about 40,000 years ago and ended about 12,000 years ago, when 40 percent of the earth's land mass was covered by ice.

What we have been seeing were the remains of that ice age. How much longer it will take for the glaciers to melt, and when the next ice age will begin, are still being debated. For certain, the warming effect created by celestial forces is being exacerbated by the depletion of the ozone layer at the South Pole. Scientists disagree on the degree of impact created by fossil fuel burning. After all, volcanic eruptions and meteorite collisions have also contributed to the gunk thrown into the atmosphere over the millennia since the last ice age ended.

On this cruise through the "Gallery of Glaciers," as the Beagle Passage through the Straits discovered by Magellan in the early 16th century is called, one sees all kinds of glaciers. Some, like Pia, are masses that cover entire valleys with ice to a depth of 1,500 feet or more. The pressure of such snow weight is what produces the blue surface in some glaciers. At the same time, some stretches of ice are stained a dirty black, like a giant snowbank against a shady wall during a thaw. This, I learn, is debris captured by the slowly moving ice – boulders, trees and soil caught in the flow of these frozen rivers.

So, what's the big deal about glaciers melting? I'll elaborate on some of the effects in a subsequent report on my trip to the end of the world.

Climate Changes May Tip Delicate Balance in Patagonia

P UERTO WILLIAMS, CHILE – Western "civilization" wiped out the indigenous Yaghan people who once roamed the rugged islands of Tierra del Fuego, a nomadic people who traveled these treacherous waters in tiny canoes in search of game and fish, the entire clan totally naked in sub-freezing weather.

I wonder, as I visit the national parks of Chile and Argentina at this remote edge of the world, whether it will do the same to the natural beauty that remains.

As I noted in a previous column about a recent trip through the Straits of Magellan, the glaciers are melting. You can see it in then-and-now photos showing dramatic glacier retreat in recent decades. One taken in

1928 of the Upsala Glacier in Santa Cruz, Argentina, showed a vast ice field encompassing the entire field of the photo. A recent photo taken from the same location shows snow only on the top third of the photograph; the rest is bare rock and soil.

An Argentine scientific expedition in January-February sponsored by Greenpeace documented that just from 1997 to 2003 Upsala lost five square miles of its surface. A recent article in *Science* magazine reported that all of the 63 principal glaciers in Patagonia have shrunk in the last 30 years, with the rate of shrinkage doubling since 1995.

Why is this important? Here in the gateway to the Antarctic, the glaciers represent 90 percent of Patagonia's fresh water supply. When they are gone, the area could be virtually without water to meet the needs of its people, industries and farms.

As the glaciers melt, sea levels rise – by an average of 19.5 inches for every degree of increase in global temperatures. During the 20th century, scientists say average global temperature has risen by 1 degree Fahrenheit. They project that, without any reduction in emission of greenhouse gases, the average temperature will rise between 2.5 and 4.5 degrees over the next 100 years. It doesn't take a scientist to understand how such a sea level rise will affect waterfront communities like the islands of Patagonia or, for that matter, a slender peninsula like Florida. Beaches will be underwater and buildings on stilts will be flooded. Entire economies will be wiped out.

In addition, glaciers affect weather patterns. As the Antarctic's fierce winds blow across shrunken ice fields, the result will be higher temperatures and lighter snowfalls. That will change conditions for cattle, sheep, crops and even Argentina's burgeoning ski resort industry. Similar glacier melts going on at the North Pole will affect climatic conditions in North America.

And biodiversity will be altered. Sara Larran, president of Sustainable Chile, a non-government agency doing research here, estimates that for every degree rise in the average global temperature, ecosystems shift 62 miles away from the equator.

"This is an issue that directly affects biodiversity and the biological wealth of nations," she said in a report in the English-language weekly *News Review* published in Chile. "In these shifts or migrations of ecosystems, species that are unable to swiftly adapt to the changes swill be lost." That will mean significant changes for agriculture, forest management and a host of natural systems.

In the forests of Patagonia, it isn't hard to see how such climatic changes will affect the delicate ecosystem. Here at Puerto Williams, a Chilean naval base on the island of Navarino in the Beagle Channel, scientists from a number of countries and universities are studying biodiversity changes in some of the very lands that Charles Darwin trod 180 years ago in formulating his theory of natural selection. In the Omora Ethnobotanical Park, they have established a primitive outpost both to learn more about the delicate balance of life in this sub-Antarctic region as well as to teach visitors the importance of respecting natural forces.

Having walked through a mature forest on a glacial mountainside just days ago, I have been made aware of just how tenacious nature can be in establishing plant and animal species – and how easily a small shift in climate can alter that process. The deposits of rocks and boulders left on the shores and sides of towering mountains by melting glaciers starts as bare stone. Over time lichen spores, carried by the fierce Patagonian winds, take hold as little orange clusters the size of a quarter. As more of them develop, they become tiny "nets" that trap nutrients and salts. Over more time the lichens transition into moss, which eventually will cover most of a boulder. With more time and more wind, seeds and grains of soil are deposited in the moss, producing ferns and other native plant species.

Over hundreds of years, if left alone, those plants will become a forest such as the one near Marinelli Glacier that we tramped through on a cold, misty morning. Standing in the ancient glade a few hundred yards from shore, I was reminded of Longfellow's opening line, "This is the forest primeval" from "Evangeline." Longfellow wrote of "the murmuring pines and the hemlocks," but here in this isolated wood there was utter silence, save for the sound of water dripping from a fern cluster on a rock cliff high overhead.

Comparing these soaring trees and fern-covered cliffs to the tiny spore clusters on the boulders recently deposited on the shore, I could only imagine the millennia it must have taken for the forest to develop to this stage. I thought also of the Yaghans who inhabited Tierra del Fuego (Land of the Fires) before Magellan "discovered" it in the early 16th century. Like the plants, they adapted to nature in one of the most hostile environments that exists anywhere, covering themselves with seal oil to ward off the cold.

These are the people that "experts" like Darwin considered subhuman, a label that gave the Europeans license to cruelly exploit and kill as they fought one another for control of the land and waterways of Patagonia. Disease took its toll among the Yaghan tribes, and by the 20th century their culture had basically ceased to exist. Modern-day research has proven that the Yaghan culture was incredible complex: Their vocabulary had at least 35,000 words, far more than any of the European languages. Today only two Yaghans who speak the language are still alive, according to the *New York Times*, and I was privileged to meet one of them, Emelinda, an elderly, snaggle-tooth woman, during a brief stop at her tiny village in Puerto Williams.

On this trip I've thought a lot about the relationship between lichen spores and towering beech trees, between global warming and shrinking ice fields, between "civilized" western societies and primitive indigenous ones. It won't take much to tip the balance here. The Kyoto Protocol would reduce production of greenhouse gases that are tearing apart the ozone layer at the South Pole. The Andean countries of Chile and Argentina are responsible for just 0.02 percent of the greenhouse gas problem. The United States' share: 25 to 30 percent.

Guess which country refuses to sign the protocol.

BACK TO MY ROOTS, IN THE PAMPAS

Re-reading these observations 16 years later, I am struck by how little progress has been made in addressing the causes of global warming and climate change. While one president committed the U.S. to significant reductions in production of greenhouse gases, his successor revoked that commitment, pronouncing climate change as little more than a hoax, a liberal plot to destroy the economy. While other nations, including some of the worst polluters, like China, have begun to take measures to reduce hydrocarbon pollution, the U.S. continues to deny any role in the climate changes occurring in front of us, in the form of longer-lasting and more severe hurricanes, prolonged droughts that lead to deadly forest fires, record-high temperatures that cause high numbers of deaths among the old and fragile, especially in poorer countries lacking air-conditioned shelter.

*Back to Patagonia for one more vacation report, this one taking me close to my farm roots, but thousands of miles away on an estancia in Patagonia. This was published on **April 18, 2004**.*

Pampas Guest Ranch Visit Stirs Memories of Youth

SAN ANTONIO DE ARECA, ARGENTINA – It is harvest time in the Pampas.

As the late March arrival of autumn tinges the sycamores and beeches in pale yellows and golds, the farmers work late into the night to gather their crops. Wheat and corn fields have already fallen to the reapers, their yellow stubble providing lush forage for herds of fat cattle. Giant self-propelled combines crawl through the soybean fields, stripping wide swaths through the waist-high brown beanstalks. Under the shade of tall trees on the fence lines, field hands wait with trucks and trailers for the signal from the combine driver to unload his hopper-full of beans.

The dusty roads leading to San Antonio, the largest city in this district, are full of truck tandems heading for the huge grain elevators on rail spurs in town. On the outskirts, implement dealers display their wares: shiny Massey-Ferguson tractors, gleaming John Deere Harvesters poised to catch the lustful eye of a farmer with crisp peso notes in his pocket.

It is a surreal déjà vu experience for me, a visitor at La Bamba estancia (ranch) in this province some 120 miles northeast of Buenos Aires. This was the life I lived as a youth in Texas, following the combines, hauling the hay bales, driving the truckloads of grain to town, praying for Dad to trade our primitive tractor-pulled combine in for a self-propelled model.

Only here I am on the other side of the world, where fall begins in March and spring in September, as a paying guest on Argentina's version of a Texas dude ranch, reminiscing about a rural way of life I couldn't wait to get away from 50 years ago.

I revel in the serenity of this place, where the most audible noise is the chatter of wild parakeets, doves and assorted hawks in the soaring trees on the back lawn. Fifty years ago, I hated the loneliness of rural life; now I am paying $200 a day for it.

Amazing how our perspectives change as our circumstances do. Now a lifetime removed from the sweat and stink of the dairy farm I grew up on, I can nostalgically reminisce on the simple life of those days as I watch others toil in the dust and heat of the harvest field. From this vantage point, sipping a cool drink in La Bamba's shady backyard park, it is a delightfully pastoral scene, not the backbreaking, dawn-to-dusk job I remember from my youth.

I am torn, as I sit here watching the harvesters creep steadily through the fields, by the contrast between there and here, then and now. I have just finished a delightful lunch with La Bamba's owner, Isabella Aldao, whose late father is credited with starting the estancia guest house industry in Argentina 18 years ago. Over a traditional asado (barbecue) featuring five types of meat, I learn how much land means to Argentines and how fiercely they cling to traditions.

La Bamba dates to 1830, when it was an inn on the ancient road from Buenos Aires across the Andes to Lima, Peru. It has been in the Aldao family for three generations. Originally huge spreads of 5,000 to 10,000 acres, many Argentine ranches like La Bamba have been broken up into smaller farms as one generation died and its heirs split up the acreage. By the 1980s farming on such a small scale – La Bamba is now barely 400 acres – was no longer profitable, and Aldao's father faced the prospect of losing his beloved estancia.

It was then that he turned to renting rooms in his colonial manor house to outsiders, a move that earned him scorn from his neighbors for commercializing their somewhat aristocratic way of life. The criticism didn't last long, however, as others saw the opportunity to generate additional income and hold onto their lands, even if it meant moving out of their stately homes. Today there are more than 600 estancias in Argentina that open their doors to paying guests; it has become a mainstay of the Argentine tourism economy.

But the love of the land remains. "If I ever had to sell this place I would die," said Aldao, wife of a Buenos Aires attorney and mother of five. "It is a part of my life. My husband doesn't understand. When you have a house and sell it you move on. But when you have land, it is different. It is a part of you."

A twinge of conscience pulls me up at that statement. For even as she speaks, I know that, back in Texas, my sister is making arrangements to sell the farm that has been in our family for 70 years. When she and her husband decided to retire from the dairy business last fall, there no longer seemed to be a good reason to keep paying taxes on the land. My two surviving siblings and I had no interest in farming, and none of our children did, either. So just days before leaving on this trip to South America I had agreed to the two offers that would split the farm in half and put it in the hands of strangers.

What is wrong with me, I wonder? Why do I not revere my roots as Isabella does? Why am I so eager to sell my patrimony?

The answer is all around me – in the imposing, antique-filled manor house with a watchtower topped by a widow's walk and graced by a lovely courtyard and veranda. In the staff of white-coated waiters who bustle between kitchen and alfresco lunch table bringing fresh entrees, refilling wine glasses, removing used plates. Indeed, in the dirt-caked workers on the combines and trailers in the nearby fields.

This is not the farming experience I knew. I was not sitting under shade trees sipping wine and savoring choice meats. I *was* that dusty field hand. I *was* that gaucho driving cows out of the field at dusk. My home was that humble, jerry-build stucco house on a gravel road, not a mansion at the end of a tree-lined park. My family's was not the gentleman farming operation of the owners of estancias like La Bamba. It was back-breaking, hard-scrabble, sweat-and-blood toil that never ended.

So my second thoughts about selling my land don't linger long as I listen to Isabella describe the loving restoration projects she has in mind for La Bamba. My life has been so much different than hers; my memories aren't of carefree days playing with cousins on manicured lawns.

But it certainly has been delightful to savor such a life for two days.

I INVENTED THE 'STAYCATION'

*I may not have had a clever term for it, but I figured out the benefits of vacationing close to home years before that became a thing clever and thrifty people do to take time off without traveling long distances. Living in a coastal community, less than 10 miles from the sugar-sand beaches for which Manatee and Sarasota counties are world-famous, I just thought it made sense to head for "the islands," as we fondly referred to the barrier islands that fringe much of the west coast of Florida. And decided to share my views with readers. This column was published **Oct. 30, 1977**, just five months into my career as an editorialist at the* Bradenton Herald.

Getting Away from It All – But Not Too Far Away

"Every now and then, go away and have a little relaxation. When you come back to your work, your judgment will be surer. But to remain constantly at work will cause you to lose power of judgment. Go some distance away, because then the work appears smaller. More of it can be taken in at a glance and lack of harmony or proportion more readily seen."
--Leonardo da Vinci

Having read Da Vinci's advice in a recent column in the *Herald*, I decided to take his advice and go away for a little relaxation. Now, Lennie may just have meant to stand back from your easel a bit when he suggested "go some distance away" so that "a lack of harmony or proportion" could more readily be seen.

I, however, interpreted the advice to mean: Get the hell out of town. Away from the telephone and the newspaper. Leave it behind.

But not too far – not so far that the Master Charge would become a disaster area this close to Christmas. Say, The Islands, maybe?

No, not Jamaica or Bermuda or St. Thomas or San Juan. Not the Caribbean Islands – the Manatee Islands. Say Anna Maria Island-Longboat Key. Not so glamorous, perhaps, but not even Freddie Laker can beat the fare.

A vacation in Manatee County sounded ridiculous, at first. I mean, it's a nice place to live and all, but you wouldn't want to just visit, would you?

That's what I thought, until I really *thought* about it. Hadn't I, before moving here permanently in 1975, spent $150 to $200 a crack to fly here for a vacation – twice in one year? Don't thousands of people do the same thing every year? So why, now that I live here, isn't it good enough for me to vacation in anymore?

That was the kind of rationale I was using as I debated with myself over where to go. Actually, it may have been mere rationalization for not being able to afford a trip to a glamorous hideaway like Pago Pago or Jamaica or some such tropical isle.

But it wasn't until I got firmly ensconced in a pleasant little nook on the north end of Longboat Key that I realized I was *in* a tropical hideaway on a beautiful isle that had as much going for it as Martinique or St. Croix.

The faint sound of the surf and a salty sea breeze lulled me to sleep in the evenings. A breathtaking vista of blue sky and softly lapping sea greeted me each morning as I breakfasted in my private dining room or under a cheery umbrella on my outdoor patio. A sweeping expanse of white sandy beach, backed by softly rustling pines and tall stands of sea oats, beckoned from my front door.

A dozen comfortable lounges and rustic chairs, almost always empty save for the one in which I plopped, awaited my pleasure. A gentle sun and soft breeze gave constant ministration as I day-dreamed or snoozed the afternoons away. Visiting seagulls, sandpipers and the resident great blue heron provided all the companionship I needed. An occasional jogger or stroller on a shell-hunting expedition gave assurance of other human habitation without disturbing the tranquility.

For local color there were commercial fishermen from Cortez running their crab traps or netting for mullet, and a sailboat now and then. For diversion there was a stack of books that had collected during the last six months of the rat race (one of which I actually read), or, if I really needed it, TV.

This was the kind of vacation I had wanted, not the if-it's-Tuesday-this-must-be-Belgium rush of beautiful sights, ancient ruins, exotic foreign cities, exciting nightlife. For those I would journey to Mexico, Europe, South America or wherever. But just to take Mr. Da Vinci's advice and "go away and have a little relaxation," it would be hard to beat my vacation in Manatee County.

I think it is important to get away from home. You just can't relax as well at home as you can in a strange place. You're always tempted to do some chore you've been putting off. And there is the aggravation of the telephone to contend with.

No, Lenny was right when he urged, "Go some distance away." But that's why my destination was so perfect. You see, I packed in rather a hurry and forgot my toothbrush, tennis gear, sunglasses and other essentials. But it wasn't the crisis it would have been in, say, glamorous Acapulco. I simply drove home the next day and got the items and was back on the beach within the hour. Hard to beat that kind of convenience.

TWENTY-FIVE YEARS LATER, ANOTHER KIND OF ISLAND VACATION

*I would wind up spending many vacations either on Longboat Key or Anna Maria Island over the next four decades – along with the wife and family I acquired just a year after the above column was published. It was the only kind of vacation we could afford in those years, but it served nicely for all of the reasons stated in that column. But 25 years later, when we were empty-nesters, we went "up North" to Philadelphia for a niece's wedding and accepted the offer of Jo Anne's ex-brother-in-law of a week's stay at his vacation home on an island in central Maine. What a difference from the sandy beaches and semi-tropical climate of southwest Florida. Bone-chilling water, rocky beaches and folks speaking with a strange accent were among the differences we noted. Plus one other biggie, which was the focus of the following piece, published **Aug. 25, 2002.***

Livin' Is Easy on This Island -- But a Tyrant Rules

ISLEBORO, MAINE – A gentle breeze bearing a strong scent of the sea wafts through the car windows and open sunroof. At the dock, lobstermen in chest-high yellow waders unload the day's catch into huge plastic bins. The sun pokes weakly through gathering clouds, and a curtain of fog far off at sea awaits the chance to move in with a few-degrees drop in temperature.

You notice things while waiting in the ferry line – things you miss in the mad rush of normal commuting. The ferry forces you to stop, to follow its schedule instead of yours, to move from the fast lane to the wait lane.

Here in coastal Maine, the offshore islands are much different than those off coastal Florida. Most of the islands of Penobscot Bay are reachable only by boat. My vacation refuge, Islesboro, is a 20-minute, $8 ferry ride away from the mainland, redefining the meaning of "island living" for this recent Anna Maria transplant. It truly is a world unto itself, enabling one to literally "get away from it all."

Here there are no shopping centers. No movies. No traffic lights. Not even a real supermarket – two small general store-type groceries provide the necessities, but few frills. One up-scale bed-and-breakfast offers dinner by reservation only, and one diner offers sandwiches and ice cream.

And that's basically it. Once on the island, there literally is *nothing to do*.

Except sit on the shore under sighing pine trees and watch sailboats crisscross the bay. Or watch the squirrels, such as the one I've named Fearless Freddie, do incredible acrobatics to get at the bird feeder. Or take a long afternoon nap in a shaded porch chair. Or watch the setting sun turn Penobscot Bay into a sea of gold, with seabirds wheeling through the dazzling rays.

An island vacation here truly is an escape. But it has its price in the lack of convenience when the notion to do something different strikes. You don't just hop in the car and go into town to browse the shops. You look for the ferry schedule and begin calculating. Can we make the 9:30? If not, what if the 10:30 is full? There won't be another until 1:30 since they close for lunch.

And what about the return trip? Should we plan on the 3 or the 4? Should we pack an overnight bag in case the 5 is full?

I think back to years of Anna Maria Island vacations when, sated by days of beach-sitting and perfect sunsets, we often have driven into town for dinner and a movie. Here, you bow to the tyranny of the ferry.

But there are compensations for that bondage. With just 10 crossings a day and a capacity of 34 cars (fewer if there are trucks) the ferry guarantees Isleboro will have no traffic jams. It doesn't even need a traffic light. Bicycling is a popular form of transportation, as are boats, if you can afford them.

Animal habitat isn't threatened by overdevelopment; deer abound in the forested hills. The town retains much of its 19th century charm, though the pace of mansion-building lately causes some to fret about the changing landscape.

After almost a week here, I begin to understand why island residents guard their way of life with such passion. The feeling of being isolated, removed from the daily rat race, is very comforting.

Back at work in Manatee County, as I take up a new way of life in Anna Maria, I try to imagine what it would be like catching the ferry to downtown Bradenton every weekday. And I have a whole new respect for the Palma Sola Causeway, traffic-jam-producing drawbridge openings and all. I don't think I would make a very good islander in Maine, but I think I can handle it in Florida. I'll provide an update on that in a few months.

POST SCRIPT: SIX MONTHS LATER

Well, I learned a lot about island living during the months that followed that Maine vacation. Having sold our beloved home on McLewis Bayou in Bradenton in June to build our dream home "Out East," we rented a duplex on Anna Maria Island while our new home was being built. We took a one-year lease, thinking that would be just about the right amount of time to complete the new house and get "the island" out of our system once and for all. Little did we know how long – and how short – a year could be ("long" being a story for another time). Though it's not connected to a *vacation per se, here is my follow-up to that Maine island vacation article above, published in **early January 2003**.*

Thank You, Anna Maria, for the Memories

Now I know. For more than 25 years I have wondered what it would be like to live at the beach. For all of the years my family and I have vacationed at the beach – Anna Maria, Holmes Beach, Longboat Key – I have wondered: What would it be like to live here permanently? To know that, after a glorious Saturday under an umbrella on those sugary sand beaches followed by a golden sunset and romantic beachside dinner, I didn't have to pack up the car Sunday and regretfully say farewell for another year.

Now I know. For six months I lived the island life – or tried to. Regular readers of this column will remember that I announced last summer I was moving to the island after selling my beloved home in northwest Bradenton. They will also remember that I promised a progress report in three months.

I didn't quite fulfill that promise, but I can explain. For the past two months, I have been preparing to move again – back into town.

Don't jump to conclusions! I loved the island, especially the city of Anna Maria, where my wife and I lived from mid-July until January. But we didn't fully enjoy it. We got a little taste of what is so special about island living. There were a few glorious weekends of lazy Saturdays on the beach followed by golden sunsets and romantic moonlit dinners with no car-packing the next day.

But not enough – not enough to compensate for the downside of island living: the long commute, heavy seasonal traffic, bridge openings and bridge accidents, family emergencies in town. And work. Always work.

The lesson I learned about island living is that it's for vacationers and retirees, not career people in demanding jobs. The pace of life is ideal for an unhurried lifestyle, especially in Anna Maria's north end where we lived. It was like entering another plane of existence. Cars slowed to 25 mph. People walked or rode bikes or the trolley. They visited at the Post Office and on street corners. They got to know each other at the various restaurants and pubs. They were – are – a real community, not unlike the tiny Texas town I come from where everybody knows your name.

But it was so frustrating to be there in the middle of that serenity and – I hate to say this – *not have time to enjoy it.* But that was our reality. With demanding jobs and family, including an ailing parent in town, the island became just a place to eat and crash – and then a chore. Traffic. Going to the Post Office for mail. Slow driving speeds. Bridge delays. A three-mile drive to the closest grocery. And always, the nagging awareness of the Gulf of Mexico, with its beautiful beaches within easy walking distance, and no time to enjoy it. It was depressing.

So we gave up the dream. But we take away many wonderful memories. I especially will remember: the bicycle lady with her "one-less-car" vest making her rounds every day at dawn, the "good morning" exchanges with total strangers on their morning constitutionals, the trips to the Post Office where you always ran into someone you knew, the burger-and-fries dinners on "I-don't-feel-like-cooking" nights at Hurricane Hank's, Tip of the Island, City Pier and other delightful eateries too numerous to mention. (My favorite hideaway: Rod & Reel Pier restaurant.)

I got to know Anna Maria quite well on my jogs and dog walks, especially the north end whose beaches are so coveted these days. I understand the conflict the city is going through as the cottages and modest ranch-style homes yield to the pressure of the McMansion-driven real estate market. Every block contains charming little homes on tiny lots with cleverly designed side or back yards creating hidden refuges, many with nautical themes.

I marveled at the ingeniousness of the owners in creating little Shangri-la's in such small spaces, with steppingstones disappearing into shaded backyard recesses. But on virtually every block, those modest beach hideaways are dwarfed by new stilt homes – grand two-and three-story monsters built above federally mandated flood heights that overwhelm their old-fashioned neighbors and create an architectural disconnect throughout the city.

That transition is most obvious on North Shore Drive, where million-dollar mansions line the beach side of the street, but it is noticeable throughout the city. And it's really quite sad to see the future of Anna Maria, as hard as its residents try to preserve its "old Florida" look and feel. I doubt that they will succeed in the long run. The combination of market forces and private property rights is like a rip tide sweeping an unsuspecting swimmer out to sea.

Someday I will be able to say: This is what it was like, for one brief season in 2002. Meanwhile, I have the comfort of knowing that I can always return for a week or a month, if not forever.

THE BIG APPLE, 40 YEARS LATER

I had been to New York briefly, in the early 1960s, with a couple of my Oklahoma City friends. I was of course awe-struck by the city's enormity and its beauty, but I didn't fall in love with it. It was just too much for this small-town guy – too congested, too noisy, too expensive, too in-your-face. I couldn't wait to get back on the road and see open spaces, and the sky. So, when returning from our week on Islesboro in Maine, we planned a five-day stopover in New York en-route back to Florida. It would be my first trip back to New York in almost 40 years, only this time it would be with my wife. I wondered if I would have a different reaction. Here is what I wrote, in mid-2002.

Big Apple's Charms Can't Compete
with 'Our Little Secret'

NEW YORK – I *liked* New York City. I'm surprised to be making that statement after a recent vacation trip to the Big Apple, for I was prepared to hate it. As a nearly life-long small-town guy who shuns traffic and crowds, I had unpleasant memories of both from my last trip here some 38 years ago. But New York has changed a lot in almost four decades. So have I.

I was poorly prepared for the profound cultural shock I experienced upon emerging from the bowels of Penn Station into the heart of Manhattan on a sweltering Sunday afternoon. A gypsy cab driver pestered me to avail myself of his services. Bumper-to-bumper traffic inched noisily down Seventh Avenue, the heat and fumes exacerbating the merciless humidity. Throngs of people rushed past, ignoring my wife and me and our mound of luggage at curbside. The queue for cabs was endless. And I couldn't find the name or address of our hotel.

We were in the middle of a classic "Out of Towners" experience, but the hilarity of the mishaps of the small-town bumpkins played by Jack Lemmon and Sandy Dennis in that '70s movie was lost on us at this particular moment.

But thanks to the quick thinking of my wife and the miracle of the cell phone, we managed to confirm the address and were soon in a cab headed to Midtown and our lodgings.

And that was the worst experience of our trip. New York truly has changed – for the better. The streets are relatively clean and graffiti-free. So are the subways. The city is quite visitor-friendly, with well-defined street signs and easy-to-follow maps. Even the legendary New York attitude seemed to be at a minimum. Passers-by offered to help when they saw us huddled over our maps. Servers were as friendly as those at home. I assume it's a pleasant by-product of 9/11; the we're-all-trying-to-get-along feeling was quite strong throughout the city.

295

Never did we feel threatened by crime. Police officers were everywhere – on foot, on horseback and in cars.

To this provincial, the most vivid impressions of New York are the crowds and the traffic. As streams of people flowed out of Penn Station on a weekday morning, I guessed there were more people in that one building than in the entire city of Bradenton. At night, when the theater curtains dropped on Broadway, rivers of people flowed through the theater district, spilling into streets jammed with cars and limousines. Hundreds of restaurants beckoned post-theater diners; for many, the evening was just beginning – at 11 p.m. If we could have just one block of this in Bradenton, I thought.

In Times Square, the heart of the theater district, a Monday night seemed like New Year's Eve. Street vendors hawked watches and jewelry. Street artists did sketches. Spike-haired teens eyed each other. Electronic messages crawled across dozens of buildings, and several-story-high electronic billboards flashed their pitches. Entire building facades were turned into electronic screens, with multiple images crawling along the walls in a weird panoramic effect.

On a hot afternoon, Central Park was a cool green oasis from the steamy city. Mothers strolled the shady paths with baby carriages and toddlers or relaxed on blankets under towering trees. In the sprawling Sheep Meadow, sun-bathers scattered through the vast space gave the velvety lawn a dappled effect. The importance of parks in an urban setting is made crystal clear here. Bradenton developers, please note.

As to traffic, too many cars and too much rule-breaking turn most street travel into a dysfunctional mess. Theoretically, the city's alternating one-way grid on most north-south and east-west streets, with synchronized traffic signals, would create a smooth flow. But trucks double-parked in curb lanes force drivers to blend into interior lanes, creating constant interruptions. Pedestrians ignoring crossing signals block intersections, preventing turning cars from clearing intersections before oncoming traffic moves. The result is frequent, maddening gridlock. A bus ride from Times Square in Midtown to Battery Park in lower Manhattan takes upwards of an hour – in non-rush hour periods. A cross-town ride can take half an hour. Manatee Avenue at its worst in morning rush hour is a picnic by comparison.

A few days of this, though culturally enriching, is plenty for this out-of-towner. Even as I marvel at the glitter of Fifth Avenue stores and the excitement of Broadway plays, I keep thinking back to "our little secret."

The corny truth is: I (heart) Bradenton.

THE ILLUSION OF TV STUDIO SHOWS

Now, 17 years later, I look back on that perspective and think: Am I still such a provincial? I have been back to New York several times since 2002, and each time the city has grown on me a bit more. My wife and I have even established our own favorite bistros and pubs in Midtown. The Round Table at the Algonquin Hotel on 44th Street is one of them, for its history as a hangout for famous journalists, writers and actors of the mid-20th century. I fantasize about bumping into Dorothy Parker, Heywood Broun, Robert Sherwood or Alexander Woolcott as I enjoy my overpriced prime rib, though of course the literary crowd has turned over several times since their heyday and has moved to other hangouts in the city. We have even toyed with the idea of finding an inexpensive rental – or maybe arranging a home exchange with a New Yorker desperate to escape to the sun – for an extended stay in the city, maybe a month. I would love to have the time and freedom to just walk the city at my leisure. Most of my visits are so time-constrained that I don't feel free to do that. But just the fact that I'm willing to consider living there for a month must mean I have lost at least some of my provincialism.

We returned to New York in 2003, to join Jo Anne's cousins from Honduras who were in town to meet old friends and included us in their plans. It was on this trip that I had my first live studio audience experience. In was the winter of 2003, and the debate about Iraq's role in the 9/11 terrorist attacks and its feared possession of weapons of mass destruction was raging. I was outside the United Nations *the morning that Secretary of State Colin Powell was to address the General Assembly on that issue, trying to get in to hear what I knew would be – and did become – a historic speech promoting America's invasion of Iraq, which would occur a few months later. Sadly, I failed to gain entry to the spectators' gallery. I knew no one and had no clout. So, I settled for the taping of an NBC TV talk show hosted by a has-been and staged in the studios of a little-known NBC cable offshoot called MSNBC. The following is my account of that adventure, published around **Feb. 17, 2003**.*

Live Talk Shows: Lots of Heat, Not Much Substance

NEW YORK – So, you want to be in the studio audience for a nationally televised show?

It's no problem, if you're in New York on a cold weekday in February and you have a few hours to kill. But don't expect "Saturday Night Live," "Jay Leno" or "Oprah." We're talking B-list talk shows on cable, like Phil Donahue.

Yes, that was me trying to get a sensible answer out of Phil's guests the night Colin Powell made his big presentation at the United Nations. And yes, sadly, Donahue, the man who practically invented the daytime talk show, has fallen to a nighttime slot on a little-watched cable offshoot of one of the big guys, MSNBC. Eager young men, doubtless interns, were practically begging people in front of NBC at Rockefeller Center to take tickets to the Donahue show on Feb. 5. My wife and I, having completed a tour of NBC studios that morning, thought it would be interesting and fun to be part of a live show.

It turned out to be interesting, but not especially fun. The whole studio audience thing is quite disillusioning, sort of like going behind the curtain at Oz to discover there's not much to the Wizard. The studio itself is tiny, and the sets are rather disappointing: a cheap desk and four chairs with some cheesy skyline backdrop. For this show fewer than 20 ticket-holders showed up at the announced check-in at 7; a few more straggled in to total, by my count, 32 by air time.

NBC staff, both on our morning tour and in the audience arm-up, made no secret of the fact that much of TV staging is an illusion. We were told to sit close together in the center section and to clap extra fast and loud "to make it sound like there are three or four times the actual number in the audience." Staff members sat in another section to our left to give the illusion of a much larger crowd than was actually there.

Donahue came in about 7:50, all silvery-maned, blue-eyed, gray-suited and amazingly smooth-skinned for a man of his vintage (a facelift?). He came over to rev us up, informing us it would "be a better show if you get involved. Get in early and often" with questions, he urged. An assistant followed him, handing out portable mics. I took one.

The opening topic was, of course, Iraq, and Powell's UN presentation that morning. The guests were a former colonel, a prominent peace activist, a gung-ho pro-war advocate and, by remote hook-up, the former governor of Virginia. I didn't recognize any of their names.

It quickly became evident to me that the purpose of the show was not so much to debate the merits of Powell's evidence as to start an argument. Guests took turns attacking each other's positions. Then Donahue would take a question from a caller or look to the audience hoping for some fiery barb to be tossed out.

After a couple of such exchanges I stood and asked what I thought was a very relevant question: "Which of the three guests in the pro--war camp would be willing to join the front line of the troops headed for Iraq or to have their son or daughter in that line?"

Apparently, that wasn't on Donahue's agenda. Only the retired officer answered. Of course he would be happy to go except his physical condition would surely disqualify him. Neither of the other two hawks bothered to answer, and Donahue didn't press them.

He certainly wasn't shy about baiting the anti-war guest, though. He allowed the right-wing hawk to sharply attack her without much chance to rebut. A few hawkish members of the audience got riled up, and scattered boos erupted behind me. Donahue seemed pleased.

I felt used. Certainly, it was a long way from the hooting, ranting audiences of Jerry Springer or Maury Povich. But I could see how the talk show hosts goad people into overreacting to a guest's answer and how certain audience members might try to do something outrageous to get on camera. I had no desire to have my views on something as important as war exploited for mass entertainment.

I wanted to leave right then but decided to stick around out of courtesy.

The second and last segment was on missing California mom-to-be Lacy Peterson, which didn't produce much heat –or new insights. Mercifully, Donahue finally announced he was out of time, and the show ended.

Well, like much of New York, it was a new and unique experience and I'm glad I did it. But I probably wouldn't do it again. SNL or Leno, maybe – they look like more fun. I like serious debates. However, in my opinion, most talk shows are too much like sucker fests, setting someone up for a cheap punch. I don't want to waste my time.

Years Before the I-Phone, Technology Dazzled

*Enough of the Big Apple. It's time to head for another favorite vacation spot, from a much earlier era. The next one takes us to Orlando once again, this time for the opening of Walt Disney's Experimental Prototype Community of Tomorrow – EPCOT. The theme park opened on Oct. 1, 1982, to much hype about its futuristic view of the world in 2050. From the perspective of almost four decades' passage of time, in a Digital Age with mobile devices capable of performing almost any electronic function one can imagine, the entire concept seems almost quaint. But it was a very big deal at the time. This is my account of my family's visit, published on **Oct. 10, 1982.***

Epcot: Fantasy-Chasing, Minus Fairy Tales

The "newest wonder of the world" Epcot Center is not. Such exaggerations are to be expected from overambitious press agents trying to drum up a good crowd for opening day.

An interesting, entertaining, provocative production it is, and if you go there with down-to-earth expectations, you'll probably enjoy Epcot Center immensely.

"Walt Disney's greatest dream" is something less than the Buck Rogers-like working prototype of life in 2050, which advance billing had led us to expect. In spots it approaches Disney's vision of a real-life community evolving in harmony with ever-advancing technology, such as in the experimental agricultural section of The Land pavilion. There experimental farming methods that may one day help feed a starving world are on display for visitors to either ride or walk through.

But much of Epcot is pure Disney animated gimmickry, merely elevated to a more mature level than the storybook displays of Disney World. As *Time* magazine put it: "The adult toy of the future. . .a mind-pummeling assault of electronic ingenuity, historical fact, fancy, showmanship, faith, hope and goo."

The much-touted ride through the 18-story geosphere Spaceship Earth, which most opening-weekend visitors missed because of technical problems, is a hybrid of the best of 20,000 Leagues Under the Sea, the Haunted House and It's a Small World as it depicts man's progress from cave-dweller to space explorer. The finale of that journey, a ride by a futuristic space city glowing from what seems the darkness of outer space, brings ohs and ahs from awestruck visitors.

Another highlight of Epcot, the World of Motion sponsored by General Motors, resembles nothing so much as the Pirates of the Caribbean exhibit at Disney World – except that the 24 Audio Animatronic scenes are not storybook adventure tableaus but authentic depictions of man's progress from the invention of the wheel to the invention of the space rocket. True to Disney standards, all are superbly done, especially the elaborate scene depicting the first traffic jam. Here horses rear in fright, drivers yell and shake their fists at each other, a plump matron scolds her hapless husband, a fruit vendor bemoans his ruined produce, and a cageful of chickens overturned in the middle of the street adds its frightened clucks to the din. It is priceless.

World Showcase, the much-talked-about collection of nine international pavilions around a 45-acre lagoon, was to me the least impressive part of the park. They may in time become the cultural microcosms of the lands they represent, but so far the pavilions seem mere facades around which to display expensive souvenirs – some of them high-quality items, to be sure – but souvenirs nevertheless. Perhaps more cultural aspects will be added as time passes, but on opening weekend the emphasis was on shopping – which is fine, if that's your thing. It isn't mine.

What is most striking about Epcot – aside from sheer scope of the endeavor –is the influence of the computer. Here, in mind-boggling variety, is the essence of Disney's "prototype community of tomorrow," though perhaps not exactly as Walt envisioned it. In exhibits like Communicore and Journey into Imagination, banks of video screens allow Epcot visitors to confront the computer one-on-one in many different formats: game-playing, learning, communicating, retrieving information. Touch-sensitive screens permit anyone able to read to interact with computers that, it is obvious, will someday be routine household appliances performing precisely the functions shown experimentally at Epcot.

This is far more exciting to me than the contrived thrills of cute animated figures or thrill rides. That's because while so much of Disney's empire is based on fantasy, this seeming fantasy of the computer world is real, here, today. The fantasy of only a few years ago is a reality today in a way that Cinderella and Mickey Mouse can never be. And what you see here you know is only a sample of what is serving man in a thousand ways now and a fraction of what is in store in the future.

Not that there's no place for fantasy at Epcot. Journey into Imagination is pure computer-age fantasy housed in a geometric puzzle-like building of glass, steel and purple walls whose design itself is exciting. Here, the "playground of the future," is fantasy – but fantasy that can be formed, felt, experienced, rather than just observed, as in Disney's other creations.

You want to paint an electronic picture in colored lights? The Magic Palette's laser pen makes it possible.

You want to have your own symphony, create original music to accompany you in an interpretive dance? Step into the eerie glow of the Stepping Tones room listen to the other-worldly music created by the movement of your feet.

Or perhaps you've always dreamed of creating and starring in your own movie. At the Dreamfinder's Drama School you can step into a set and dance, sing and even fly just like Mary Poppins, while your friends applaud or hiss from the sidelines, as appropriate.

This is where Epcot comes closest to both fulfilling Walt's dream of an Experimental Prototype Community of Tomorrow AND capturing the Disney magic. I thought our 11-year-old daughter aptly summed up Epcot when, amid the electronic marvels of the purple-and-glass Journey into Imagination, she said, "This is sort of like a fairyland, isn't it?"

Yes, I conceded. It is. Sort of.

AN OLYMPIC EXPERIENCE

Atlanta's successful bid to host the 1996 Summer Olympics gave me the chance to fulfill a life-long dream of attending the Olympic Games. The fact that our son Max had obtained a paying job on the Olympic Planning Committee staff made it all the more imperative to plan a week's vacation in Atlanta. He provided us free lodging in a city of booked-up hotels and gouging homeowners renting out their modest homes at exorbitant rates, although sleeping on a futon on the living room floor of his garage apartment was not my idea of a three-star experience. Still, it was free, so I didn't complain. Much.

His job – he served as a liaison between various law enforcement agencies providing security for the Games – entitled him to two free tickets to – unfortunately, not the coveted Opening Ceremony, but – the dress rehearsal for the Opening Ceremony. Which was almost as good, for we were able to see the entire spectacle for the sold-out event the following evening. The column I wrote for the July 28, 1996, edition of the Herald had nothing to do with the games themselves but was all about the spectacle of them as well as the experience of being part of a truly global event.

Olympic Games Transforms Atlanta into a True Global Village

ATLANTA -- Home never looked so sweet as it did at mid-week when my wife and I returned from a week's vacation in Atlanta.

Yes, Atlanta, Georgia – Olympic-crazed Atlanta. The Atlanta of $3.50 Cokes and $4 water. The Atlanta of more than 10,000 world-class athletes – and a million street vendors. The Atlanta of chrome-plated Chevy pick-ups and dime-a-dozen celebrity sightings.

Hotlanta, as we Floridians are fond of saying in deprecation of our big-city neighbor to the north. Hot-hot-hot Atlanta. Ho-boy, so sweltering you might have thought the Yankees had come back and started another fire in the middle of Peachtree Street. Don't believe that old weather line about it being not the heat but the humidity that makes you uncomfortable. A 94-degree July day in Atlanta is as wilting as anything a steamy southwest Florida July day can throw at you.

But if this is starting to sound like another diatribe against the heat, hype and hustle of either the Centennial Olympics or their host city, that is not my intent.

Home looked so good to us because the Atlanta Olympic experience was so exhilarating and overwhelming that we were left drained and exhausted by it. After a week of rubbing shoulders with people from around the world in an environment charged with the emotion of a shared adventure, we needed a vacation – to the normal world. Lots of people thought we were crazy for going to Atlanta during the Olympics. The heat, the traffic, the crowds and the gouging would make the city unbearable, friends said in discouraging our trip.

We saw it as a once-in-a-lifetime opportunity that folks so close to the host city would be crazy to pass up. Our experience convinced us that we were correct. And Friday night's bomb incident does not alter that view.

It is difficult to describe the excitement that has overtaken Atlanta since the opening ceremonies July 19. It stems from the fact that these are, indeed, the best athletes in the world and that the people around you represent virtually every nation in the world. The sense of the commonality of humankind was palpable in Atlanta – at the opening ceremony, in the packed MARTA trains, at the athletic venues and in Centennial Olympic Park, through which hundreds of thousands of visitors pass each day.

Watching faces, eavesdropping, or starting up conversations of your own, you are struck by the mosaic of nationalities united in this quadrennial coming together, as the ancient Greeks intended, in peace and human bonding. Here is a TV news crew doing a standup in front of Centennial Park while waiting for the torch to pass on its final swing through downtown. They inform you they're from Indonesia. A few blocks away, the talk between members of another TV crew setting up in front of the High Museum sounds like German. The nametags on the two mountains of muscle in front of you on a MARTA car tell you they're weightlifters from Great Britain and Pakistan, respectively. In the CNN Center food court, a Chinese family stops for a cup of tea. Nearby a weary Korean couple sit on a planter wall to rest and check their maps.

In the stadiums, the tiny flags waved by cheering sections for the competing teams indicate more nationalities: Russia, New Zealand, Netherlands, Ukraine, France, Italy. And everywhere there are the wonderful Atlanta volunteers in their color-ringed polo shirts, khaki shorts and Crocodile Dundee straw hats inquiring in their distinctive Georgia drawls: "May I help you?"

What struck me about this panoply of humanity was how quickly we all ceased to be foreigners and became simply fellow adventurers, coping with the heat, crowds, prices and disorientation of an unfamiliar city not as people of specific nationalities but simply as people. We're here from every corner of the world and we're talking to each other as pleasantly as if we've run into neighbors at the mall.

In NBC's TV coverage of the games, many sponsors have built their commercials around the global village theme: credit cards, phone services, copiers, underwear, to name a few. For 2 ½ weeks, Atlanta has become a global village, and the people who make the trip are having a global village experience.

And it is one that most will never forget, regardless of which nation wins the most medals. On the streets, especially those wide downtown avenues like International Boulevard that Atlanta officials have blissfully closed to vehicular traffic, a festive mood permeates the sea of humanity coursing to and from the venues and into Centennial Park.

Vendors hawking T-shirts, souvenirs, food and drink add a carnival touch to the scene. Tawdry, kitschy, noisy, commercial – yes, it is all of these, but it is also an almost surreal display of Americana that I'm glad foreign visitors can see.

This is us, folks, including chrome-plated pick-ups, and Atlanta, the capital of the South, has done a great job of representing us to the rest of the world.

Of course, it hasn't been without problems: overcrowded MARTA trains, computer glitches in reporting results, high prices for everything, and the oppressive heat. But I can't imagine staging an event of this magnitude without some problems. What city in the world could handle a tripling of its mass transit ridership without crowding problems?

It's not too late to have an Olympic Experience for yourself. If you have any vacation time and vacation money left, I recommend making the trek up I-75 for a few days.

There is still a week's worth of Olympic competition before the closing ceremony Aug. 4. At mid-week the *Atlanta Constitution* had 2 ½ pages of ads for housing and tickets. I can't vouch for the prices or quality of any of these, but, based on my experience, I would take the chance.

CHAPTER SIX
TRIVIA OF LIFE

Many of the topics I chose for my Sunday edition columns don't fit into any category. The inspiration would come from something that happened to me in my personal life, or that I had observed and thought worthy of commentary. I grant you that some may seem trivial today, but at the time they seemed very important to me. Or else they had special poignancy that I felt readers would identify with.

*The first one has special meaning for me. It was an account of a road trip from my hometown that allowed me to revisit the lonely landscape of my childhood, to experience the mood set in one of my favorite movies, and to briefly delve into the mind of a world-famous author. That's a lot to ask from one article, but I believe the following, published in **April 2002**, accomplished that in its longer-than-usual format.*

Lonely Landscape of 'Last Picture Show'
Changing into 'Book World'

ARCHER CITY, TEXAS – "The Last Picture Show" has been one of my favorite movies since its release in 1971. That's because it so perfectly captures the bleak landscape of a small west Texas town circa 1950s. The fact that it was filmed in Archer City, a mere 80 miles southwest of my hometown, made it especially relevant for me even though the landscape changes drastically in those 80 miles – from the rolling black-soil farming country of my native Muenster to the sagebrush-filled ranchland of Archer City.

The movie's small-town Texas culture also was evocative of my own town's. "This is what my youth was like," I tell anyone who shows an interest in my background. So much of it *was* my life – the cattle-and-oil-based economy, the tiny, struggling high school, the aimless, Main-Street-cruising youth, the café with lusciously greasy hamburgers and gravy-smothered chicken-fried steaks, the ramshackle pool hall and, the title landmark, the "picture show" doomed by the invention of television.

The movie, based on a book by Larry McMurtry and directed by Peter Bogdanovich, became something of a classic for its film noir black-and-white imagery and emotionally raw representation of the desperation, resignation and hypocrisy of small-town life. It starred the young Cybil Shepherd, Jeff Bridges and Timothy Bottoms, along with Ben Johnson as the town sage and Eileen Brennan as the hard-bitten, heart-of-gold waitress. And it established McMurtry as a serious novelist who later would go on to international fame with the classic western "Lonesome Dove," the sad mom-daughter terminal-illness tale of "Terms of Endearment," and many more.

Indeed, almost everyone connected with "Last Picture Show" got famous – except Archer City. This tiny town, which was called "Anarene" in the movie, sat in obscurity for 20 years and saw lots more than its "picture show" close as the oil boom went bust.

But because of McMurtry, that is beginning to change. Thanks to McMurtry's idiosyncratic relationship with his hometown and his love of books, Archer City is becoming a Mecca for book lovers. In the last few years McMurtry, a world-renowned collector, has closed his bookstores in Houston, Los Angeles, Dallas and Phoenix and moved the collection to Archer City. He adds to it regularly by purchasing other collections, even entire bookstores that are going out of business. His Booked Up store now occupies four buildings in Archer City, a mind-boggling 400,000 to 500,000 volumes. McMurtry has literally put Archer City on the map as the home of the best second-hand bookstore in the country and is well on his way to achieving his goal of making it "a book town."

It is that anomaly, along with my 30-year interest in its fictional representation, that has brought me to this wind-swept hamlet to stand under the marquee of the Royal Theater (the "picture show" of the movie title) and to ask the waitress in the café, just as Ben Johnson did to the slatternly Genevieve in the movie, "How 'bout chikin-fryin' me up a steak?"

Alas, the café is one of the few landmarks of the movie on Archer City's main drag that's still identifiable. In fact, grabbing lunch there is like stepping into the 1950s, so little is it changed from the movie: red-leatherette booths, chrome-edged tables and chairs, black and white fake-marble floors, pressed tin ceiling, and locals in grease-stained overalls and jeans ordering "burger baskits" (with fresh-cut, not frozen, French fries), chicken-fried steaks or today's special, all-you-can-eat tortillas.

The pool hall, much like the one I learned to shoot 8 ball in 45 years ago, still stands, but it is now an upholstery store. The flapping screen door, which Bogdanovich used as a metaphor for the bleakness of Main Street, appears to have been replaced. The marquee of the Royal is about all that's left of the movie house; the rest of it burned down a few years ago. Now the bright Texas sun shines down on the spot where Sonny (Bottoms) and Duane (Bridges) watched Grade B westerns in the film.

The Dairy Queen is still there, seemingly as little changed as the café, and the imposing stone courthouse dominates the courthouse square as a strong symbol of the town's resilience and rugged independence.

To call Booked Up a mere bookstore does not do justice to its four emporiums here. They are libraries – huge, sprawling spaces lined with 12-foot-high shelves crammed with books of every style and variety imaginable. Each building is dedicated to certain subject areas, much like the floors of a multi-story university library. Some of the books appear brand new, some are old, and many are rare. A small leather-bound book with a metal clasp in not-so-perfect condition, picked off the shelf at random, has a $400 price tag. Many first editions and other well-bound or rare books are in the $60 to $75 range.

McMurtry personally presides over this book empire, dressed in jeans, boots and a plaid work shirt. He politely but coolly responds to visitors' questions while sorting through books and preparing a loading dock for another shipment in Store One, a former Ford dealership. This would seem to be an ideal marketing opportunity for his own books, but like much about this town, logic has its own native terms in Archer City. Books he penned aren't for sale, and don't even think of bringing your own copy of, say, "Lonesome Dove" and asking him to autograph it. He doesn't do autographs. "After signing my name about 60,000 times, I just got tired of it," he explains.

"But why all of this way out here?", I ask, gesturing at the 10-shelf-high stacks of books as far as the eye can see. "Is this your way to lure the big-city literary sophisticates to your world?"

"No," he answers, without a trace of irony in his voice. "This is for the local people – for West Texas. This is their bookstore." He takes my speechlessness as a signal that this interview is over, finishes stacking boxes of books on a dolly, and wheels it across the street to Store Two.

Like much of McMurtry's literary work, there is more than a little exaggeration in that statement. If every living human in West Texas descended on Archer City in a day and left with an armload, they would scarcely make a dent in his collection. And, though there may be pockets of literary-minded folks in Archer and neighboring counties, this is not exactly a hotbed of bibliophiles. There is some speculation that his book project represents a sort of personal closure for the writer, an attempt to make peace with the locals resentful of the depressing image he gave the town in "Last Picture Show."

I want to believe that McMurtry is sincere about fulfilling the literary needs of his hometown. After all, he has taken an interest in the writing courses at Midwestern State University in nearby Wichita Falls, which has established a McMurtry Writing Center, and he has hosted some gifted high school student writers.

But as I head east out of town past the Royal Theater marquee, I can't help but wonder if Booked Up is the ultimate expression of irony by a literary genius whose characters represent many degrees of irony. A world-class bookstore in a God-forsaken town like this – it's a plot twist straight out of a McMurtry novel. If you've read much of his work, you know what I mean.

TAKING NOSTALGIA FOR A SPIN

Curious about the state of Booked Up and Archer City today, almost 20 years later, I googled McMurtry. I learned that he decided in 2012 to downsize his collection and conducted an auction in August 2012 that drew hundreds from across the country, including dealers, collectors and gawkers. He sold off some 300,000 volumes of his collection and downsized the remainder into just one store. And after its brief fling as a book capital, Archer City reverted to pretty much as it was depicted in "The Last Picture Show": a bleak, Godforsaken town that offered its residents little hope of anything better.

The next piece contains quite a bit of nostalgia, too. In 1999, the year leading up to the changing of the millennium, the Herald *sought reader input on how the country had changed in the century that was about to end. On the Opinion Pages, I asked readers to recall how the culture had changed in their lifetimes, and I primed the pump with a series of personal recollections that fell under the title "The Things We Used to Do." Here is one from* **Jan. 3, 1999,** *that brings in my beloved father-in-law for a much-deserved bit of attention.*

The Things We Used to Do: When Savings Accounts Had Real Meaning

On Dec. 10, 1946, a proud young father stopped in at the Wheeling Dollar Savings & Trust Co. on Market Street in Wheeling, W. Va., to open a savings account for his baby daughter, Jo Anne, aged six months.

He handed six dollars and seventy-eight cents to the teller, who took out a little dark-green passbook, stamped the number 87030 in red on the front cover, then wrote in the name "Gerald Patterson, trustee for Jo Anne Patterson," at the top in blue ink. The initial deposit of -$6.78 was dutifully noted in the first column beside the date – the beginning of this father's 50-year-long ritual of saving spare change for a daughter's yet-undreamed future.

It wasn't at all unusual to save money like that in those days. People didn't have much – $40 a week was a decent salary for a young family man just getting started after the war – so putting aside a few coins each week represented tangible progress toward achieving goals, whether it was college tuition or a bridal dowry or just. . .well, who knew what? Savings meant security.

The passbook filled painfully slowly. On March 11, 1947, the second entry was made: $2.50 – in the same blue ink, by a different hand. And on May 1 the first interest was recorded: two cents. On July 3 there was another $2.50 deposit, and on Sept. 25 a third, bringing the total saved in nine months to $14.30. By Nov. 1 the interest accrual had more than doubled – to five cents.

Gerald Patterson continued adding money to his daughter's savings account, in pennies, nickels and dimes, for 49 more years. In 1956 the records show the account moved to the Upper Darby National Bank when the family moved to Philadelphia, then back to the Wheeling Dollar Savings and Trust in 1962 when the family moved back to West

Virginia. By 1978 it went with him to Florida, where retirement did not keep him from adding $5 every month or two.

On June 24, 1996, as he presented his daughter – now Jo Anne Klement, my wife – the gift of that savings account on her 50th birthday, there was more intrinsic value connected to it than the $965 it contained. The packet of little savings passbooks – six in all – that he had so faithfully kept since the year of her birth represented a little hidden bond between father and daughter, a symbol of devotion that required no reciprocation or acknowledgment.

Though I am of the post-war generation that also counted nickels and dimes as precious savings, it struck me then that this was something younger generations might not even know existed. Banks today are too busy to record two cents' interest; they don't even like to be bothered with children's saving accounts, certainly not in two-dollar-and-fifty-cent increments. If they even still have passbooks, it's certain a gracious teller isn't writing out the entries in blue ink.

Those little passbooks represent a nostalgic link to the past, a reminder of the way we used to live before computers, credit cards and a new consumer philosophy changed the way we save, spend and bank. The neat columns of carefully printed figures are symbols of a vanishing way of life, a reminder of a culture that our children barely knew of, and that their children will never experience for themselves.

How about you? Do you have stories from the past like this that tell the younger generation About the way we used to live, about the things we used to do? If so, we invite you to share them with readers as part of our year-long millennium project of looking back at the past while looking ahead to the next century.

Not Everything Has Changed

I probably could write a similar column about the changes in banking, computerization and attitudes about money today, 20 years after that lament. Forget piddling savings accounts and gracious tellers, you're lucky if you can even find a branch bank, let alone a friendly teller to take your deposit. So much has changed in every aspect of our culture, especially anything connected with commerce. But there is one institution in Bradenton that remains true to its tradition, 20 years after I celebrated its old-fashioned virtues of customer service and professional knowledge. The store remains virtually unchanged from the one I described along about spring 1999.

Neighborhood Hardware Store: A Treasure for Do-It-Yourselfers

I hate filling out those forms where there's a blank for "hobbies."

What do I put? I don't play golf, fish, hunt, roller-blade, surf the internet or collect beer cans, baseball caps or green crockware.

The thing I spend the most of my waking, non-working hours on is home repair. So do I write in the hobby blank: Keeping a 70-year-old house from falling apart?

Sigh! It's neither hobby nor obsession but survival that has caused me to spend inordinate amounts of time studying O-rings, grommets, toilet-tank flappers and spackle compounds, to cite a few of my recent home-repair challenges.

Fortunately, there is a store close by that keeps me from going bonkers when I am stymied by a leaking faucet, broken toilet or cracked drop-ceiling panel where an errant champagne cork rocketed through last New Year's Eve. You probably have a similar place in your neighborhood; mine is Crowder Brothers, a Bradenton institution for more than 40 years, a mom-and-pop hardware store that has carved out a niche for itself with a simple formula: carrying the supplies and offering the know-how to help people solve their home-repair problems.

Crowder's is a home-grown, family-owned institution which generations of Bradenton residents have grown up trusting to have just the part they need for any job. A trip to Crowder's is part of the Saturday ritual for countless residents who have moved far from its original location in the Westgate Shopping Center, 3933 Manatee Ave. W. As of last weekend, I also have to go farther afield to visit Crowder's – not because *I* moved, but because *they* did. But since their new location is all of 15 blocks west of the old one, it's not a big deal.

True do-it-yourselfers like me know that, if Crowder Brothers doesn't have it, you probably can't find it. My revelation came a number of years ago when I noticed the kitchen sink was in need of new caulking. Peering under the sink, I discovered that it was held in place by metal clips, some of which had rusted, causing the sink to sag and creating an unsightly gap on the countertop. Naturally, I headed to Crowder's and described my problem to Bob, Spencer, Carl or one of the other know-almost-everything middle-aged guys who are on duty to help technology-impaired customers like me.

"Sink clips," he answered. "What kind?"

Basic Lesson No. 1 for the do-it-yourselfer: Always bring the defective part with you, for any guess will inevitably be the wrong one. When I returned with a rusted clip I learned why it was so important to have it. There are trays and trays of sink clips – fat, skinny, long, short – but only one fits your sink opening. And Crowder's has it.

It also has multiple trays of dozens of other items, from mirror clips to hose bibs to sprinkler parts to drill bits to fuses and much more. In the new store, which almost doubles the square footage, they will probably have dozens of other trays of parts I still haven't discovered after 35 years of home repairs.

Though my wife will protest, it's OK to go there in your grubbiest, sweatiest work outfits, for you'll inevitably run into someone you know who looks just as grubby. There are few pretensions in Crowder's. You're there to do a job, and you're not afraid to admit that you need help. The middle-age guys in the red vests are the most knowledgeable; the handful of young hardware-gurus-in-training are eager enough, but they have a lot to learn about grommets and toilet flappers and sink clips. You are truly blessed when you get a real *Crowder* to help you.

I admit it, there's probably something of Tim "The Toolman" Taylor from "Tooltime" in me, for I just enjoy hanging out in Crowder Brothers. I love handling the tools, and every home repair problem I tackle teaches me something new about things mechanical. To a desk jockey like me that's as satisfying as turning out a well-crafted editorial.

Fortunately, there's a place nearby like Crowder Brothers to help me through the rough spots. If you have such a place in your neighborhood, it wouldn't hurt to tell 'em how much they mean to you. They're a treasure.

A Different Neighborhood – and a Wake-Up Call

As previously noted, we made the decision to leave our beloved house on the bayou in 2002. That was the year I turned 62, and maintaining a 73-year-old house and nearly-acre-sized yard had simply become too much. By then I had repainted the house three times, risking my life on 20-foot extension ladders, and I just didn't want to do it again. The 50-some palm trees on the lot were in perpetual need of trimming, and I didn't want to keep doing that, either. The seawall needed to be reinforced, the ancient wiring and plumbing – original to the home's construction in 1929 – needed to be updated. Manatee County real estate – indeed, most of Florida – was enjoying boom times after the dot.com recession, and we decided to take the money and run.

It took quite a while to figure out where we would run to, for all of the real estate in west and northwest Bradenton also was hot, even off the water. Eventually we decided to take the radical step of moving "Out East" – the term Bradenton folks used for the previously undeveloped region of eastern Manatee County that was *burgeoning with growth since the launch of the Lakewood Ranch planned development in the early '90s. In fact, our son-in-law was developing a small subdivision of his own in East Manatee, a community of 25 homes nestled among 26 acres of pristine woods on the banks of the Braden River, just west of I-75. It wasn't Lakewood Ranch, with its cookie-cutter homes on tiny lots without a tree in sight. It was like moving into your own private forest, with old-growth trees and thick clumps of palmettos forming the natural landscaping, a far cry from the manicured St. Augustine turf and puny palm trees of Lakewood Ranch. It took four full years to make the move, during which time we tried renting on the beach and bought and refurnished a "temporary" home on the near west side. But finally our new dream home in River Forest was completed in **September 2006**. Three weeks later, here is what I had to say about the move.*

Out of the City to Quiet Suburbs — and a Crime Wave

East Manatee – Ah, the very name evokes images of tranquility, quiet and – except for certain stretches of State Roads 64 and 70 during rush hour – safety.

So why, on my ninth day of residence in this tranquil zone of alleged peace and quiet, were platoons of sheriff's deputies with flashing lights parked outside my door and a noisy sheriff's helicopter buzzing my subdivision as dawn broke? Was this East Manatee or East Bradenton? Or maybe Southeast Los Angeles?

That was, indeed my introduction to suburban living last weekend as I stepped outside for my morning jog around the neighborhood. I hadn't even had time to completely unpack my socks and underwear, and here was *CSI* unfolding in my front yard. A polite deputy filled me in on the case as I stood with jaw agape at the surreal scene. It seems a burglary team had been interrupted inside a neighbor's home and, in attempting

319

to elude Manatee Sheriff's deputies, had fled on foot through the nearby Braden River High campus after abandoning their car – in my driveway.

Well, at least I had the assurance that this was one run that wouldn't be boring, as they usually are. With patrol cars discreetly parked in several driveways along the route, I felt sure the burglars wouldn't leap out of the bushes if it turned out that they hadn't left the neighborhood. Besides, I had my trusty Rhodesian Ridgeback Lily with me, and I was sure she would protect from any evil-doer. Wouldn't she?

Along the back side of the subdivision I happened to notice an object leaning against a neighbor's mailbox. I stopped to check it out. It was a golf bag, full of golf clubs. Wow! I thought, I am living in a high-class neighborhood if they're throwing out perfectly good golf clubs like these. I made a mental note to swing back by the house on the way to work and pick them up before the garbage truck made its rounds. Of course, I forgot.

Back home, I showered, ate breakfast and dressed for work. The officers were still checking out the white car at one end of my driveway as I moved to get into my car. Then I noticed something wasn't right. The driver's-side door was ajar, and the glove box was open. The thieves had either tried to steal my car or strip it. Fortunately, no damage was done, but keys and a remote control were taken from the glove box.

On the way into town, I considered the irony of this incident. For 31 years I had lived in the urban core, the last four inside "The Box," the area of Central Bradenton in which police say the majority of crime occurs. I have never experienced a break-in, although once someone stole a ladder from my carport and another time someone rifled my car. Now one week in a sparkling new suburb full of security-wired homes and I come face to face with crime at its most frightening: Home invasion while occupants are inside.

Nowhere, it appears, is anyone safe from crime. Officers said the suspects probably were looking for cash or pawnable items to exchange for drugs.

That's a common element in this kind of crime: Addicts desperate for a fix taking foolish chances to get their hands on something of value.

I could only thank God that the burglars had turned left instead of right when seeking a potential target. For later that morning, as a contractor was working on our "punch list" of incomplete items on our new home, he discovered two sets of sliding glass doors had been left unlocked during the night, including one to our bedroom. Of course, we know better, but the home was so new to us we hadn't yet established a routine for checking the doors before going to bed.

The what-ifs of that discovery were chilling, although there was comfort in the knowledge that Lily would have heard any noise and alerted us. Wouldn't she?

Oh, and the golf bag? It turned out to be part of the loot from break-ins in the adjacent neighborhood that the burglars had stashed there with the intention of picking them up when they finished in ours.

Our neighbors and family are still trying to deal with the shock of this invasion. No doubt it will make everyone doubly careful to lock cars and home doors. Security companies doubtless are doing a brisk business in the area.

And I'm waiting for the first person to say: Welcome to the 'hood.

MY PET PEEVES, FOR ALL TO READ

*The beauty of a personal column is that it gives one a chance to gripe about things that bug him. Assuming readers care, of course. I seldom passed up the chance to air my pet peeves, for I assumed that I wasn't the only one who wanted to scream at certain behaviors or conditions which one is powerless to control. In fact, early in my career I launched an entire column about my pet peeves – and invited readers to share theirs as well. I believe the inspiration for this column came from the late Andy Rooney, who always closed his stint on "60 Minutes" with a pet peeve. This column was published in **October 1978**.*

Pet Peeves: Little Annoyances
That Keep on Festering

Peeve (noun): *An object of dislike; annoyance. Peeved (adjective): "Irritated; annoyed."* – Webster's New World Dictionary

I looked up "peeve" because I wanted to be sure I had the right word to describe something that bugs me. Yep, "peeve" does the trick. I've been bugged by so many things lately I started to make a list. My Pet Peeve List. Little things, mostly; pet peeves have to be little things or they're no longer peeves – they're major issues suitable for weighty editorials.

Anyhow, right up there at the top of my Pet Peeve List is the driver who pulls into a left-turn lane ahead of me and won't pull up far enough to activate the electronic eye that tells the green arrow to come on. So there you sit in the turn lane while the traffic light goes through sequence after sequence, and the timid lead driver in the turn lane can't understand why everyone's honking at him or her.

Another pet peeve of mine is trying to carry on a conversation with people who can't speak without asking a question. You know, those who, after almost every statement they make, add, "OK?" or "Right?" Even the most innocuous statement requires the added interrogative for these people. For example, "I picked up the phone to call my mother, right? And the line was busy, OK? So I couldn't get through for an hour and was worried about her, understand?" The questions drive me mad! I never know whether to answer them or ignore them and let the speaker continue. I want to scream: "Simple declarative statements don't require questions!" But I don't.

You want a real peeve? Coming out to fetch the newspaper in the morning and finding that dogs or raccoons have tipped over the garbage cans and strewn the contents over the front yard. Arrrrgh! All I can think of in such circumstances is what great bodily harm I would inflict if I could catch them in the act.

Another big peeve of mine is having to search for a desired object that the last user neglected to return to its proper place. Whether it's the kitchen scissors, the family telephone directory, my Phillips screwdriver or the toothpaste tube, I get upset when I go to the place it's supposed to be and can't find it. Why can't people put things away?

Oh, and you should see the smoke come out of my ears when I read the morning paper (yes, *this* one) and find spelling and grammar errors. Not on *this* page, of course, but elsewhere in the paper. Doubtless a few readers may share that pet peeve.

Humorist Andy Rooney is a great one for peeves. He writes several-page articles about one peeve, and then combines a series of the articles into a book and makes millions. My Pet Peeve List probably isn't worth writing a book about, and you'd probably be peeved if I did. But noting them in writing makes me feel a little better about them. It's a reassuring experience – even if the source of the peeve utterly fails to shape up.

How about you? Do you have pet peeves? Here's your chance to tell the world about life's little annoyances: Our first – and perhaps last –Pet Peeve Contest. What's the thing that irritates you the most? How do you cope with it? Is there any hope for a solution? Best letter will receive a free copy of Andy Rooney's latest collection of peeves and provocations.

I DEMAND TO SPEAK TO THE EDITOR

*Well, that was my first but not my last expression of my pet peeves. From time to time I would devote a column to a single peeve, one that, as the piece above suggests, deserves a full-blown editorial. The following column, published on **Oct. 4, 1998**, qualifies as such. As an editor with his name on the masthead, I was part of the public face of the newspaper. And as the guy responsible for the majority of the newspaper's editorial viewpoints, I was the one called upon to answer to the public when there was a complaint. As a result, I spent a fair amount of time – precious time that I could better have used to write or polish tomorrow's editorial – talking to readers.*

One of the most memorable of such calls came from the wife of a county commissioner who was running for re-election. The paper had chosen his opponent in its editorial endorsements, considering the incumbent an incompetent elected official. The wife was furious at the paper's failure to support her husband, and gave me an earful. Then she informed me that the paper owed her for a visit to a chiropractor's office. "Why would we be responsible for your medical bills?" I meekly inquired. "Because when I read your editorial, I was so angry I threw the paper across the room and doing that threw my shoulder out of joint," was her dead-serious reply.

But sometimes a phone call wouldn't do. A fair number of them dropped by for a personal chat, assuming I had nothing better to do than listen to their complaints. That was the inspiration for the following rant, which recounted a particularly irritating visit by an irate reader.

Nothing Is Worse Than Being Trapped in a Corner by a Time Thief

You would never know the little old lady was a terrible thief, but she was. As prim and proper as she could be, she smiled as sweetly as any angel and invoked the name of the Lord reverently several times as she stole from me. You could tell from her self-assured bearing, her precise diction and her smart summer outfit of a white linen skirt and white and blue sailor top that she had good breeding, as people used to say about such older women. She reminded you of your favorite grammar school teacher, now long retired, whom you might run into at church and pass a few reminiscences with.

So sweet. So precise. So endearing. But a thief.

Of what? Of my time. And, no doubt, of everyone around her who was raised to be respectful to older people and not show rudeness even when it's being shown to you.

Which is why she was in the *Herald* lobby a while back, demanding to see "the editor." She came carrying a two-page letter of complaint about an employee who had been "rude" to her over the phone when all she had wanted to do was let the paper know about a story opportunity – about herself. The employee had said she was too busy to see the woman in person but would look at the materials if she left them with the receptionist.

That the visitor would not do, because you don't want to let important papers in the hands of receptionists; you want to give them to the editor in person and talk to him or her face to face. "Is it too much to ask for a few minutes of an editor's time to talk about a story?" she wondered.

Well, yes, it can be, but I didn't think that she cared to hear a monologue about the time demands of newspaper editors, so I gave her the audience she craved. In those 20 minutes I learned about the writing award she'd won (the reason she'd come to the paper), her professional career, many of her likes and dislikes, her religion, and details of her move to Florida.

At one point, when my deer-in-the-headlights eyes must have given away my anxiety at the approaching deadline I faced in the newsroom she asked, "Am I boring you?"

"No," I lied, "but I do have a meeting coming up in a couple minutes," which was the truth.

Though that could have been a natural break in the pointless discussion, the one where even a boor gets the message and takes his or her leave, it hardly fazed her. Time thieves never get it. She made motions as if to go, but never stopped talking for a second, merely shifting the conversation slightly. Soon I was deep into the careers and marital history of both her children. I signaled my desire to break off with body language – feet inching to the exit, eyes desperately searching co-workers passing by, nervous glances at my watch. Finally, she left just enough of a pause in her conversation – the first since she'd arrived – for me to beg the urgency of my meeting and end the conversation.

I felt angry at that sweet little old lady. She robbed me of 20 minutes of precious time for what should have been a two-minute exchange of information. Sadly, she isn't so rare. Time thieves lurk everywhere – at work, at the supermarket, in church and especially at family gatherings. They pay no attention to what you are doing, what you last said or what subject is being discussed. They seize the conversation, turn it inwardly to focus on themselves and ramble on, oblivious of the glazed eyes of those around them. They assume that what they have to say is of the utmost importance and that others have nothing better to do than listen for as long as they decide to talk. And they seldom leave a pause long enough for the trapped listener to insert the slightest disclaimer of more important business.

"The way to impress people is not by telling them how wonderful you are. If you want to impress people, you need to listen to how wonderful *they* are," Natasha Josefowitz, Ph.D., wrote in "Too Wise to Be Young Again."

It's advice from which we could all benefit – including sweet little old ladies who would die before taking so much as a grape from the supermarket produce shelf but steal precious minutes from the people in line by gabbing with the cashier.

&%$#@ FLORIDA WEATHER

*I had many other peeves, of course. One Sunday in **August 1998** I simply had had it with Florida's wilting summers and felt the need to share that sentiment with readers. I grant you that it may be somewhat hyperbolic, but if you've endured a Florida summer, you'll know it's not a lot.*

Summer in Florida: The Good Life
– If You Are an Amphibian

S ummertime, and the livin' is easy.

Yea, right. It may have been cushy enough in some moonstruck song-writer's idyllic image in June, but in reality, summer ain't so easy in Florida – especially the damp, dark days of late August.

You think it's easy keeping a starched white shirt crisp while walking in 300 percent humidity from the parking lot to the office? I don't think so. Nor is recreating four hours of work after a lightning strike zapped your computer any Fourth of July picnic, let me tell you.

You want to talk weather-induced stress? Try watching the brown stain on the ceiling spread another foot after each downpour. Or worse yet, wake up and find the ceiling crumbled in the middle of your bed or desk. For real trauma, there's nothing like having to cock an anxious ear out the back door every half-hour or so to see if the aging air handler has expired – especially at the beginning of a three-day holiday weekend.

No, summertime in Florida during the rainy season is anything but easy, in case the last week of monsoons hasn't sunk in yet. It's so tough I'm going to recommend it to the Marines for advanced survival training after Camp Lejeune. You want to test the mettle of these elite troops? Here's a sample drill instructor command:

"Listen up, you (expletive deleted) wimps, I want you to get out there behind that lawn mower and push it through that tall grass for the next two hours." Believe me, they'd wash out the weak ones in 20 minutes of Florida heat – especially when they denied them a towel to mop their sweating faces.

Or, how about this:

"Awright, you (blanking) sissies, see those cars in that treeless, asphalt parking lot? I want each of you to go over to one, open the door, slide across the nice warm leather seat, grip the nice warm steering wheel and pretend to drive it away." I'd be surprised if half the squad didn't file a class-action suit for abusive training practices.

Yet we Floridians are supposed to carry on in this manner day after day, week after week, and still pretend that life in Florida in August is beautiful. Yea, right, just like Roberto Benigni did in "Life Is Beautiful," this year's smash Italian movie set in a Nazi concentration camp. Benigni, as the loving father of a 5-year-old son, managed to convince the gullible boy that the camp's brutal regimen is part of a game.

It's a game in Florida, all right – of survival. If the alligators don't crawl from their flooded sewer pipes to make you their next meal, the hordes of mosquitoes swarming off backyard lakes will happily oblige. If the bolts of lightning zipping out of thunderclouds don't fry you en-route to your car, the buckets perched on ceiling beams to catch leaks will clobber you when they tip onto your head. If the carnivorous vines in your back yard that grow not by inches but by feet per day don't grab you as you dash between carport and front door, the giant spiders that come out of invisible crevices will.

Not to mention the assorted snakes, snails, walking catfish, lizards and frogs – oh, the frogs! – that pop up out of every cloudburst to scare the bejeebers out of the hapless Floridian.

And the aromas! Nothing like the stench of rotting mangoes carpeting your side yard and aswarm with flies and gnats to rev up the old appetite – unless it's the distinctive odor of rotting wood from your aging deck floorboards. Of course, the mildew buildup in your air conditioning conduits will eventually dominate in the offensive odor department, since you spend the most time breathing the (hopefully) chilled air that pours from the vents.

Newcomers are taken aback by the ferocity of our rainstorms. "Does it always rain like this?" asked one new arrival after a particularly heavy rainstorm recently.

"No, just during the rainy season, which lasts from June through September," was the answer.

Which means . . .what? Only another five weeks or so of hot, wet days and clammy nights, of computer-killing lightning flashes and ear-splitting thunderclaps, of mushrooms growing in the patio and green algae growing in the recesses of your closets, of flooded streets and water-logged lawns, wet dogs and crabby spouses. And, if we're very lucky, only a couple more months of waiting for an Andrew or Georges or some other deceptively-named, God-awful freak of nature to decide this spit of sand is the one he or she wishes to feast on this year. At this writing, there are not one, not two, but three potential candidates for the role lurking out there in the Atlantic and Caribbean.

Ah, yes, summer time, and the livin' is easy – anywhere but Florida. Still, I can't think of anywhere I'd rather spend August than right here in Bradenton, where if you sweat enough and get grubby enough and adapt enough you eventually qualify as a semi-native. That is a title I claim after 25 years – and wear with pride.

UP-CLOSE-AND-PERSONAL VIEW OF MEDICINE

There were plenty more rants like that over the years, but I think I've made my point. Lots of things ticked me off, and I had a chance to let off steam by writing about them. But now I'd like to move on to a more serious issue – and one that's still very much in the news 32 years later. That issue is health care. In 1988, the Manatee County Medical Society, anxious to counter the image portrayed in the media of doctors as money-grubbing mercenaries, announced an initiative called the Mini-Internship Program. In this pre-HIPPA era, the program exposed volunteer laypersons to the day-to-day routine of the practice of medicine. Mini-Interns would shadow one or more doctors for two full days, watching them perform surgeries or other invasive treatments and sitting in on patient consultations and examinations. Such a thing could never happen in the current era of patient privacy, but it was no big deal three decades ago.

Naturally, I was first in line to become a Mini-Intern. I was always eager to have new experiences. (I still am.) Members of the Medical Society had a low opinion of the Herald *because they felt it took sides in an internecine war among doctors 15 years earlier when a group of 30 young doctors – who became known as the Dirty Thirty – staged a coup against the good-old-boy medical establishment and built a second hospital – a for-profit one that competed with the county-owned Manatee Memorial. They also felt the press seldom showed much empathy for the medical profession, too often portraying its practitioners as. . .well, money-grubbing mercenaries and invariably sided with plaintiffs in medical-malpractice lawsuits. I was honored that the Medical Society chose me to be the first media representative in the program. I felt it represented a measure of trust in my ability to be an objective observer and reporter on their profession. Plus, it gave me a chance to polish my long-form journalism skills, not often employed in a role that called for turning out 850-word opinion pieces every day.*

So here is that very long account of two grueling days following around a surgeon and a GP, published on **Dec. 4, 1988.**

Doctor's Job Is Tiring, Risky, Tough – and the Most Rewarding in the World

Medical science has produced life-sustaining technological advancements bordering on the miraculous. Some, however, have questionable benefits for the elderly and drain resources from the entire medical system.

Medical practitioners are tenacious workaholics who deeply love their profession but who feel besieged by a system that demands perfection while constantly questioning their judgment and putting barriers in their path.

330

Medical care users – all the rest of us – demand too much of the profession and its practitioners without taking our share of responsibility for staying healthy and without facing up to the true cost when we don't.

Broadly stated, those are my chief observations from a brief but intensive behind-the-scenes study of the medical profession in Manatee County. As a participant in the Manatee County Medical Society's Mini-Internship Program, I got an eye-opening view of health care by walking in the footsteps of doctors for two days. The Mini-Intern program, which originated in Oregon some five years ago, is designed to broaden the public perception of medicine by exposing laymen to the day-to-day, real-world practice of medicine for a short but intense period.

"We have invited you literally to become a doctor for a short time," Dr. Bernard Seidenberg of Volusia County, chairman of the Mini-Intern program for the Florida Medical Association, told Manatee's first four mini-interns at our orientation session Nov. 18. We want to be totally open for the first time . . .to show you the practice of medicine as it is, totally realistically. . .We want you to see it all. We have nothing to hide."

The Medical Society stood by Dr. Seidenberg's pledge. For 26 hours – doctors routinely work 12-hour days, I learned – I followed local surgeon George R. McSwain and family practitioner E. P. Dickerson through their daily routines. I trailed them on morning and evening rounds at the hospitals, witness to more pain, gore, despair, frustration and hope in two hours than I had experienced in two years.

I stood beside them through some 30 patient consultations during office hours, bewildered at the variety of ailments they were called upon to correctly diagnose and treat on a minute-to-minute basis.

I went behind the scenes in Intensive Care, X-Ray, Recovery Room, Emergency Room, nurse stations – everywhere the doctors went, I was by their side.

Including surgery. I sat self-consciously in shapeless green scrubs in the surgeons' lounge of Blake Memorial Hospital as doctors came and went, amazed that they could chat about sports, weather and misguided newspaper editorials while waiting to cut someone open. My own mind was filled with dread at the major surgery I was about to watch Dr. McSwain and his partner, Dr. Paul Prillaman, perform: a duodenoplasty and an aneurysm repair. In laymen's terms, the first means opening up a blocked section of the digestive system, and the second replacing an enlarged section of the aortal artery with a dacron tube.

Miracle of Surgery

This was the part of my internship I was not sure I could handle. Just the thought of cutting people open gives me the willies. But I had resolved I would have this experience or pass out trying. To me, this was the most mystical aspect of doctoring. How could they ever know enough to have the confidence to cut open a fellow human being? And how did the mechanics of it actually work – how did they make the incisions, staunch the bleeding, keep open the incision and cut around on living organs without destroying them?

Now I know. I stood transfixed through nearly three hours of surgery and marveled at what I saw. There were times when my nerves were so on edge I thought my knees would buckle, but I forced myself to keep watching. Here, in this stark room with green tile walls, white floor and glaring lights, I knew that a life was literally in suspension. The snipping and sewing of the surgeons and the minute adjustments on the machines of the anesthesiologist would determine whether this person lived or died.

While Muzak played! Somehow, "Girl from Ipanema" seemed out of place here, but someone definitely was humming along to that tune as the patient lay spread-eagled on the operating table, his trunk sliced open from breastbone to groin, his pulsating internal organs sprawled out in a neat pattern of reds, pinks and yellows.

At times I had to remind myself: These are not mad scientists doing experiments on captive prisoners. These are trained doctors who know precisely what they are doing, who perform these operations routinely, who are helping this patient. As he watched the digital readouts on the computerized machines measuring the patient's blood pressure, temperature, pulse and other vital signs, anesthesiologist Dr. Richard Wynkoop tried to explain to me how doctors so coolly handle what I was near to fainting over:

"Well, if you know it's going to make the patient better, you can do it. It's an attitude. You just do it." Of the gaping incision I had exclaimed over, he said nonchalantly, "Wounds don't heal from end to end; they heal from side to side." The patient's belly would knit back together, he said, about as quickly as a bad cut on my finger.

As the surgeons removed the aneurysm and began stitching the artificial tubes—actually a soft dacron material – in its place, I got an insight into what makes doctors run. The diseased section of this approximately inch-diameter artery had ballooned into a fist-sized lump of yellowish gray gunk. Cholesterol in its raw form. What if they hadn't operated? The patient gradually would have deteriorated, said Dr. Wynkoop and, "Next stop, Griffith-Cline" (funeral home).

Top Challenge

Healing. Or the challenge of healing. That's what it's all about. That's what motivates doctors to get up before dawn to check on yesterday's patients, to work past their kids' bedtimes and frequently in the wee hours, to battle endless red tape, to deal with cases so hopeless and conditions so disgusting as to turn the stomach of most of us, to put their reputations and indeed their own health on the line every time they see a patient.

Yes, they do it for the money, too. I don't know any poor doctors. And some make much more than others. Nationally, according to the American Medical Association, the average family doctor made pretax net income of $80,000 in 1986, the average surgeon $162,0000, the average radiologist $170,000.

By my standard, that's a very comfortable living. But is it too much? I can't say that it is. I know I would not, could not, trade places with them. I know that many corporate executives with far lighter responsibilities make far more than most doctors. And few people squawk about greedy CEOs.

Dr. Dickerson, who has been a family practitioner for 31 years and who is one of the busiest GPs in Manatee County, explains it this way: "Medicine isn't a job – it's a way of life. Sure, I could breeze through my visits, spend less time with each patient, and be home by 6 o'clock. So what? You don't do it for money – it's a miserable way to make a living. You do it because you enjoy the practice of medicine."

Paperwork Nightmare

Money is, however, an ever-present factor in the lives of doctors – not *their* money, but the government's. Medicare has been a blessing and a curse to the medical profession, producing a stream of elderly patients with an endless variety of ailments – and a red tape nightmare for the harried doctors forced to justify to government watchdogs their every move.

Dr. McSwain grimaces contemptuously as he flips through the chart of an elderly patient at Manatee Memorial who is having complications after removal of a tumor of the colon 13 days earlier. On the chart's plastic jacket is a blue strip from "the PRO" stating, "Please sign cost outline certification." That is a warning to the surgeon from the hospital's Professional Review Organization that the patient is nearing the end of her allowable 20-day maximum for this procedure that can be covered by Medicare, and he must justify her continued hospitalization. He scribbles something on the chart and explains, "That will be checked by some bureaucrat clerk, probably a high school graduate. You can't imagine how much this adds to the cost of medicine."

The Medicare rules setting limits on designated medical procedures not only waste personnel but insult doctors by forcing them to justify their treatment – as if their professional judgment about what's best for the patient isn't trustworthy.

"I just want to be able to take care of sick people – but it gets discouraging," said Dr. McSwain at the end of a 13 ½ -hour day. "The long hours, the high malpractice insurance, the fear of being sued – and then all the extra work that contributes nothing to patient care, by people who are worried about money, not the patient – yes, it gets discouraging."

Next day, on rounds with Dr. Dickerson, another example of the wasteful bureaucratic maze appears. Here is an elderly woman with osteoporosis – softening of the bones – who has broken her pelvis by coughing. She is extremely thin and in terrible pain. But Medicare says a broken pelvis is not a hospitalizable ailment because its only cure is bed rest, and theoretically one can rest at home as well as in a costly hospital bed.

The patient has no one at home to care for her and is plainly a very sick woman. Medicare will deny her admission, the hospital will have to write Medicare a letter defending the admission, Dr. Dickerson will have to squeeze a few minutes somewhere between the 35 patients he will see today to write a letter defending the admission, and eventually Medicare probably will allow it. If it doesn't, Blake "will have to eat" the bill – as both hospitals frequently are forced to do. And hundreds of dollars' worth of manpower will have been expended to defend Dr. Dickerson's judgment that she needed to be hospitalized.

Down the hall, meanwhile, is an example of the reverse – Medicare rules abetting the misuse of the system. The patient is a diabetic who has a gangrenous foot. She has lost all feeling in the foot and ignores the doctor's instructions to stay off it. The pressure of her walking on it has spread the poisons into her bloodstream, so she must be hospitalized until the infection has cleared up. Since May, this one infected foot has cost Medicare about $250,000. But, says Dr. Dickerson with an air of resignation, "She is entitled to Medicare, and it's her right as an American not to listen to my instructions."

Costly Cures

Many of the feeble elderly patients with multiple ailments I saw during my Mini-Internship caused me to question some of the miracle technology that has vastly increased life expectancy for Americans in recent years. I kept asking myself, "Why? What is the point of staying alive to die here in a near-vegetative state?"

One of the best examples I saw is kidney dialysis, which has made it possible to live with kidney failure that just a few years ago would have meant sure death. One of Dr. McSwain's most common surgical procedures is implanting of artificial "shunts" in the arm to facilitate the thrice-weekly dialysis process that cleanses patients' blood. One of his first patients that morning is a frail elderly man whose shunt is clotted; the surgeon will have to work him into his surgery schedule sometime today in order for the patient to receive dialysis tomorrow. He has had three operations since his kidneys failed six months ago, and also suffers from blindness, arteriosclerosis and low blood pressure.

If this were England, that patient would be dead, said Dr. McSwain, for England, with its highly regarded socialized medical system, has decided it cannot afford dialysis for anyone over 65. As it turns out, by week's end the patient is dead – of kidney failure. And complications from his multiple ailments. Was his extra six months of life worth the "phenomenal cost" that it placed on Medicare? I don't know. Dr. McSwain isn't allowed to make such a judgment; his job is to keep the man alive. But it seems clear that as long as the government is paying the bill, we as a society will avoid making these kinds of tough decisions. And until we do the quality of our health-care system will keep going down and its costs keep going up, putting decent health care out of the reach of more and more low- and middle-income people.

Highest Praise

I was struck during my Mini-Internship by the respect in which all of the doctors are held by their patients. Not just respect – trust – trust that the doctor is going to figure out what's wrong and make it right. That trust, and the challenge of earning it, must be one of the unspoken fringe benefits of being a doctor. That point was brought home to me late in the afternoon of my stint with Dr. McSwain as he examined a patient with whom he'd performed an aneurysm repair here weeks earlier. It was the very same type of operation I had witnessed that morning, except that this man's had burst before surgery.

As Dr. McSwain checked the incision and gave the good news that the stitches could come out, the patient's wife, seated beside the examination table, said softly, "Thank you, doctor, for saving my husband's life."

It was the high point of my experience. Despite the frustrating red tape, the punishing schedule, the missed family activities, the grisly messes and the 10,000 details of his job, the doctor could go home today knowing that, because of him –his knowledge and skills – a man is alive. Few of us will ever find that kind of job satisfaction.

Can't They Get Anything Right?

I read the above with amazement that so little in the health care industry has changed in more than 30 years. Doctors are more stressed at work overload and paperwork than ever. The system continues to be top-heavy in caring for senior citizens like me, while too many younger people are denied adequate and sometimes any health care services. And paying for it has become much more costly, exceeding the annual Cost of Living index by several points. Like so much of America's social fabric, inaction, neglect and bad policy have left us with a second-class system compared with much of the rest of the developed world.

However, it's time to move to a different topic. How about sewage? Yes, I wrote a personal column about that stuff when it impacted my life in a very real and personal way. In the process, I got a few valuable insights into how it feels to have a newspaper write about you – and get it wrong. For reasons that I never understood, one reporter, who covered the county government beat, had a particular dislike for me, occasionally expressed openly in the newsroom. He chose to reflect that dislike in a report on a county dredging project of McLewis Bayou, in which I as a homeowner had a personal interest.

*The following piece is from **Sept. 20, 1998**.*

When the News Is on the Other Foot,
the Results Can Be a Shock

A cardinal rule of journalism is: Report the news. Don't make it.

I have always tried to follow it, for being the subject of news stories in your own newspaper is about the worst predicament a journalist can face. For one thing, no matter what the story is, readers will wonder about your paper's objectivity if a member of its staff is involved.

Worse than that, though, it's very uncomfortable being in the spotlight. As you're talking to a reporter, you become aware that he or she is writing down your every word, and you think: I have been talking like a blithering idiot. Please don't put that in the paper.

And the inevitable concern: Will the reporter get it right?

But being on the other side of the fence once in a while also has given me a different view of some of the people and institutions I editorialize about every day. That especially applies to local government. I write about government issues in the abstract all of the time. But when my personal life intersects with a local government agency in a direct way, I gain a new understanding of the frustrations that ordinary citizens run into in dealing with government.

The best example has been my neighbors and my 20 years of frustration in battling pollution of the stream on which we live, McLewis Bayou. The bayou, a natural tributary of the Manatee River between 38th and 40th Streets NW, became badly silted in the '60s and mid-'70s when trenches for the laying of the county's water and sewer systems went unprotected for months during the rainy season, allowing tons of dirt to wash into the bayou. This collected on top of years of silt from stormwater runoff that had created small deltas at several stormwater discharge pipes.

Then, starting in the late '70s, we began noticing raw sewage floating down the bayou on many occasions. The sewage was easily traced to a malfunctioning sewer lift station behind the Manatee Plaza shopping center at 39th and Manatee.

But county officials would do nothing about it, blaming the problem on vandals prying the manhole cover off and stopping up the line with rocks and sticks. Besides, the lift station was on private property, so the county had no jurisdiction to force any changes to it even though it was tied into the county sewer system, we were told.

County pollution control officers called occasional overflows "a fact of life" and "minor in comparison to other discharges" and would do nothing to remedy the situation even while admitting that the lift station was substandard and needed substantial upgrading.

Finally, in 1983, after years of neighbors' complaining to county officials and some *Bradenton Herald* coverage of the sewage spills, a county utility engineering crew equipped with a video inspection tool was sent to check the lift station and lines. They found five structural flaws, including:

- An eight-inch clay pipe from the shopping center to the lift station was badly cracked.
- A six-inch, gravity-fed line connecting the troublesome manhole to another manhole was broken and sagging.
- Another six-inch line temporarily blocked and impeded by a reverse grade, i.e., the sewage was supposed to flow uphill.
- The alarm system on the lift station was malfunctioning, so no one knew when the system was overflowing - except residents of the bayou when they saw feces floating by.

The county commissioners at last intervened, working out an agreement with the shopping center owner to repair the malfunctioning sewage system and drafting a policy that enabled them to deal with future sewage discharges, whether by county-owned systems or not.

Fast-forward to August 1998. The commission unanimously agreed to split with us the cost of dredging the bayou, now so badly silted that boats cannot use the channel at low tide. This decision was the culmination of almost five years of neighbors, county staff and county commissioners working to create a uniform county dredging policy to correct past neglect and to prevent re-silting of streams once cleaned out. It came after my neighbors and I chipped in to hire our won consultant, who offered scientific evidence disputing the county consultant's finding that just 21 percent of the silt was the county's responsibility.

The 50-50 split of the $500,000 dredging tab, most felt, was a reasonable compromise in the years-long battle to restore McLewis Bayou. Although most of us felt a fairer split would have been 80-20 county to homeowner, we walked out of the meeting in jubilation that we had achieved at least a modicum of justice for the degradation of the bayou by the county's negligence.

What a surprise, then, to read the *Herald's* version of that decision next day. In a two-sentence item in a roundup of commission action, my newspaper reported that the county commission "spent $134,000 more of taxpayers' money than an engineering consultant recommended for dredging in McLewis Bayou in west Bradenton and canals in the Manalee subdivision in Ellenton. The decision means property owners bordering McLewis Bayou will save thousands of dollars in dredging assessments. . ."

Technically, that was an accurate report of the commission decision. But it overlooked the fact that I and every neighbor affected by the decision are also taxpayers – taxpayers whose property values had been degraded by the county's negligence for more than two decades. It made us out to be freeloaders taking advantage of the county instead of injured property owners who would have to fork over $17,000 to $20,000 per household to complete the project. And it overlooked the general public benefit of having a source of pollution to the Manatee River cleaned up.

In two misleading sentences, 20 years of frustration and work to correct a health-menacing pollution problem were dismissed as a group of whining west-siders getting favorable treatment.

Getting this close to a story certainly helped me understand why some of our readers accuse us of slanting the news.

BACK IN COLLEGE – AT AGE 52

The year 1992 marked a turning point in my life. Through the philanthropy of the Knight Foundation's Visiting Journalist program, I was offered a one-month sabbatical at Duke University. Having by this point worked for 30 years with only my brief interruption between leaving Detroit and hiring on at Bradenton, I was ready for a real break. Duke offered that. I was told there were no expectations of me. I could use the time in any way I chose: Audit classes, research or write a book, catch up on sleep, whatever. Knowing my background, the company brass had no fear that I would choose the latter. The next two columns offer highlights of how I spent my time – and what I learned. This one was published Feb. 2, 1992.

30 Years Later, 'Student' Relives Joys and Anxieties of College

DURHAM, N.C. – I am having one of my recurring dreams. I am back in college, hurrying to a class for which I am late and facing a test for which I am totally unprepared. As I hustle across the campus, I pass a few friends and acquaintances – people whom I've sat next to in a previous class, a prof or two I've had before, some people from my dorm. I nod absent-mindedly at them, absorbed in my worry about the test and the unread assignment. I can see the F coming, which could well mean a D in the course, which will knock my grade-point average down under a 3.0, which will make my parents question why they're spending all this money on my college education if I can't show my appreciation by making better grades than that, which will cause a big fight, which will . . .

Wait a minute! By now, I should have awakened to find it was all a bad dream. Usually I sit up in bed and think how silly it is that this dream keeps recurring, now fully 30 years since I faced my last anxiety-ridden exam. But I'm not sitting up in bed in pajamas drenched in perspiration. I really am walking across a college campus, absorbed in my concerns about course schedules, unread assignments and a heavy schedule, nodding absent-mindedly at those I pass whose faces look familiar. I'm fully dressed, and the bite on my face and fingers is from real winter winds, not those of my dreams. This is reality; I *am* living a nightmare!

Or a fantasy, depending on one's point of view.

A week into my Visiting Journalist Fellowship at Duke University, I still have to pinch myself occasionally to see if I'm dreaming or really here within the granite-walled quadrangle that defines Duke's distinctive Gothic heart. As I have walked the Duke campus for the past week it has been a continuous déjà vu experience, taking me back across three decades as if it were yesterday. Memories come rushing back as I learn the routine that will enable me to attend classes with students the age of my own children. The smell of bacon and scrambled eggs wafting across the early-morning air from the back door of a student dining hall takes me instantly back to my first college job in a dorm cafeteria. As I stand in line at the Bursar's Office to cash a check I recall the long registration lines of my undergrad days. A shortcut through a dorm brings a pungent, nerve-jangling reminder of the trials – and carefree atmosphere – of communal living. A search for a book instantly delivers memories of long, pleasant afternoons lost in a carrell in the library stacks.

And now, rediscovering – along with all that is good about being an undergraduate student, but without most of the pressures that make it a less-than-exhilarating experience when one is 19 or 20. That is, no tests. No worries about missed homework. No incompatible roommate who plays his music too loudly and stays up all night. And, thank God, no crisis over dating! For me this has been a rare chance to go back and live

342

part of my life over again – but knowing everything I have learned from having lived for the past 30 years, and without the responsibilities of the first time around. Not many people get a chance to do that.

Yet I can't help feeling that the students I'm encountering know a lot more than I did at the same age – and perhaps much more than I do *now*. I am impressed at the level of intellectual discussion I hear in philosophy and literature classes. How do these kids know so much when they can't even legally buy a beer? It is, of course, a far different generation from mine – which I should know from having helped rear two of its members. But I am still struck by Duke students' sophistication in intellectual matters, a reflection, no doubt, of the superior education and family support they must have had for acceptance into this extremely selective university. These kids mean business. I feel better about the future of this nation.

Students have been uniformly polite and respectful, holding doors, apologizing for an elbow bump, prefacing questions with sir, showing tolerance for conflicting opinions.

I've seen no evidence of the hostility I expected as a result of the "political correctness" movement in which Duke has reportedly played a leading, early role. Professors have acknowledged the movement in lectures, where non-PC views are intrinsic to the lesson, which indicates a sensitivity to its positive aims without sacrificing intellectual honesty. I found encouragement in that discovery, too.

As I delve deeper into the undergraduate experience, I gain a new appreciation for the strength and durability of young people today and wonder if I could have done as well had I faced similar stresses. They are under tremendous pressure to excel, both from their parents and their professors, which puts a heavy workload on them. They face social pressures that my generation didn't cope with until well into its 20s, if at all. They see a future with a shrinking horizon instead of the world of limitless possibilities I took for my birthright in 1962. While many have come from affluent families for which Duke's $20,000 annual cost is no problem, others face severe stress over financial matters – guilt over their parent's' sacrifice to send them here and worry over whether they 'll have enough money to come back next semester. I compare my own undergrad financial problems and smile at the contrast: all four years totaled less than the cost of one semester at Duke.

I'm hoping this visit will purge from my subconscious the memories of unfulfilled academic ambition that I blame for my recurring nightmare of uncompleted coursework. In any event, it is a joy to be able to relive those days from this perspective. But would I trade places with one of the students? No way. That would be a *real* nightmare.

You're Doing What?

*So that was after one week of my sabbatical. Here's what I wrote about the experience upon returning home. Don't miss the surprising outcome. It was published on **April 5, 1992**.*

Duke Sabbatical a Time to Rediscover Value of Intellect – and Self

What was it like to be back in college? And what did you learn?

Those are the two questions I'm most often asked about my month's sabbatical as a Visiting Journalist at Duke University. They're not easy to answer. The month was an opportunity to recapture a bit of lost youth, freed from the responsibilities of being husband, father and employee, to slip back in time 30 years into a carefree world that I had long forgotten.

But it was also a reminder of how truly lonely and isolated a student can feel, even on a campus as magnificent as the Gothic-themed Duke. Far from home and family, the student is captive in a totally artificial world where grades and social status assume extraordinary importance and the stuff of ordinary life, like nutrition, hygiene and work, become inconsequential bothers.

What I learned – or relearned – is the value of real intellectual exercise. I couldn't suppress the surge of exhilaration at first hearing a world-renowned scholar on John Milton read and discuss the English poet's sonnets. I couldn't help wondering what the poor (working) people were doing as I listened to a Goethe scholar theorize about the meaning of life as depicted in the epic German literary work *Faust*. And I reveled in the luxury of dawdling for hours on the symbolism in Marcel Proust's *Swan's Way*, or projecting the economic consequences of a purely hypothetical policy in a class on micro-economics.

It was all terrible exciting intellectually, but against my working world experience it was all so unreal. And I tried to imagine how the real students felt, motivated not so much by the intellectual challenge as the need to pick up three hours' credit, where the grade came first and knowledge second. And they were doing this in four or five other courses, each with its own reading load, report expectation and exam schedule. It's no wonder they obsess on trivial issues and drink so much beer. And no wonder they're constantly counting the days until their next holiday break. They couldn't wait to be gone. I couldn't get enough. The difference was that I was pleasing myself and they were pleasing someone else. Also, they were taking the exams; I was not.

The chronology of college ought to be reversed, I thought: Let young people go to work earning money right after high school, and when they're settled down and ready for serious study in about 20 or 30 years, then let them enroll in college. The month certainly made me aware of the importance of continuing education throughout one's life. Rediscovering works I'd brushed over lightly in my own undergrad days, discovering vast gaps in my knowledge of the humanities, I was reminded how important it is never to lose one's curiosity about the world.

I approached this venture into the strange world of academia with considerable trepidation. Surrounded by people I considered my intellectual superiors, this small-town editor with a state-college education feared being found unworthy of a prestigious private university like Duke. The fact that the other Visiting Journalists in my group represented the nation's top three print media didn't help that anxiety. It always seemed a bit incongruous to see the flyers posted around campus announcing our presence: *The New York Times, the Washington Post*, TIME magazine and. . .the *Bradenton Herald*.

But I got over being daunted by names and titles and discovered I need apologize to no one. I realized that as a generalist responsible for all subjects on a small newspaper's editorial staff, I was better informed on many issues than the writers from *The Times* and *Post* who are limited to one or two specialties. It was a heartening validation of my own abilities and talents – and of my decision years ago to pursue small-town journalism instead of heading for the Big Apple. My job, I decided, is at least as fulfilling as theirs even though I don't have the prestige and clout of a national medium. I have vastly more variety in choice of issues and much more editorial freedom.

In my free time away from classes and colleagues, I also rediscovered myself as a person, distanced from the roles of husband, father and employee by which I have grown accustomed to thinking of myself. Without anyone around attaching those labels to me I could be just me – the me that I was 30 years ago before I started acquiring all of my roles and the baggage of other people's expectations.

I liked what I found; I was happy to learn I hadn't changed that much. In the humdrum routine of daily life we forget who we were and what we stood for. Life becomes a routine that wears us down into mindless conformists, much like a river turns jagged stones into smooth pebbles. I discovered I still have a few sharp edges left, and I've been trying to accentuate those since returning home. I'm not quite as anxious to please others as I was; I give more thought to what I want to do. I actively seek new friends and new intellectual opportunities. And I am more jealous of my time, especially time for reading. I am putting less time into reading periodicals and more into books, especially classics.

Perhaps most importantly, I discovered that dreams need not die because one is over 50. At Duke, I renewed old visions and found inspiration for new ones – like teaching, writing a novel, making a documentary film, working in a key policy-maker's office in Washington or Tallahassee. I still *can* do any of those things if I want to, I realized; before, I assumed I was over the hill and cruising to retirement.

And already I have been motivated to make at least one of those dreams become reality. The week I returned home I wrote the University of South Florida for a graduate school application and this summer I hope to begin the first semester of study toward a Master's Degree in Journalism. After 30 years I will be going back to academia in pursuit of new goals. Unlike my Duke sabbatical, though, this time I'll have to read all of the coursework and pass all of the exams.

YOU'RE HOW OLD?

The sabbatical did indeed prove to be life-changing. I followed through with the grad school application, somehow passed the GRE to be admitted to USF's Master's program, and by mid-May I was sitting in a night class at USF's St. Petersburg campus, enrolled in its brand new Master's in Mass Communication program. For the next four years I plugged away at that degree, two classes per semester, all in the evening after work with a one-hour commute from downtown Bradenton. The degree, conferred in May 1996, got me no more in my paycheck at the Herald *and no more recognition in the community. But it would turn out to be the key factor in two future job applications – job opportunities I pursued because of the lessons learned at Duke. But that's another chapter.*

Moving ahead to 2005, as I was about to turn 65, I took the opportunity to warn my fellow senior citizens and those heading for that label – which every single reader actually was doing – about preparing for retirement. I wasn't ready to call it quits just yet, but I could see the horizon, and it caused quite a bit of angst for me and my wife as we contemplated the future. This was in early March 2005.

Fledgling Geezer Fears 'Poor House' for Future Retirees

O K, it's done. I'm officially a geezer.

The transformation occurred last week when I went to the Social Security office to sign up for Medicare, upon the approach of birthday No. 65.

I know, some – most – people probably considered me a geezer 15 years ago, when I got my first AARP card. Trust me, 50 is *not* geezer-hood.

The Big 6-5 is. Big time. You walk into the Social Security office and start filling out forms, and it hits you: This is for real. This is *Medicare* and a *pension* they are talking about – *my* pension. This is for life – what there is left of it, that is. The pension calculations are no longer hypotheticals; this is your paycheck for the rest of your life, give or take a few bucks for Uncle Sam's generous cost-of-living raises.

The experience was relatively painless, once through the teeming, noisy waiting room where a security guard acts as the receptionist. Once ushered into the inner sanctum of counselors' modern, carpeted cubicles, I felt like an honored guest rather than a "client." The intake adviser, a wonderfully accented woman, could not have been more gracious and helpful. She had all the time in the world to answer my questions and elicit my vital information. She was, it seemed, bending over backward to ensure that I got every penny I was entitled to. There aren't many places where you receive such courteous treatment these days.

The fact is, I signed up only for Medicare for now. I don't intend to retire for awhile, and besides, the full retirement age for my birth year, 1940, is 65 ½. Boomers, just wait. It gets progressively higher with each year or two, the result of a previous reform to keep Social Security sound.

Of course, President Bush's current Social Security reform plan is on my mind a lot these days. I wonder how much I'd be getting if part of my

43 years' worth of deductions had been invested in the stock market. Doubtless it would be more generous – provided I hadn't put everything on Enron, Tyco and high-flying dot-com companies in the '90s. But I wonder: What if my investments hadn't done especially well in recent years? Would I have a choice about retiring? Or would I have to ride out a bear market to regain some equity?

There is a great deal of comfort in knowing that a certain amount of money will be deposited in my checking account each month – enough to pay the rent and buy food, at least.

And that's the essence of Social Security: a basic benefit to assure retirees of a minimal life. That was the promise of the new Deal. Not a windfall to pave the golden years with gold, but a meager living. And if you have lived prudently over the years there should be savings to supplement that basic pension.

It's a compact between generations. I'll take care of you (older generation) if you (younger generation) take care of me when I'm too old to work.

The Bush plan, I fear, weakens the compact, turns it into an every-person-for-himself mindset. Not for my generation, those 55 and older who have been assured the system will continue intact for us.

But what about the Gen X'ers and Y'ers who aren't prudent investors or savers and who job-hop too much to earn a pension? How will they live at 65? What security will be there for them at 65?

What I can't understand is why the president is getting away with it. Are there so few people who remember the New Deal and appreciate what it did for older Americans? I'm old enough to remember talk about the "poor house." In my parents' generation that was the place that old people were sent when they had no resources and were too feeble to work. It was a terrible place – a human warehouse maintained by the county to keep impoverished oldsters from starving in the streets, but little else. My parents, even in their younger years, worried about being sent there if there was another Depression or the farm failed. If we kids didn't work hard enough we could all wind up in the poor house, we were told.

I fear those days will return in a few years if Bush succeeds in weakening Social Security to the point that it will collapse, which appears to be his strategy. For all of the talk of "reforming" the system to make Social Security sound, there is no reform in his plan. His plan to allow younger taxpayers to divert portions of SS taxes into individual savings accounts takes away revenue the system will need to remain fiscally sound. It does nothing to alter the formula to assure that revenues match obligations as boomers retire in large numbers and life expectancy rises.

It wouldn't take a major overhaul to put Social Security back into balance. Delay the full retirement age a bit more. Raise the maximum salary level at which workers stop paying SS taxes. Inch up income penalties for early retirement. A combination of these minor tweaks would be relatively painless and would apply only to future retirees And Social Security's integrity would be assured, through at least my grandchildren's generation.

Sorry, here I am, sounding just like a geezer, telling everybody else how to run things as if I had nothing better to do. Well, don't listen to me. I've got mine and likely won't be around when the whole thing collapses. But don't say I didn't warn you,

POST SCRIPT

As it turned out, that birthday did turn out to be a turning point in my life, at least the beginning of a very wide turn. After 65, the job that had so consumed me for almost 30 years began to become tedious. On many days I felt like I was merely going through the motions. And I started thinking more and more about retirement. Or, at least, reducing the workload. I knew I would need to keep working part-time for a few more years, because our pensions and savings simply were inadequate to support us for 20 or more years without a drastic lowering of our quality of our life. At the same time, the newspaper industry was beginning to hit really rough water after years of seeing its ad revenue and circulation base shrink. Corners were being cut everywhere to reduce the payroll and cut newsprint costs.

So I came up with a plan to retire but to continue writing editorials as a part-time free-lancer. For a 50 percent cut in pay, with no benefits, I would produce five editorials a week. All of the administrative work of producing an editorial page – editing letters to the editor, laying out pages, proof-reading, selecting syndicated columnists and cartoons – would be handled by a copy editor. It would save half an FTE position while still providing five locally-written editorials a week. Since Saturdays and Mondays were not big opinion page days anyway, the readers might not even notice the difference.

I wrote up a formal agreement spelling out the terms described above. After quite a bit of back and forth with the publisher and my editor, they bought it. They signed off on the deal in spring of 2007, and I set my retirement plans for fall of that year. But then, my plans changed. I learned through the grapevine that the University of South Florida's Sarasota-Manatee branch was looking for a person to head up a think tank it was planning to establish through an endowment provided by former Congressman Dan Miller of Bradenton. It so happened that I knew Dan Miller quite well. He and his wife Glenda had been friends of Jo Anne's even before I met her, and we had maintained a cordial relationship through the years. The newspaper had enthusiastically endorsed his candidacy for Sarasota-Bradenton's seat in Congress for every one of the five terms he had served. I had even entertained the idea of working in his district office. That, however, never panned out for several reasons, not least of which was the pay cut I would have had to make to accept such a job.

Anyway, I called Dan and got a full run-down on the new think tank. The vision statement that had been drafted said it would "help shape the conversation on issues that influence the lives of citizens – especially in the South Tampa Bay region – by collaborating, communicating, deliberating, educating and facilitating."

According to Dan, the Institute for Public Policy and Leadership "was created to help the Sarasota-Manatee community manage in a rational and purposeful manner the triple challenges of rapid growth, social change and an aging population."

"Wow!" I thought. "That sounds a lot like what I have been doing the last 30 years as editorial editor, except in a different format." It seemed too good to be true. I hastened online and filled out the application for the director's position. I passed the initial applicant screening and was invited to campus for a personal interview. That went well, and a few days later the campus Chancellor called and offered me the job. It wasn't a great salary, but it was more than I would have made in my planned part-time editorial free-lancing gig for the Herald. *And it came with full benefits: health, dental, pension, vacation credits, the works. I accepted without hesitating.*

And for the second time in my career at the Herald, *I submitted my letter of resignation. Yes, second. Unbeknownst to all except four people – me, my wife, my editor and the then-publisher – I had resigned 15 years earlier to accept a job working for the competition, the* Sarasota Herald-Tribune. *And the irony of my wife having worked for John Hamner, the man who had been fired from my job at the* Bradenton Herald *years earlier, grew. The position I had accepted at the Manatee Bureau of the* Herald-Tribune *was John's former job as bureau chief and editorial writer. I kept following in this man's footsteps.*

Except this time I didn't. The publisher refused to accept my resignation. He asked me to sit tight for a few hours, even though I had cleared out my desk early that morning, before anyone else had arrived in the newsroom, because I knew that "traitors" who went over to the Dark Side were escorted out of the building by a security guard as soon as they gave their notice. I didn't want to go out like that.

But I didn't have to. By around 10 that morning the publisher called me into his office and said if I would agree to stay, he would more than match the pay offer of the competition. I was too valuable to the paper to lose. His offer would mean a salary increase of roughly one-third. Making more money was the main reason for my plan to jump ship. It was an offer that was too good to refuse. I stayed.

But now, in 2007, it was much harder to resign. I was leaving a job I loved and co-workers whom I regarded as a second family. I was walking away from a profession that had consumed me for 45 years, into the world of academia, about which I knew nothing. I had never let the Great Unknown keep me from taking on a challenge before; I certainly wasn't going to start now. My notice sent shock waves through the newspaper, and the community. I was the longest-tenured newsroom employee of the Herald and had become something of an institution in town. People actually read my editorials and knew who wrote them even if they weren't signed. I had more institutional knowledge than anyone else on staff.

To my surprise, the publisher threw me a grand retirement party. He invited 100 or so movers and shakers in the community to a reception in the South Florida Museum, complete with hors d'oeuvres and open bar. Most of them came – and a few even gave commendatory speeches. These were people who had felt the sting of my editorial whip more than once, whose development projects or political causes I had opposed. In my early days in the job a few of them had even shunned me, literally turning their backs at parties if I approached their conversation groups. Now, 30 years later, they were openly paying me respect. Former Sheriff Charlie Wells, who himself had retired the previous year, summed up the reason for the respect: "Even if you didn't agree with him, David was always fair. He always called to get your side before he wrote his editorial."

It was the greatest thing anyone could have said, for it validated my work for all of those years. It made worthwhile all of the verbal abuse I got for taking unpopular stands, the names I was called, the threats made to sue, the dirty looks I got in the grocery store and in church. I was fair. That was enough.

I don't remember what I said at that community party, besides thanking everyone for putting up with me for 32 years. But I still have a copy of the speech I wrote for the retirement party thrown at the newspaper. Here are excerpts:

How does something like this happen? Beats me! You just keep going to work every day and having fun, most of the time, and the next thing you know 30 or 40 years have passed. There's probably a lesson there somewhere.

I've been to plenty of these gatherings over the years, but never really thought that someday it would be my turn. Now it is, and I have to say it's a surreal feeling. You don't just end something you've done for 32 years as easily as turning off a light switch. It's a huge decision, and that's why I have procrastinated about it for the last couple of years.

But as a wise king said a very long time ago, there is a season for everything. And it is time for a new season for me. I leave the *Bradenton Herald* with very mixed emotions, to be sure — excitement for what's ahead, and elation at the freedom from a daily deadline — the heavy burden of trying to come up with something meaningful, interesting and provocative to say every day, holidays included, week after week, month after month, year after year. I figure I have written something like 12,000 editorials, give or take a few hundred, in 30 years as Editorial Page editor. And I'm happy to turn that job over to someone else. Good luck with that, Chris.

But it is hard to leave a place I consider home and a group of co-workers I consider family. I've known a few of you for all of those years and many of you for most of them. We've gone through many changes, survived many challenges, and celebrated quite a few successes together. I'll miss you -- but I also am not going very far away. I hope to return often, especially for gatherings like this. And I'll still be calling and emailing my newsroom colleagues to pass on tips and ideas.

As Jim Smith wrote in his superb feature on my retirement last Sunday, don't look for me on the golf course, or on the porch rocking and whittling, or in front of the TV watching daytime soaps and Oprah.

I'm still going to be working, still involved in the community, and still writing. My farmer parents embedded the work ethic in me too deeply to allow me to just sit around while I have energy and health. So I'm not retiring from work -- just from daily journalism.

Then I thanked a few people: the publisher my editor, a couple of my cronies, my wife, daughter and finally the entire staff, quite a few of whom I had known since joining the paper in 1975. And it was done. It took a half-dozen boxes to pack up all of the personal stuff I had accumulated in 32 years. But I got it done, wheeled the boxes to my car on a hand cart, and walked out of the place I had found my calling for the last time. I left behind my farewell column, and was honored by two other farewell columns, one printed the previous Sunday and the second a few weeks later. Herewith, the farewell column penned by Managing Editor Jim Smith, published on **Sept. 9, 2007.**

THE LONG GOODBYE

David Klement, *Herald*'s institutional voice, leaving after 32 years
By Jim Smith
Managing Editor

When he arrived for his first day of work at the *Bradenton Herald* on Sept. 22, 1975, David Klement planned to give the newspaper two solid years.

And that he did. Followed by two more, and two more, and two more after that. When you total them up – and we must do that now because his last day at Manatee County's daily newspaper is Friday – you come to 32 years of exemplary service. Incredibly, all of Klement's years at the *Herald* were solid ones.

How many 67-year-olds can you say that about?

"I have ink in my veins," says Klement in discussing his farewell to newspapering, a rewarding career that spans 45 years – 47 if you include the time in college when the journalism bug first bit him. Leaving, he admits, "will be very hard, extremely hard. I'll be like an addict withdrawing."

Now there's the real corker: Unlike most retirement-age workers who are racing out the door to spend their twilight years golfing, fishing or gardening, Klement is changing careers. He has another job waiting, and it's a good one – perfect for him, it seems: Director of the Institute for Public Policy and Leadership at the University of South Florida's Sarasota-Manatee campus. It will easily be the longest job title he has held.

Klement certainly appears up to his new challenge, which will find him directing workshops and community forums for the university – the same kind of work that helped distinguish his tenure at the *Herald*. Don't let the age fool you. "I don't feel 67," he insists. "I'm not going to acknowledge that age in my mind. I'm more like 57, maybe 55."

He still has a healthy crop of hair and boasts the belt-tightening weight of his high school days. And there's still that wry smile and twinkle in the eyes when he's immersed in something he really enjoys.

Hiking the Grand Canyon with his wife of nearly 29 years, Jo Anne – whom he met through a church group in Bradenton and has shared a born-again relationship – will have to be put on hold. So will his goal to write and publish a successful novel. (He has three in his mind, two partly outlined and one chapter written, and a first draft of a screenplay completed.)

Consummate Crusader

Klement has served as the *Herald*'s Editorial Page Editor for more than 30 years. He has been the consummate journalism crusader, serving as the institutional voice of the paper and watchdog for the community. If you have ever been a regular reader you have probably experienced the full range of emotions reading his editorials and columns. You laughed with him, cried with him and pounded your fist – either to affirm your support of a strong stance or to display your disagreement with it.

Klement never took it personally. Unless a caller was particularly mean-spirited, he listened to every complaint. And there were more than a few calls over the years, considering that he has written in the neighborhood of 11,500 editorials for the paper.

"Mostly I think we set a tone, and people came to understand that the *Herald* stood for the town's best interests," says Klement. "We're trying to call them as we see 'em, like the umpire, and most people can understand that."

Just one year at the *Herald*, Publisher William Fleet has been able to witness Klement's passion, courage and dedication to the job.

"I've been in the newspaper business for 30 years and I can say unequivocally that David Klement is the finest editorial writer I've known," says Fleet. "More than that he is a great guy and has been a pleasure to work with. We will miss him here, but I'm happy that he will continue to be an integral part of our community. I wish David and our friends at USF all the best."

Last year, Klement was named the *Herald*'s Employee of the Year. It was a year during which readers were exposed to one of his most gratifying projects: chronicling the six-month anniversary and aftermath of Hurricane Katrina in a stirring week-long series.

Earning His Way

Raised on a Texas dairy farm in a devout Catholic family, Klement developed important qualities that would reveal themselves in his journalistic work: integrity, humility and fairness. He put them to work early in his first job at the *Daily Oklahoman* in Oklahoma City, and later at the *Detroit Free Press* before joining the *Herald*.

Somewhere along the way he developed a layer of thick skin, which came in handy. "I was called a communist pinko when I was in eighth grade," says Klement, "so I was used to being vilified."

Klement's first job at the *Herald* was Business Editor, a position he secured after a visit to Manatee Memorial Hospital where then-Editor Wayne Poston was being treated for a bleeding ulcer. "David was vacationing from Detroit, and I interviewed him from my hospital bed," recalls Poston, now Bradenton's mayor. "He wanted to move to Florida, and it was a great opportunity to hire somebody of his caliber."

"He conducted the interview in his hospital bed gown," smiles Klement. "Maybe he hired me because of my chutzpah."

Klement quickly moved up the ranks, becoming News Editor and then City Editor within a year, before moving into the Editorial Page slot in April 1977. And he soon was earning accolades for himself and the *Herald*.

After a January freeze in the early 1980s left migrant workers without clothing and food, Klement's appeal for help generated a caravan of vehicles packed with donated food, blankets and clothing.

During the exodus of the refugees from the killing fields of Cambodia in 1980, Klement's editorials helped spark a wave of refugee sponsorships among Bradenton church groups that enabled 150 to resettle into new lives here. Klement personally signed for a family of 10 through his church.

In 1997, Klement's editorials went a long way toward securing the Pew Center for Public Journalism's prestigious James K. Batten Award of Excellence for the *Herald's* coverage of a new city hall. And in 1999 he made significant contributions to Project Safeguard, a grassroots look at safety in local schools that was a Batten finalist.

Redefining Retirement

Klement talked about retiring from the *Herald* for the past few years but kept putting if off. A new retirement date would change every few months – and every time he extended his tenure, Executive Editor Joan Krauter would express relief.

"I'd argue, 'You can't leave us – you're the institutional soul of this newspaper.' But now that he is really moving on, I know he is leaving that wealth with us," Krauter said. "I'm honored to have been David's colleague here for almost nine years. I've learned more from him about community journalism than anyone in my career."

Klement plans to spend two weeks relaxing with his family – a brother and sister are coming to visit this week – and "getting my bearings" before starting his second career at USF on Oct. 1.

Features Editor Chris Wille, who has occasionally written editorials at the *Herald*, will assume the newspaper's editorial duties Sept. 17.

Klement's final week at the *Herald* comes during the sixth anniversary of 9/11. Klement had been back home less than two days from his mother's burial in Texas when the planes struck the twin towers and the Pentagon. He had also endured the deaths of a sister and brother-in-law earlier that year. And his 13-year-old German shepherd had to be put down in the spring.

The hectic, chaotic hours and days that followed 9/11 – including a direct hit on Bradenton from Tropical Storm Gabrielle – were among the most trying of Klement's career, and his column the following Sunday was perhaps his most self-revealing.

The headline: "Since Sept. 11, real men DO cry."

Klement spilled his emotions onto the page, showing readers once again that he was human and vulnerable like the rest of us. That was always the purpose of his columns, to show that he was a real person, with humble roots, not some loud voice shouting down from an ivory tower.

"My life experiences led into what I wrote," says Klement. "Growing up on a farm and shooting calves when I was 14 because my Dad told me to, that helped make me who I am. And getting up at 5 o'clock seven days a week to milk cows figured into my work ethic."

Those revealing columns, along with Klement's intelligent and thoughtfully constructed editorials, helped the community he has called home for 32 years.

"It IS my life, second to my family, thankfully – I tried to keep that from happening," he said. "It's been a home you don't just lightly give that up, and I wouldn't.

"But I just feel in my heart that it's time."

WORDS FROM THE WISE WOMAN

I cherished that column a great deal, for Jim Smith had been one of our sharpest writers before being promoted to an editor's job. But a tribute that followed a few weeks later meant even more. It came from Patricia Glass, considered the Wise Woman of Manatee County for her role in shaping public policy for 28 years. She broke the gender barrier on the Manatee County Commission in 1978 and went on to serve seven terms. She also made an unsuccessful bid for Congress one year. She was known for advocating for more affordable housing, protecting the environment and improving the local healthcare system for the indigent. The newspaper had

*endorsed her candidacy in every election campaign. So well thought
of was she that the Board of County Commissioners in 2018
renamed its meeting chamber in the County Administrative Center
for her. This column was published on **Oct. 10, 2007**, in Pat's role
as Citizen-At-Large, a feature the newspaper had initiated to bring
outside voices into the paper.*

No Goodbyes for Klement in Public Discourse

By Patricia Glass

Hail and farewell hold the same meaning in every language. We greet and depart, but what happens in between "hello" and "so long" gives real meaning to our various encounters in life.

I don't remember the first time I met David Klement, nor am I ready to say "sayonara" just because he relinquished his role at this newspaper. It is well that this community expressed its gratitude and applauded a remarkable man and the significant impact his career has had upon our lives.

How great for me, your citizen-at-large, to make contact with his readers from a different vantage point and to define, if possible, that age old relationship between politician and editor.

Money may be the mother's milk of politics, but rest assured the press is the ultimate yardstick of performance. Reporters may come and go, but good editors tend to stay. And in the case of David Klement they know well whereof and of whom they speak.

Aside from elections, endorsements and peccadilloes of candidates and officeholders, I know that there is a whole world of requisite knowledge and understanding inherent in the work of editors like David. Can we truly comprehend the length and breadth of the mission undertaken or the scope of his commitment to truth, justice and decent journalism?

There is not enough ink in this moment to recount all the war stories, earthshaking events and daily drama of things good and bad that fueled his opinions, giving us the energy to make a decision. Good editors don't just tell us; they challenge our judgment. They create that bridge between newspaper editorial board and the reader without compromising their own convictions.

Mark Twain anticipated the likes of David Klement when he wrote, "Imagine what a library an editor's work would make after 20 or 30 years of service. How editors can continue this tremendous labor, this exhausting consumption of brain fibre (for their work is creative, and not a mere mechanical laying up of facts), day after day and year after year, is incomprehensible." Twain labeled it "unspeakable hardship." Hard it may have been, but the writing part reflected an unspeakable joy.

Before 9/11, I was able to run up the stairs at the *Herald* and find an open door at the editor's office. No matter the topic, I felt welcome as we exchanged information and ideas.

David is a listener, a person sensitive to matters of community well-being and civic concern. This may be why he has offered up yet another gift to all of us.

David Klement will take his talent and ability to a new office at the University of South Florida, where most likely letters on the door will read "Executive Director, Institute for Public Policy and Leadership."

The underlying goal is to foster informed decision-making and responsible and ethical governance. How fortunate it is to find a perfect match in the perfect role.

Let me be the first to say, "Hello, how can I help?"

END OF A CAREER

What an eloquent tribute, from someone I so respected. I especially loved her reference to Mark Twain, one of my favorite authors. He summed up my role far better than I ever could have.

Now, I fear it's time to wrap up this chapter of my life, with my own reflection on that career at the Bradenton Herald. *Here is my farewell column, published on* **Sept. 16, 2007.**

Klement's Farewell to a Career in Newspapers

It was early spring, 1977 – a Monday, about 5 a.m.

Bleary-eyed editors and reporters filtered into the old *Bradenton Herald* newsroom on13th Street West, most bearing steaming cups of 7-Eleven coffee.

Time to gear up for another week of publishing Manatee's hometown newspaper – to refill the news pipeline that had been drained by the Sunday edition. For afternoon newspapers, which the *Herald* was in those days, that meant getting the street edition out by mid-morning. For the home-delivered edition, the deadline was noon.

As City Editor, I was working feverishly on the scant advance copy that remained from the weekend while perusing the news agenda, or budget, for that day's coverage. The Managing Editor paced nervously through the newsroom, muttering to himself and stopping often at the teletype machines furiously clacking out news from the Associated Press. He also paused to look over my shoulder and that of the News Editor to see what we'd added to our news budgets.

"Man, I need something for an editorial," he said. "I don't have a single idea."

Wearing two hats since the departure of the Editorial Page Editor some months before, he seldom wrote ahead – perhaps because his other hat involved managing 25 or 30 newsroom employees, perhaps because he worked best on deadline.

Which was approaching as the sky outside our window began to brighten with dawn.

"I just wish I could find somebody to write editorials," he said. The help-wanted ads had produced no viable candidates.

"I'll do it," I blurted. "I wanted to write editorials in Detroit before I came here."

Our eyes met – and held for a long time.

Tension drained from his face, replaced by a big smile, as he said, "You're on."

And that was it. That was my beginning as the *Herald's* Editorial Page Editor, 30 years and six months ago. Of course, we went through the formalities: Get buy-in from the top editor, Wayne Poston, and be interviewed by the publisher to establish my political bona fides. I must have passed, for I got the promotion.

And now it is over. Friday marked my last day of work at the *Herald*. My retirement is official Sept. 30, but I've elected to spend the last two weeks using up remaining vacation, resting up for the next phase of my life. Which is NOT fishing, golf or daytime TV.

It's hard to believe my newspaper career is over. The 45 years since I began as a cub reporter in Oklahoma City have flown by. The news business has been so much a part of my life all that time I can't predict how its absence will affect me.

I won't miss the pressure of a daily deadline and the need to produce a thoughtful, provocative and relevant piece of writing every day, regardless of whether the muse was around or not. I won't miss the phone calls from readers telling me how biased, stupid, narrow-minded and off-base I am. I won't miss the emails from readers complaining about the delivery of their paper, which many assumed must be part of the editor's job.

But I will miss the daily engagement with the issues of the day, the challenge of making sense out of complex issues and debating my conclusions with open-minded people. I'll miss the calls and emails from regular letter-writers, who seem like old friends though I've never met most of them. And, of course, I'll miss friends at the *Herald* I've worked with for years, and the familiarity of a work routine that has changed little in 30 years. Not many people have been so lucky.

Work has defined my life since my earliest memories. You started working at an early age on a farm. But unlike many in today's high-stress world, I haven't made work my life. I tried to put my family first. When the children were young, I coached soccer. I attended games, recitals, concerts. We went on long family vacations, weekend campouts, church outings. My life was balanced.

But work never was far from my mind. The burden of responsibility I felt – I used to say I was responsible for *anything* going on in the world, in a sense – never left, even on vacation. I always felt "on call."

Friends who know me well say, why quit now if you still enjoy what you do, your boss still wants you around and you are still healthy?

Good points, all. I've thought about them a lot in the last couple of years. One image that comes to mind is from the movie of two years ago called *About Schmidt*. Jack Nicholson played a mid-level insurance executive on the cusp of retirement, not yet ready to go but being gently edged out by management. He enjoys the warm farewells and basks in the accolades of the young hot shots who are replacing him.

But as he walks to his car carrying a box with his personal belongings on his last day, he happens to walk by the office dumpster in back. There, awaiting removal to the landfill, are boxes of his files, sales manuals, contacts – the accumulated wisdom of his career, thrown out with the garbage.

It was a powerful metaphor for any senior citizen. Age, like the foxhole in war, has a way of concentrating the mind. I don't want to wait to be gently pushed toward the door. I want to believe that the accolades are sincere. Coincidentally, this realization comes at a watershed moment for journalism. The daily newspaper is undergoing seismic change. The internet is as revolutionary to journalism as the automobile was to transportation a century ago.

Could I adapt to this new world of journalism? Absolutely. I have been testing its waters for several years now. I am not hostile to change.

But I also realize that it is a new era, one I couldn't imagine 30 years ago when I said, "Editorial writer? Hey, let me do it." That era is over for me. As Solomon said around 3,000 years ago, there is a season for everything. This season has ended for me.

But as I also know, one season follows another. And a new one is beginning for me. Next month, I will become the director of the Institute for Public Policy and Leadership at the University of South Florida's Sarasota-Manatee campus. In that role, I'll still be focusing on the issues of concern to Manatee and Sarasota residents. The new job offers me the chance to keep thinking about government and social policy issues without a daily production deadline. It permits me to leave at the top of my game instead of in its fading moments while still contributing to the causes for which I have fought for the last 30 years.

What more could anyone ask?

To all my readers: Thanks for all of the kind words expressed since my retirement was announced last week. They have meant more to you than you know.

THE END

ABOUT THE AUTHOR

David Klement is a self-labeled naïve optimist who enjoyed a 45-year career as an old-school journalist, reporting and writing about some of the most important news events during the golden years of newspapering: the second half of the 20th century and beginning of the 21st. He spent the majority of that career as Editorial Page editor of the *Bradenton Herald*, a member of the McClatchy (formerly Knight Ridder) news organization. In that capacity he wrote one to two editorials per day, published anonymously as the newspaper's voice, seven days a week – a total he estimates at around 11,500. For about half of those years he operated as a one-person shop, writing all of the editorials as well as laying out the pages, selecting the op-ed columns, cartoons and letters to the editor, and proofreading.

To establish a personal identity as the newspaper's opinion editor, he wrote personal columns for the Sunday editions on alternate weeks. It is the reprisal of the best of these columns that forms the core of this book. He currently is working on a more comprehensive autobiography that will encompass his early life growing up on a Texas dairy farm and his early journalistic experience at the *Daily Oklahoman/Oklahoma City Times, Chicago Sun-Times* and *Detroit Free Press*, where he shared a Pulitzer Prize with the news staff for coverage of the 1967 Detroit riot.

After retiring as the *Herald's* opinion editor in 2007, he enjoyed a second and third career, one as a think-tank director for local colleges and another, briefer one as a member of Florida's utility regulatory board, the Public Service Commission.

He lives in Bradenton with his wife of 42 years, Jo Anne, also a retired journalist.

Made in the USA
Coppell, TX
18 February 2022

73753565R00217